THE
JAPANESE AMERICAN
COMMUNITY

THE
JAPANESE AMERICAN
COMMUNITY

A Three-Generation Study

Gene N. Levine
Colbert Rhodes

PRAEGER

PRAEGER SPECIAL STUDIES • PRAEGER SCIENTIFIC

Library of Congress Cataloging in Publication Data

Levine, Gene Norman, 1930-
   The Japanese American community.

   Includes bibliographical references and index.
   1. Japanese Americans. I. Rhodes, Colbert. II. Title.
E184.J3L48   305.8'956'073   81-1134
ISBN 0-03-055691-0   AACR2

Published in 1981 by Praeger Publishers
CBS Educational and Professional Publishing
A Division of CBS, Inc.
521 Fifth Avenue, New York, New York 10175 U.S.A.

© 1981 by Praeger Publishers

123456789   145   987654321

Printed in the United States of America

for John Modell,
without whom, not

ACKNOWLEDGMENTS

After well over a decade of work, the list of persons and institutions to whom thanks are due by me personally, and by the Japanese American Research Project at the University of California, Los Angeles, is lengthy.*

I thank, first, the Japanese American Citizens League as an organization, and its members individually, for having had the vision to instigate the project and the patience, at times tried, to see it out. Shigeo Wakamatsu, chairman of the league's History Committee for nearly two decades, has provided continued support. The same can be said for Mike Masaoka, even though his role was less official. In Los Angeles, Frank F. Chuman worked with us to clarify many issues while fashioning his own study of the legal difficulties of Japanese Americans.†

I am deeply grateful to the late Joe Grant Masaoka, long the public symbol and efficient manager of the project. He officially served as liaison between the project and the league. In fact, he was drawn considerably into the research work itself and recorded scores of oral histories on our behalf.

T. Scott Miyakawa initiated the project's sociological research endeavors and, with consultation, gave them their early shape.

Robert A. Wilson played a day-to-day role in our activities. Absent Wilson, as administrator and as historian, we would have functioned with hardship.

In the early stages of the project, Yasuo Sakata prepared the mainland-wide list of some 18,000 surviving Issei from which the first-generation sample was drawn.

---

*The present work has been conducted through grants from the Japanese American Citizens League, the Carnegie Corporation, and the National Institute of Mental Health (Grant no. 5-R01-MH12780). Computing assistance was obtained from the Health Sciences Computing Facility, UCLA; from the UCLA Campus Computing Network; and from computing facilities at the University of Texas, Permian Basin. A list of Japanese American Research Project publications completed and in progress appears as Appendix A. The historical and survey materials collected provide for many secondary analyses, some already conducted and others under way. The historical materials, including oral histories, are stored and indexed in the Special Collections section of the Graduate Research Library at UCLA, as are the survey interviews and questionnaires (excluding respondents' names). Coded data from the latter, including codebooks and computer tapes, are stored at the Institute for Social Science Research, UCLA. With my permission, they are available to the interested scholar.

† Frank F. Chuman, *The Bamboo People: The Law and Japanese Americans* (Del Mar, Calif.: Publishers' Inc.,]976).

I acknowledge the contributions of the Survey Research Center (now part of the Institute of Social Science Research) at UCLA. Its director then, the late Leo G. Reeder, had a long and essential relationship with the project.

Imaginatively guided by Eve Weinberg, interviewers from the Survey Research Service of the National Opinion Research Center, University of Chicago, conducted our interviews with Nisei. Paul B. Sheatsley played his usual remarkable role in helping us to refine the instrument and its specifications.

My staff at UCLA was devoted. My good friend, former student, and present colleague, John Modell, shepherded the project through from mid-1966. He was responsible for instrument construction, coding and processing, and data analysis. There cannot be many historians who are so adept at survey research. Edna M. Bonacich joined the project in its later years, and brought her brilliance to bear in the analysis of the data.

In sequence, Michael Edlen, Donald M. Long, Michael Rudd, Sheila Henry, Darrel Montero, and Ford Waite mediated between me and the computer. Henry and Montero, then sociology graduate students, themselves played important roles in the analysis.

Among early consultants, I wish to thank Raymond J. Murphy, Tomatsu Shibutani, Harry H. L. Kitano, Frank Miyamoto, Ralph H. Turner, Roger Girod, and Kurt B. Mayer.

Project officers at the National Institute of Mental Health—first Lorraine B. Torres, then Joyce Lazar—were helpful and encouraging over the protracted run of the enterprise.

Among a list of able secretaries, I should like to single out Keiko Watanabe.

In preparing the final manuscript for publication, staff members at the University of Texas, Permian Basin, have been especially helpful. Thanks are due programmer William Hackos, librarian Cathy Clayton, and typist Clara Jenkins. Joseph W. Malley served as technical assistant in Texas.

Finally, I thank former students of mine at UCLA whose thinking influenced my work—among them Hilla Kuttenplan Israely, Susan McCoin Kataoka, Ronald T. Tsukashima, and Jess M. Carrillo.

Gene N. Levine
Los Angeles

CONTENTS

THE
JAPANESE AMERICAN
COMMUNITY

1

INTRODUCTION

THE CENTRAL QUESTION

Most ethnic minorities in the United States have undergone similar fates: The immigrant generation adapted economically, but not socially, to its surroundings, while keeping its group boundaries closed. The second and third generations have become more or less acculturated, a condition brought about largely through the mechanism of education.[1] Assimilation, commingling with the host society, has been the outcome for some.

With acculturation to the host culture occurring in other-than-economic ways, the walls among groups have fallen or at least have become permeable. Irish and Italians, Jews and Poles, Armenians and Scandinavians—all have undergone the same experiences. The tradition that opposed acculturation, blocking the way through community elders, other leaders, and parents, was not strong enough to keep sizable numbers of the young locked in.[2]

Adapt to America? Get ahead? The routes were clear: the pursuit of education or of business enterprise, or of both—and, correspondingly, more diffuse relations with outsiders ensued. For many groups, not just the white, the engine of intermarriage was unstoppable, its consequences viewed by the older generation as disaster.

For the later generations, ethnic communities have inevitably become transformed. But the many in these groups have not totally disappeared. They flourish in a different guise, and new life has been breathed into cultural remnants thought to be irrevocably lost or moribund as one generation has succeeded another.

Is America the melting pot to which erosion of minority cultures and communities would attest? Or is it, rather, pluralistic, as shown by growing interest in old forms among the third and fourth generations of some ethnic groups? And why should such interest grow? Has assimilation, at least in white America, succeeded? Or has the complex class and ethnic mosaic made for a persistence of many Americas, interlocked but not entirely welded together?

For all the erosion of subcultural forms and their wedding with the host culture, they have not entirely vanished. Antique allegiances still hold, even if sometimes weakly. Appeals on ethnic grounds assuredly work. Politicians are ever sensitive to the ethnic character of neighborhoods they enter when campaigning.

We have elected to study one ethnic group, and a colored one at that: the Japanese Americans, now nearly 600,000 in number.[3] They, like others, have undergone cultural erosion in generations succeeding the immigrant. They have been phenomenally successful in terms of education and have made great strides occupationally.[4] The same disturbing signs of ethnic amalgamation that have occurred in other groups have shown themselves among the third generation—most notably, a pronounced predilection for exogamy.[5]

Withal, a community (or multiple communities in a spatial sense) very different from the Issei, or first-generation, community persists, albeit transformed. It is, for example, now far more urban. Our data do not allow us to foresee the disappearance of Japanese Americans as a community. But the conflicting forces ought to continue: on the one hand, centripetal, drawing men and women more closely into its net; on the other hand, centrifugal, influencing them to doff the remnants of old ways.

The central problem of this volume is to attempt to discover how the Japanese American community has managed to retain its solidarity as it has, considering all the contrary pressures toward acculturation and assimilation. Community social control, exercised largely by the family, vies with simultaneous participation by the many in the larger society. How is potential conflict resolved? The close-knit family persists, and close ties with Caucasians exist. This anomalous situation forms the core of questions we address with our data. We concentrate on the Nisei (second generation), use Issei as the basis, and employ Sansei (third-generation) data to gauge outcomes and offer prognoses.

A NOTE ON THE JAPANESE MIGRATION TO THE UNITED STATES AND ON OUR SAMPLE

The sample of Issei and their offspring under study forms part of a migration from Japan to the United States that began in 1868, increasing as the Meiji restoration set out to modernize Japan with vigor. Tiny in any case, the immigration was officially cut off when Congress set out to limit Asian (and other) immigration in 1924. A few Japanese continued to gain entry after 1924. Then, with new legislation in 1965, Asian immigrants were made more welcome. War brides were, of course, free to come before that date. Our study limits itself to pre-1924 immigrants and their progeny, although we speculate later on the communal consequences of this new blood from Japan. We further restrict ourselves by using mainland Japanese Americans, though a minority (some 10 percent) of the Issei arrived by way of Hawaii, where they had usually spent less than a year.

According to William Petersen (who remarks about the faulty statistics kept on both sides of the Pacific), 298,457 Issei migrated between the opening up of Japan and 1924.[6] During these years, there were many "birds of passage," as Robert A. Wilson puts it and as Petersen affirms.[7]

During 1962-64 we attempted to list every living Issei on the mainland. Some 18,000 names were obtained. A sample of 1,047 was eventually drawn for interviews. (Two-thirds were men. Women were taken in part to provide occupational data on unavailable or deceased spouses.)[8] We have eliminated Issei who did not marry, who bore no children, or whose children did not become respondents. Our effective sample of Issei was thus 907.

Thirty-six percent of our sample arrived before the Gentlemen's Agreement of 1908 restricted migration from Japan. This compares with Petersen's figure of 47 percent.[9] That our respondents form a somewhat younger cut of all immigrants merely attests that they are among the survivors.

The Issei under study came young, to be sure. Fully 62 percent entered the United States before their twenty-first year. The later the men came, the younger they tended to be (see Table 1.1). The reverse holds for women. This is of course due to the fact that men arrived first—and single. Once settled, they sent to Japan for mates (thus the famed "picture bride" method of selection).

TABLE 1.1

Issei Age at Arrival, by Time of Arrival and by Sex

Age at Arrival	Percent Who Arrived		
	Before 1908	1908-15	1916-24
Men			
Under 18	28	50	46
18–20	38	24	31
21 or older	34	26	23
Total number	(290)	(129)	(161)
Women			
Under 18	33	11	9
18–20	30	37	32
21 or older	36	52	59
Total number	(33)	(131)	(159)

Source: Data for this and for subsequent tables are derived from the authors' samples, unless otherwise specifically noted.

A HISTORY OF THE PROJECT

The Japanese American Research Project at UCLA sprang from a decision made in June 1960 by the Japanese American Citizens League (JACL), an organization of some 20,000 Nisei. They raised funds from JACL members initially to prepare a written history to pay tribute to their parents, Issei, who were then largely in their seventies and eighties. The project began at UCLA early in 1962, after which its goals became elaborated. During 1963–66, data were collected on a national sample selected from national lists of approximately 18,000 surviving Issei. An oral history program was also established within the project. Upon its completion, this program had obtained interviews with over 250 key figures, both Japanese American (largely Issei) and non-Japanese (especially men who figured in the relocation actions). Survey data from the Nisei and Sansei generations were collected for the period 1966–67. The study includes 1,047 Issei, 2,304 Nisei, and 802 Sansei.[10]

During the life of the project, students undertook related inquiries. One compared men in the Nisei sample with a sample of second-generation Armenian American men. Another directed a second query to members of the Sansei sample in order to assay dimensions of ethnic identity. A third reanalyzed the Issei replies in order to delineate the role of the immigrant women. Later, a student fashioned a survey, parallel to ours, that was conducted among Filipino migrants to Los Angeles.

The survey data collected by the project have, then, proved useful both in mounting studies of other ethnic groups, and in providing modes of interpretation that help in understanding processes of acculturation. To Armenians and Filipinos, one must add Jews, Chicanos, and Puerto Ricans. In this work, we stress the importance of reports on behavior as indicators of degree of acculturation. The data have led us to rely more upon these reports than upon attitudinal measures. There are indicators, from another data set, that the relationship between attitudes and behavior, as tapped in studies of acculturation and assimilation within ethnic groups, is complex.[11] Some kinds of behavioral change appear to be forerunners of attitudinal change. Behavioral changes have recently been found to include, for example, choice of language, food preferences, and media use. These changes antecede a shift from traditional to modern attitudes toward mental illness.

The Japanese American Research Project, over the years, provided us with a laboratory in which to test various notions about American ethnic processes. The work begun there is being continued among other minority populations.

NOTES

1. The experience of Russian Americans is a good case in point. See Alex Simirenko, *Pilgrims, Colonists, and Frontiersmen: An Ethnic Community in Transition* (New York: The Free Press of Glencoe, 1964).

2. The process is not confined to the United States. Groups in other plural societies have behaved similarly. In Brazil, for example, younger generations of Japanese Brazilians have little in common with the older immigrant generation or its offspring. Interestingly, young third- and fourth-generation Japanese Brazilians have just as little in common with sophisticated Japanese who have arrived since World War II to trade and to instigate industrial development. Leonard Greenwood, *Los Angeles Times*, pt. IV, October 20, 1974, p. 6. There are, by the way, some 730,000 Japanese Brazilians, more than the number of Japanese Americans in the United States (including Hawaii).

3. The actual figure of Americans of Japanese origin or descent was 591,290, according to the 1970 census count. Sixty-three percent of them live in the 48 contiguous states; the rest, in Hawaii (except for 854 in Alaska). U.S. Department of Commerce, Bureau of the Census, *United States Census Population: 1970* (Washington, D.C.: Government Printing Office, 1970), table 1; "Japanese, Chinese, and Filipinos in the United States," Subject Reports, Final Report PC(2)-1G, mimeographed, p. 1.

4. The type and character of these strides are discussed in the companion volume to this one, Edna M. Bonacich and John Modell, *The Economic Basis of Ethnic Solidarity: A Study of Japanese Americans* (Berkeley and Los Angeles: University of California Press, 1980).

5. See Gene N. Levine and Darrel M. Montero, "Socioeconomic Mobility Among Three Generations of Japanese Americans," *Journal of Social Issues* 29, no. 2 (1973); Harry H. L. Kitano, *Race Relations* (Englewood Cliffs, N.J.: Prentice-Hall, 1974), p. 229.

6. Between 1925 and 1940, 6,156 came. William Petersen, *Japanese Americans: Oppression and Success* (New York: Random House, 1971), table 2-1, p. 15. He uses U.S. census data and draws also upon Yamato Ichihashi, *Japanese Immigration: Its Status in California* (San Francisco: Marshall Press, 1915), p. 9.

7. Petersen, *Japanese Americans*, p. 16: "From 1908 to 1924 (that is, from the Gentlemen's Agreement to the law barring Asian immigration), the 160,000 Japanese arrivals resulted in a new movement into the country of only 90,000."

8. Admittedly, we notoriously underestimated the role of Issei women in bolstering economy and society. This fault has been repaired by Susan McCoin Kataoka's secondary analysis of our data on Issei women: "Issei Women: A Study in Compliance-Noncompliance" (Ph.D. dissertation, University of California, Los Angeles, 1977).

9. Petersen, *Japanese Americans*, p. 15.

10. The results of an analysis of trigenerational familial data are not included in this work.

11. Fernando Parra, "Chicano and Anglo Attitudes toward Mental Illness" (Ph.D. dissertation, University of California, Los Angeles, 1980).

2

THE EVOLUTION OF THE JAPANESE AMERICAN CONCEPTION OF COMMUNITY: THEORETICAL PERSPECTIVES

The focus of the Japanese American Research Project's surveys of three generations has been upon the adaptation, social and economic, of Japanese immigrants and their descendants to life in the United States. If we do not emphasize the impact of Japanese Americans upon the majority culture, it is not because it has been slight. Indeed, in fields such as agriculture, especially in California, the Issei and their offspring have made enormous contributions.[1] We are more interested here, however, not in how Japanese Americans have affected America, but in how they have been able to survive in an alien culture—and in the prognosis for their survival as a distinct community in the future. Another caveat: We do not deal in any detail with the World War II relocation. There is ample literature on that subject. We do stress the remarkable achievements of the Japanese Americans, and focus primarily upon their ability and willingness to survive as a distinctive ethnic group even when these very achievements tend to tear apart the traditional fabric of their community.

In this chapter we discuss the meaning of community generally and the evolution of the Japanese American community, in particular, over three generations. We also attempt to provide a theory that explains the changes and continuities in the character of the community. In studying the community, we learn how each generation of Japanese Americans has gained an identity that defines, for the person, the extent to which he or she is Japanese or American— or both, in intricate combination. The paramountcy of ethnic identity is brought out by Erik Erikson, who argues in *Childhood and Society* that an important element of ego identity—the sense of self—is ethnic identity, the sense of belonging to, or identifying with, an ethnic group.[2]

The central thrust of this study is the denotation and the measurement of the ties that make up (and tear apart) the ethnic community. The conception of community usually includes the shared identity, group awareness, and self-consciousness that stem from common cultural patterns and experiences as well as from in-group marriages, internal friendship networks, and organizational memberships and participation.[3]

Geographical location—the clustering or dispersion of the ethnic group—must also be considered. Given clustering, occasions for group interaction are obviously increased. And the more intensive the contacts, the greater the chances for the maintenance of community boundaries.[4] Community reflects "a high degree of personal intimacy, emotional depth, moral commitment, social cohesion and continuity in time."[5] Even if a person does not live close to his or her ethnic peers, he or she can still share a sense of community. Periodic (even telephonic) contact serves to refuel the sense of belonging.

THE JAPANESE AMERICAN CONCEPTION OF COMMUNITY

In our study of the changing character of the Japanese American community, we discuss both forces that have led to the formation of the community, and forces that have served to transform each generation's idea of community. The Japanese American's conception of community is different from other minorities' in that it is highly associated with generation. The terms Issei, Nisei, and Sansei refer to first-, second-, and third-generation Japanese Americans, respectively. These labels are used in everyday life by Japanese Americans in the United States, and indicate how the concept of generation is central to their experience with the ethnic community.[6] We show how a sharp distinction between and among generations contributes to different configurations of community life. We compare the varying paths to ethnic identity that have been followed by each generation, and trace the causes for these differences. We characterize the structure of the community in each generation—those who are more active in it and those who have tended to cut ties in favor of integration into the larger society.

The concept of community refers to the existence of a real group, not merely a social category. Members of the community interact more with each other than they do with nonmembers; they share norms and values, and value-group goals; and they define themselves as members.

In considering the degree to which Japanese Americans form a community, along with differential rates of participation, there is the opposite question to be examined: the degree to which Japanese Americans are acculturated or assimilated, or both, into the larger, environing, even overpowering American society. We divide the world in which people of Japanese ancestry may participate into two categories—a Japanese American community, centered on itself, and a general, vaguely defined "American community." At the start, we can conclude that Japanese Americans have not, like some ethnic groups, wanted to maintain their singularity; generation by generation, they have been more oriented toward becoming part of the American mix.

Persons vary in the degree to which they are active in either community; and, at least in some areas of life, these two dimensions may be independent of each other. Some persons may be heavily involved in both worlds; others may be active exclusively in one; still others may have withdrawn from, or never become active in, either. We use two variables to define a person's location in the community: interaction and values.

In determining in which of the two communities, the Japanese or the American, an individual participates, we first distinguish between the social and cultural meanings of membership. The social basis of membership in either community consists in a person's interacting, to a significant degree, with other members of that community. The cultural basis consists in a sharing of common values, norms, and customs with other members. These two are related: the more people interact, the more likely they are to develop patterns of interaction and shared values; and the more similar people are in the cultural values they hold, the more likely they are to interact with one another.

Ethnic groups have an existing cultural system on which to draw. This means we can attempt to define the boundaries of the Japanese American community by the closeness of the individual to the culture of the mother country. We examine cultural continuity between generations in terms of the retention of Japanese norms and values, especially in the Nisei generation. Our primary theoretical interest, however, is social structure, an approach that leads us to emphasize patterns of interaction in characterizing the Japanese American community. We start with an examination of culture and values, and from there move to a consideration of interaction patterns. Finally, the effect of interaction on values will be analyzed to see if values help to determine interaction.

The rich heritage of contemporary Japanese American communities had its start with the Issei community. A landmark discussion of the first-generation Japanese American community is provided by Shotaro Frank Miyamoto in his study of the solidarity of the Issei community in Seattle, a community that has parallels with other prewar Japanese American communities.[7] He discusses the unique culture the immigrants brought from Japan, which served as the foundation for the formation of the Issei community. The Japanese immigrants, Miyamoto observes, adjusted to American life by forming communities that included organizations to satisfy virtually every social need, so as to produce strong internal solidarity. Thus, it is essential to study their community in order to understand their method of adapting to the United States.[8]

The first-generation Japanese Americans, like all immigrants, formed their community by viewing America through lenses derived from their homeland. Miyamoto describes the traditional Japanese cultural heritage and emphasizes the ethical system that determines behavior in social relationships.[9] The primary emphasis in the Japanese ethical system is upon the notion of social obligation. In Japan the family, not the individual, is the unit of society. Each person feels a sense of ethical responsibility to the family, to the community, and to the rest of the nation, which is seen as a larger family. Even when acting alone, the Japanese is less an individual than a representative of a larger group. These collective obligations are enforced by the superiority of the group, which dictates clearly defined rules and obligations to the individual. This Japanese heritage must be understood when interpreting the Issei community, for the collectivist system of Japan provided the basis for group solidarity among the Issei.[10]

With this foundation in values, norms, and institutions derived from the Issei, the Nisei developed their own conception of how the Japanese American community could and should satisfy their needs. The Nisei community retained many traditions from the Issei at the same time that they became increasingly acculturated to American ways. This meant that the Nisei broke away from some of the values and norms of the Issei community, and patterned their community more and more after the dominant white community. The barriers of communication, age, and culture between generations assisted the Nisei in establishing their own community organization, based on their own view of their needs, since Issei-made structures and organizations were not passed down to them.[11] Instead, there is, as Harry Kitano notes, a strong tendency for the Nisei to provide organizations for the younger generations—such as a junior unit of the Japanese American Citizens League—and to create resultant problems of goals, purposes, control, policy, and membership that might not arise if the Sansei were allowed to develop their own groups to meet their own needs.[12]

The sociocultural dimensions of community life do not play such a major role in the life of the Sansei. The third generation is virtually totally acculturated, has entered many institutions of mainstream America, and no longer reads or speaks Japanese.[13] Nevertheless, an interest in the Japanese American community is emerging as the young Sansei mature and take on responsibilities. It seems likely that they will want a more critical and penetrating understanding of who they are than did their forebears, who simply took their heritage for granted.[14]

In the coming discussion we examine the values, norms, and goals that make up the Japanese American community organizations. This will require an analysis of the institutions of the community that meet the needs of the people, an examination of community organization that best illustrates the action of the community, and changes in community expectations from generation to generation.

The Issei brought with them to America the conviction that the family is, in two senses, the basic institution in society. First, the individual is subordinate to the family. In the classical period of the Japanese American community, the family functioned as a unit and was considered to be more important than its individual members, who derived their positions in society from their location in their family. Second, primary-group relations—defined as relations in which a group holds a wide variety of common interests and values face-to-face communication—exist both within the family (widely drawn) and within the community. Unlike Caucasians, the Issei extended primary-group relations to what are typically American secondary-group relationships—relations in which indirectly related groups engage in impersonal contacts. The Issei viewed their community as a primary group—an extension of their kinship group—which acted as a solidifying factor in binding them together.[15] They saw their community as a set of interdependent families; and within their collectivist system, family functions are an intertwined part of community functions.

No disorganization appears in such a community because individual thought and action, as they develop within the family, are in accord with the community's set of expectations. Through their primary-group orientation toward the community, people are encouraged to have intimate social interactions and to share experiences. This tradition enabled the Issei to call upon the community to aid in bringing up and disciplining the young, and in exchanging collective sympathy in times of disruption. The family and community benefited from the success of the members and were adversely affected by their failures. Desirable behavior was strongly reinforced both within the family and by the community as a whole. The behavior of any Japanese was held to be a credit to or a stain upon all members of the Japanese American community. Therefore, family standards of social behavior were reflected in, and reinforced by, the community. The reason for the low rate of crime and delinquency among Japanese Americans is that the community cooperated to prevent it.[16]

When serious family problems arose—such as illness or delinquency—help came from the extended family, fellow *ken* (prefecture-of-origin) members, or professionals within the ethnic community. The Issei family seldom used outside professionals, and when it was necessary, preferred Japanese. Although in-group dependence is changing only slowly, the current generation is more likely, Kitano notes, to seek assistance from professionals outside the community. Family service organizations and community agencies in the larger society still have few Japanese clients. The continuation of ethnic patterns is much greater, Kitano observes, than would be expected from an ethnic group so highly acculturated to American life.[17]

Community and family life for the Issei continued in the traditional Japanese way because these early communities hampered acculturation to American traditions.

The modern Japanese American family has retained some of the traditional Japanese forms of family interaction that place the father in a position of leadership, and in which interaction is based on prescribed roles, duties, and responsibilities, rather than on personal affection.[18]

Economic institutions among the Issei were central to strengthening community structure and to tightening the bonds of the immigrants to the community. The Issei were dependent on the economic institutions of the Japanese community because work was not easily acquired in the white community. If not small farmers, the Issei were overwhelmingly associated with small business, either as owners or employees, so as to produce a shared identity of occupational interest and a single class orientation.[19] Since white bankers would not finance Issei businesses, their financial needs were met through an adaptation of a Japanese custom, the money pool.[20] By this custom, a loan was subscribed from friends who together contribute an unsecured sum of money without stipulated interest. The debt was paid at a later date with an expected money gift for each contributor.[21] The financing of individual business was, therefore, a collective obligation that further tied individuals to the ethnic community.

The Issei established businessmen's associations to facilitate good relations between the Japanese businessman and the white community; the social functions of these associations contributed to solidifying the community by encouraging good relations and friendship among members of the Japanese community.[22] The Issei felt obligated to buy from those of one's own *ken*. Among the Japanese settlers in America, the significant community ties were those created by *ken* affiliations arising from social organizations based on the prefectural origins of the immigrants.[23] These *kenjinkais*, or prefectural organizations, also played a leading role in watching over the economic welfare of the immigrants by providing for the needy. In the prewar years, the Japanese community took care of its people. Even during the depression of the 1930s, few applied for public welfare benefits.[24]

Economic relations among Japanese were based on kinship concepts that extended to all levels of society, including the ties between employee and employer. Issei employers included employees, particularly the unmarried, in their homes. Reciprocal obligations between employer and employees meant that the workers would not break with their employers even if it would be to their benefit.[25] The source of this behavior lay in the traditional conception of collective obligations.

The close tie to the Japanese American community was reinforced by the difficulties in acquiring jobs in the white community. When the older Nisei were attaining adulthood prior to World War II, the only jobs available to them were with Japanese American businesses, and often of a menial nature.[26] The Great Depression and their race made for limited opportunities. No Caucasian companies would hire Nisei, no matter how qualified they were. The Nisei who came to maturity before the war were thus forced to seek work within the ethnic community, at jobs incommensurate with their training—and not without bitterness, a bitterness that deepened, for many with the relocation.

After World War II, when the younger Nisei subgeneration entered the labor market, discriminatory practices in occupations, income, and education diminished with each year, a factor that contributed to a weakening of one major tie to the ethnic community—economic necessity. In the 1960s the proportion of Nisei who were laborers was about 5 percent. Fifteen percent of Japanese males in 1960 were designated as professional, the same proportion as in white groups. Income has also gone beyond that of other groups. A survey of employees in the California state civil service indicates that the most frequent civil service income of Oriental employees (primarily Japanese) was $7,400 a year, almost $3,000 more than that of other minority groups in the civil service.

According to the 1960 census, the Japanese were first among all nonwhite groups in education and income in California.[27]

In 1970, Kitano notes, the median value of Japanese American homes was $27,900, and almost no member of the group expressed concern over housing discrimination. Their primary worry was, as with their white neighbors, over inflationary prices and high interest rates.[28] Japanese Americans have successfully acculturated into American society despite their earlier difficulties.

These changing figures are primarily the result of better opportunities for the Nisei and their higher expectations. The increased assimilation into American society has reduced dependence of the Nisei on the Japanese American community for economic sustenance. More and more Nisei have found their source of livelihood to be dependent on the white society. Therefore, ties with the ethnic community have taken on a more voluntary and optional aspect in the area of economic activity.

THEORETICAL PERSPECTIVES

We now examine theories that help explain the structure and changing nature of the Japanese American community, and then provide some prognoses for its future.

Sociology uses several competing theoretical frameworks. No one theoretical position is the basis for most research. So, too, with us. The result is a manifold approach to explaining the Japanese American situation in the United States.

We focus on theories that deal with large social structures, such as a society or a community. Various theories help explain the changing nature of the Japanese American community as a totality.[29] A general theory of assimilation has been one of the central themes in the literature on minority groups in the United States. In discussing the idea of assimilation, we are stating a theory of majority conformity that maintains that group relationships in pluralistic societies show a tendency for minority groups to take on the culture—mores, life styles, and values—of the majority group.

Assimilation in America occurs along a number of different dimensions. The two most important measures of assimilation, as disclosed by Milton Gordon, are cultural assimilation and structural assimilation.[30] Cultural assimilation refers to the fact that all incoming minority groups must, to some extent, learn the appropriate and expected ways of acting, dress, language, and other norms of the culture. Cultural assimilation may also be seen as the process by which immigrant groups are transformed and take on different meanings in their new country. For instance, cultural assimilation is the process through which Japanese become Japanese Americans.

An analysis of structural assimilation discloses the extent to which minority groups gain entrance into the institutions of the majority group, especially on a primary-group level. Gordon asserts that acculturation to American ways is a one-directional process. He does not allow for conflict over values that might turn minority groups away from the values and life style of American society. He claims that once structural assimilation—entrance into American institutions—occurs, the process of group assimilation will move toward complete assimilation. We must be wary in our application of the assimilationist concept, for, as William M. Newman argues, large-scale structural assimilation has not completely occurred in the United States, and one cannot be as certain as Gordon is that structural assimilation will provide for greater minority-group integration in a pluralistic society.[31]

Today, in contrast with the assimilationist perspective, an emerging theory of cultural pluralism has arisen that contends that over time, ethnic groups in the United States will continue to support certain differences between them and the larger American society. A theory of cultural pluralism assumes that different ethnic groups in a pluralistic society maintain their unique identities while living in peaceful coexistence. The theory states that after some period of adjustment, different groups will adjust to one another and live side by side. The focus is upon those forces that contribute to the maintenance of distinctive group traits in any society. Studies of various minority groups have supported either the assimilation or the pluralism theory. It has, however, become increasingly evident that various ethnic groups in the United States are neither keeping nor discarding all their cultural differences with mainstream America. Theories of assimilation and pluralism both seem to be extreme descriptions of what is happening to ethnic groups in America.

Intermediate theoretical positions attempt to deal with the inadequacies of a strictly assimilationist or pluralist position. A prominent intermediate pluralist position states that minority groups first pass through an assimilation phase, in which they become Americanized while keeping their ethnic identity as a social category in which a person can be placed.[32] Its authors argue that the Americanized minority groups' existing together denotes a new form of social pluralism. This new form of pluralism, however, is the start of further assimilation through the established institutions. The proponents of this approach, Nathan Glazer and Daniel Patrick Moynihan, do not outline any end to this process. But they do assert that each ethnic group will, to a great extent, become (economically and socially) assimilated into American society through participation in the existing social structures. We ask: Does this position apply to all ethnic groups, especially those not of European background? It is here that their theory begins to become less useful. Not all minority groups enter into, interact in, or remain within the existing structures in American society. Thus, the Glazer-Moynihan position does not take into account minority groups that turn away from an American value system and reclaim their cultural system, asserting its divergencies from the majority society. Moreover, their theory does not take into account ethnic groups that are apt to compete socially and economically, but not within the institutions of the majority.[33]

In applying a theory of assimilation and cultural pluralism to Japanese Americans, we discover a dual process occurring. Even though our findings indicate a primary directional movement toward assimilation on the part of each generation of Japanese Americans, the community, as a formal structure and as a set of informal associations, continues to exist. The continuance of the Japanese American community, although it has an increasingly peripheral role in the life of its members, is an ongoing statement of cultural pluralism. We see an incomplete assimilation with a modified cultural pluralism. The assimilating power of American society and culture has made the Japanese immigrant and his or her descendants somewhat different from the people they had been, but still a people identifiably distinct from Anglo-American society. Differences within the majority community remain distinct but also assume a new social meaning. Membership in the Japanese American community today is not so much a marginal existence removed from the larger society as it was in the past. In particular, we emphasize that pluralism has prevailed in different ways from the original conception of community brought from Japan, and that total assimilation into the Anglo traditions, especially for non-Caucasians like the Japanese, has taken its own course.

A stress on the tendency toward assimilation and the continuance of a modified cultural pluralism implies certain assumptions regarding the nature of society. Assimilation and amalgamation require that majority groups allow and indeed encourage minority groups to assimilate or to amalgamate, and that minority groups (either voluntarily or involuntarily) attempt to assimilate or to amalgamate. Although both of these conditions may prevail in some situations, this is rarely the case. Moreover, for amalgamation to occur, majority groups must relinquish their position of dominance in society. A cultural-pluralist perspective implies that various groups will live in peaceful coexistence. This can occur to some degree; but since the existence of dominant and subordinate groups is a universal phenomenon in human affairs, conflicts invariably occur over political interest and its corollary, power.

Our data indicate that most Japanese Americans want both cultural and structural assimilation into the larger American society, where different ethnic groups will combine at most levels. The Japanese Americans also desire some degree of modified pluralism in which they will maintain some of their differences while remaining in harmony with the larger society and other minority groups.

This interpretation suggests that after some period of adjustment, group relationships in society will tend toward a consensus on social values, an interest in stability, and a gradual integration of social groups. The consensus approach typically involves studying the way in which social institutions function to maintain social equilibrium and the processes by which groups adapt to society. A consensus perspective does not provide an understanding of the diversity of opinion within minority groups or of the different kinds of majority-minority relationships—according to region—found in pluralistic societies.[34]

We cannot assume that all Japanese Americans move in a single direction. Group conflict, divergencies, and social change must be included in any social theory concerned with majority-minority relations. Subprocesses running counter to the consensus model are occurring in the Japanese American community. Some are seeking a return to their ethnicity. By reasserting their differences with the basic cultural system, they are departing from the values and life style of American society. An examination of conflict within the Japanese American community and with other communities in America shows that deviance and disharmony are not necessarily disruptive, but are important sources of social change. An intensification of ethnic consciousness among some Japanese Americans, especially among the third generation, is a confirmation, to some degree, of Marcus Hansen's thesis. Hansen asserted that the second-generation offspring of immigrants are anxious and insecure about their ethnicity, as well as about their identity as Americans.[35] The third generation are secure in their American cultural identity, and thus more likely to look at their ethnic past with pride and interest.

By noting the increased participation of some Japanese Americans, both by the second and third generation, in ethnic organizations, we are stressing that there is not overwhelming homogeneity and consensus among Japanese Americans as to the goals of their community. Change is normally activated by small numbers of dedicated people who are not afraid to come into conflict with a dominant value system. It may be that a renewed interest in the ethnic community is a harbinger of greater communal identity in the future. We reserve our prognoses for Chapter 9, after our data have been displayed.

NOTES

1. See, for example, Masakazu Iwata, *Planted in Good Soil: Issei Contributions to U.S. Agriculture* (forthcoming), for a study in this regard.

2. Erik H. Erikson, *Childhood and Society* (New York: W. W. Norton, 1963). See also Hilla Kuttenplan Israely, "An Exploration into Ethnic Identity: The Case of Third-Generation Japanese Americans" (Ph.D. dissertation, University of California, Los Angeles, 1975).

3. See Russell Endo, "Japanese Americans: The 'Model Minority' in Perspective," in *The Social Reality of Ethnic America*, ed. Rudolph Gomez et al. (Lexington, Mass.: D. C. Heath, 1974), p. 201.

4. Jesse Bernard, *The Sociology of Community* (Glenview, Ill.: Scott, Foresman, 1973), p. 2.

5. Robert A. Nisbet, *The Sociological Tradition* (New York: Basic Books, 1966), p. 47.

6. There are also subgenerations whose experiences have been divergent. Consider Nisei who came of age (and entered the labor market) before World War II, and those who reached maturity after the war. Each faced radically different societal conditions, especially a reduction in prejudice and discrimination for the latter.

7. Shotaro Frank Miyamoto, *Social Solidarity among the Japanese in Seattle* vol. II, no. 2, in University of Washington Publications in the Social Sciences (Seattle: University of Washington, 1939), pp. 57–130.

8. Ibid., p. 57.

9. Ibid., p. 59.

10. Ibid., p. 62; Harry H. L. Kitano, *Japanese Americans: The Evolution of a Subculture* (Englewood Cliffs, N.J.: Prentice-Hall, 1969; 2d ed., 1976).

11. A facilitating—if disruptive—factor was the unusual age difference between the Issei and their children. Issei men sent to Japan for brides only after they had established themselves. For many Nisei sons, the father was more like a grandfather. See Dasisuke Kitagawa, "The Japanese-American Community: A Profile," in Stephen W. Webster, ed., *Knowing and Understanding the Socially Disadvantaged Ethnic Minority Groups* (Scranton, Pa.: Intext Educational Publishers, 1972), p. 408.

12. Kitano, *Japanese Americans* (1976), p. 113.

13. About 12 percent of our Nisei respondents are *Kibei*, children sent to Japan to be educated. This is a practice the postwar Nisei did not follow.

14. Many Sansei are curious—and furious—about the World War II relocation. At some colleges (like UCLA), courses are offered on the subject, and they are always filled by Sansei.

15. Miyamoto, *Social Solidarity*.

16. William H. Petersen, *Japanese Americans: Oppression and Success* (New York: Random House, 1971), p. 140. There is increasing evidence, however, indicative of the class pattern's breakdown, that some young Sansei are getting out of control, by taking drugs or engaging in other acts of delinquency. Still, Sansei do not have a reputation for forming gangs, as do Chinese American youth. Sansei delinquency seems to be a milder form of rebellion, although some have fallen outside community control and into the hands of the authorities.

17. Kitano, *Japanese Americans* (1969), p. 73.

18. Ibid., pp. 65–66.

19. Miyamoto, *Social Solidarity*, p. 70.

20. This is known as the *tanomoshi* in Hawaii, northern California, and the Pacific Northwest, and as *mujin* in southern California.

21. Ivan Light, *Ethnic Enterprise in America: Business and Welfare Among Chinese, Japanese, and Blacks* (Berkeley and Los Angeles: University of California Press, 1972), pp. 27–30; Miyamoto, *Social Solidarity*, pp. 75–76.

22. Miyamoto, *Social Solidarity*, pp. 76–77; Light, *Ethnic Enterprise*, pp. 70–71.

23. Light, *Ethnic Enterprise*, p. 62.

24. Ibid., p. 63; Petersen, *Japanese Americans*, p. 131.

25. Kitano, *Japanese Americans* (1976), p. 22; Miyamoto, *Social Solidarity*, pp. 79–80; Light, *Ethnic Enterprise*, pp. 79–80.

26. This was true, so great was discrimination, even among many who held college degrees.

27. Kitano, *Japanese Americans* (1969), pp. 47–48.

28. Ibid. (1976), p. 90.

29. The foregoing theoretical discussion of race and ethnic-group interaction is indebted to William M. Newman, *American Pluralism: A Study of Minority Groups and Social Theory* (New York: Harper and Row, 1973).

30. This two-dimensional exposition of assimilation follows the position of Milton Gordon, *Assimilation in American Life: The Role of Race, Religion, and National Origins* (New York: Oxford University Press, 1964).

31. Newman, *American Pluralism*, p. 87.

32. Nathan Glazer and Daniel Patrick Moynihan, *Beyond the Melting Pot* (Cambridge: MIT Press, 1970).

33. Newman, *American Pluralism*, p. 86.

34. John Horton, "Order and Conflict Theories of Social Problems as Competing Ideologies," *American Journal of Sociology* 71 (1966): 701–13.

35. Marcus L. Hansen, *The Problem of the Third-Generation Immigrant* (Rock Island, Ill.: Augustana Historical Society, 1937). See also Hansen's "The Third Generation in America," *Commentary* 14 (November 1952): 492–503.

3

METHODS OF STUDY

This study is based upon three-generational data collected by the JARP at UCLA.[1] One of the early purposes of the JARP was to sample and to interview surviving members of the first generation on the U.S. mainland, most of whom were becoming quite elderly. An attempt was made, beginning in 1963, to list every known Issei immigrant still living in the United States, excluding Hawaii and Alaska. The lists were derived from membership lists of various Japanese American voluntary associations and churches, and totaled about 18,000 persons. Undoubtedly, these lists were incomplete, leaving out people who, for example, had never joined an organization or a church or temple. The Japanese immigrant community, however, was one of the most highly organized of immigrant groups, and the error is not nearly as great as it would be for some other immigrant nationalities.[2]

A systematic sample was selected from these lists, stratified by residence. For example, nearly half of all Issei live in Greater Los Angeles. We took the same proportion for interviews. They were interviewed in 1964-66. Less than 1 percent refused, producing a take of 1,047 Issei. The Issei were asked for a complete listing of their children, with their addresses. This gave us a list of 3,817 Nisei, all of whom we attempted to contact either by personal interview, telephone interview, or mail questionnaire. A 60 percent overall response rate was achieved, yielding a Nisei sample of 2,304.[3] The nonrespondents were nearly all recipients of the mail questionnaire. There were very few refusals to be interviewed among those approached in person, or by telephone, by trained interviewers from the National Opinion Research Center.

Of the original 1,047 Issei, 141 did not have children, or did not have children who responded to our questionnaire. Thus 906 Issei are parents of the

TABLE 3.1

Study Response Rate by Family Size of Nisei Siblings, for All Families with at Least One Nisei Respondent

Number of Nisei Responding	Number of Children Listed by Issei								Total Number
	1	2	3	4	5	6	7	8+	
1	78	67	59	37	11	11	1	3	267
2		71	80	49	26	16	9	6	257
3			56	57	40	16	8	4	181
4				34	27	23	10	6	100
5					12	21	9	10	52
6						6	9	9	24
7							1	10	11
8+								9	9
	78	138	195	177	116	93	47	57	901

people on whom the bulk of this study concentrates, the Nisei. An attempt was made to reach Issei families, rather than individuals; when the man of the family was alive and well, he was interviewed, rather than his wife. Thus, 64 percent of the Issei sample is male, including 75 widowers and seven men who were divorced or separated. (The unmarried did not have children and are therefore being disregarded for the purposes of this study.) The large majority of the women (90 percent) were widows. Twenty-nine women (9 percent) had living husbands who, for various reasons, could not be interviewed, and four were divorced or separated.

Since an attempt was made to include all the offspring of each Issei in our Nisei sample, many of the Nisei are brothers and sisters. Table 3.1 shows this degree of relatedness for those families in which there were any Nisei respondents. Each column represents a different actual family size. Thus, there were 78 Issei with only one child, 138 with two children, 195 with three, and so on. The rows represent the number of Nisei who actually responded to the interview or the questionnaire. Consider two-child Issei families, for example: For such families, we have 67 cases in which only one of the siblings responded, and 71 cases in which both did (meaning that there are 142 Nisei who share a single brother or sister in the sample). For three-child Issei families, of which there are 195 in our Nisei sample, in 59 cases, one out of the three responded, in 80 cases, two of the three did (meaning 160 Nisei); and in 56 cases, all three answered (making 168 Nisei). Adding these up, we find that 387 Nisei in our sample belong to three-child families.

The most important description of the interrelatedness of the sample (as opposed to the population from which it is drawn) appears in the last column of Table 3.1. Here, we find that 267 persons in the Nisei sample are not related to each other. There are 257 families with two sibling respondents, or 514 Nisei who have a single sibling in the sample. There are 181 three-sibling families, or 543 Nisei with two other siblings in the sample. Finally, there are nine families with at least eight siblings in the sample, or at least 72 Nisei with eight or more brothers and sisters in our sample.

It will be noted that five families are missing from this table. Despite correction efforts, there are still a few errors in the data, and this represents one of them. In these five cases, we have one more Nisei respondent than the Issei parent claimed was in his or her family. The number of Nisei thereby omitted from the table is 19.

In contacting the Nisei, special emphasis was placed on reaching the eldest son of the family, on the assumption that he would be the one primarily marked for a move up the socioeconomic ladder. (This presumption is not borne out by the data.) The first part of the Nisei phase of the study was conducted by face-to-face or (in a minority of cases) telephone interviews, and 95 percent of eldest sons were reached by these means. Most younger sons and daughters were reached with a mail questionnaire. This emphasis on the eldest sons has affected the age-sex distribution in the sample, since there was obviously a higher response rate for those contacted more directly. Thus, 52 percent of the Nisei sample is male, and there is a slightly higher proportion of older males than females (46 percent as compared with 42 percent born before 1925).

As with the Issei, the Nisei were asked to provide us with lists of their offspring. Although they were requested to list all their living children, only Sansei 18 or older were eligible for the third part of the study. Thus, the sets of siblings are not usually complete families. This procedure gave us a list of 1,063 adult Sansei, of whom 802, or 76 percent, responded to a mail questionnaire.

The Sansei, like the Nisei, are related to each other, this time not only as siblings sharing common parents, but also as cousins sharing common grandparents. The families of siblings are shown in Table 3.2. At the risk of being repetitive, let us go over the interpretation of this table, which has the same structure as Table 3.1. The columns represent the size of the family listed by the Nisei. Thus, seven Nisei listed seven children over 17 years of age, 14 listed six, 30 listed five, and so on. Within this potential pool of respondents, the rows show how many actually answered the questionnaire. Of the families with seven siblings, for example, in one case, only one Sansei responded; in two families, two answered; in one family, three answered; and in three cases, four responded. This means that 20 of our Sansei respondents belong to families with seven siblings over 17 years of age.

As in Table 3.1, the summation column shows the interrelatedness of sample members. Thus, 262 Sansei do not have a brother or sister in the sample (even though only 41 do not have a sibling, in reality, who might have been

TABLE 3.2

Study Response Rate by Family Size of Sansei Siblings, for All Families with at Least One Sansei Respondent

Number of Sansei Responding	Number of Children Listed by Nisei							Total Number
	1	2	3	4	5	6	7	
1	41	84	81	40	10	5	1	262
2		58	53	35	7	6	2	161
3			13	16	7	3	1	40
4				10	4	0	3	17
5					2	0	0	2
6						0	0	0
7							0	0
	41	142	147	101	30	14	7	482

included). There are, for example, 161 two-sibling families, or 322 Sansei with a sibling in the sample. Error has crept in at this stage, too, and 20 Sansei are not included in this table.

As we have indicated, the Sansei in our sample not only stand a chance of having a brother or sister in the sample, but they may also have cousins in it. Table 3.3 depicts the nature of the sample in terms of this relationship. There are 348 cousin sets in the Sansei sample; i.e., there are 348 Issei who have one or more grandchildren in the sample. Of these, 143 Issei have only one grandchild who responded to our questionnaire, and these make up the limiting case of a cousin set.

The columns of Table 3.3 show the size of the cousin sets. Each column lists the number of families of Sansei who share a common grandparent. Thus, there are 94 Issei who have two grandchildren in the sample (or 94 two-person Sansei cousin sets, or 188 Sansei who have a relative in the sample who share a common grandparent). There are 43 Issei who have three grandchildren in the sample (or 43 three-person cousin sets, or 129 Sansei who have two others in the sample who have a common grandparent).

But Sansei can share a grandparent and not necessarily be cousins. They may also be siblings. The rows in Table 3.3 show the number of nuclear families in each cousin set in the sample. Consider four-person cousin sets, of which there are 33, as an illustration. For six of these sets, all four members belong to a single nuclear family; i.e., they share a grandparent, but they also share the same parents. Thus, they are not actually cousins. For 18 families, there are two nuclear families, so that there are Sansei cousins in these families. The way they are distributed is not indicated here. It could be that each of the families has two

TABLE 3.3

Size of Sansei Cousin Sets, and the Number of Nuclear Families of Which They Are Composed

Number of Nuclear Families in Cousin Set	Number of Persons in Cousin Set*								Total Number
	1	2	3	4	5	6	7	8+	
1	143	73	13	6	1	0	0	0	236
2		21	30	18	11	2	2	0	84
3			0	9	5	4	1	3	22
4				0	0	0	0	3	3
5					1	0	0	0	1
6						0	0	2	2
	143	94	43	33	18	6	3	8	348

*Although we use the overall term "cousin set," some of the members of these sets are not actually cousins but are siblings.

Sansei, or that one has three and one has a single child. In any case, the four Sansei who make up each cousin set are both siblings and cousins. Finally, nine of the four-person cousin sets include three nuclear families. This means more cousins and fewer siblings in the families.

Altogether, of the 348 three-generation families, 236, or 68 percent, have only one nuclear family represented in the third generation. In other words, only about one-third of the families contain Sansei who are really cousins. Most of these (84 families, or 75 percent of the remainder) are in two-nuclear-family cousin sets. Still, on the individual level, there are 446 Sansei who have at least one cousin in our sample.

There are a number of problems with our sample as far as representativeness of the entire Japanese American population is concerned. First, despite efforts to make the original Issei lists as complete as possible, they undoubtedly omitted some people: those who were least tied to the Japanese American community. But even had the lists been complete, the endeavor itself still would have had built-in biases. Only living Issei were sought, meaning that the sample consists only of families in which a member of the immigrant generation survived into the late 1960s. Our Nisei and Sansei samples omit the children and grandchildren of dead Issei.[4] In effect, this means that our second- and third-generation samples are likely to be the progeny of Issei who came in the later phases of the migration to America.

Accurate comparisons with the 1960 census are impossible because foreign-born and Hawaiian Japanese are included in the Japanese American figures. Separate figures are provided for Hawaii and for the foreign born, so that we cannot assess the size of the overlap. Still, indications are that our Nisei and Sansei samples are overeducated. Among the Nisei, 43 percent did not pursue an education beyond high school, and for the Sansei, the corresponding figure is 12 percent. In the 1960 census, even if we subtract the combined Hawaii and foreign-born figures (meaning that some people, those most likely to have little education, have been counted twice), 67 percent of Japanese in the United States have a high school education or less.

The fact that the sample is overeducated means that this study cannot lay out the parameters of the Japanese American population (particularly of the Nisei and Sansei generation) accurately. We do not have the correct measures. What we are able to do is to analyze processes within the community, to explore the way certain aspects of social and economic life correlate with other aspects. Without a representative sample, such analysis must always remain tentative; perhaps the relationship would shift among the least educated.

Still, the sample was the best that could be obtained under the circumstances. Any attempt to get representative Nisei lists would have been incredibly more difficult than the already arduous task of obtaining Issei lists. Nisei are less likely to belong to Japanese American organizations, and thus, even this route would have been closed. At least we have managed to reach some of the non-member children of Issei organization members. Although the sample is far from perfect, we believe it is good enough, in an imperfect world, to enable us to draw some tentative conclusions about processes among the Japanese Americans.

A final note of caution: As may easily be deduced from our names, the authors of this book are not Japanese Americans. It is not important how we chanced upon an interest in an ethnic group that is not our own, but it does have important consequences for the nature of this work. First of all, neither of us has ever lived in a Japanese American community. We do not have a clear impression of what it would be like to do so, nor have we made any attempt to obtain such first-hand knowledge. Our main source of information is the survey data collected by JARP. This book principally reports on an aspect of the JARP surveys. It does not purport to be, nor is it, a first-hand account of the Japanese experience in the United States.

Second, as non-Japanese Americans, we do not have an Asian American perspective, if such a thing exists. And again, we have not tried to acquire one. Our position has been that of the researcher reporting the data in an objective manner. This perspective may be irksome to many Japanese American readers, who may wish for a more partisan treatment, or who believe our approach reflects a partisanship of its own. This may indeed be the case, and is probably not entirely avoidable. Certainly, we have not simply presented the facts without interpretation, but our attempts to interpret have been made, to the best of our ability, with the purpose of increasing understanding, and not to pursue political ends.

NOTES

1. We wish to thank Edna M. Bonacich for the framework, analysis, and cautions contained in this chapter.

2. Rober E. Park and Herbert A. Miller, *Old World Traits Transplanted* (New York: Harper and Brothers, 1921).

3. We did interview, by phone, some 40 Nisei nonrespondents in the Los Angeles area. They do not differ from the respondents on key variables.

4. Using death lists from the two Japanese mortuaries in Los Angeles, we did locate and interview 36 children of deceased Issei. They tend to be older than other Los Angeles Nisei respondents, but no different from them in other significant respects.

4

THE IMMIGRANTS

When we interviewed our sample of surviving Issei on the U.S. mainland in the 1960s (1962–66), they were quite old. One-third had arrived on these shores before 1908, and the rest, from 1908 to 1924. Only 4 percent were under 60 years old when interviewed, while 22 percent were at least 80 (see Table 4.1). Given their later arrival, it is, of course, true that the female respondents (36 percent of the sample) tend to be younger than the male respondents. Fifty-five percent of the men were 75 or older when queried, as compared with only 23 percent of the women. At the time of the interviews, only 58 percent of the respondents were still married, and 41 percent were widowed. Only 1 percent

TABLE 4.1

Age of Issei at the Time of Interview, by Sex

	Percent of Issei in Each Group		
Age Group	All	Men	Women
Under 60	4 ⎫		
60–69	34 ⎬ 58	45	77
70–74	20 ⎭		
75–79	20 ⎫		
80–84	16 ⎬ 42	55	23
85 and older	6 ⎭		
Total number	(902)	(579)	(323)

TABLE 4.2

English-Language Proficiency of Issei as Rated by Interviewer,
by Sex

Fluency in English	Men	Women
Fluent	22%	6%
Hesitant	26	19
Broken	44	49
No English	8	26
Total number	(562)	(314)

were divorced, a rare phenomenon among the Issei.

With their advanced years, it is remarkable that the Issei would devote so much time to the interview. Four out of every ten sessions lasted eight hours or longer; 13 percent took at least 12 hours. Surely, feats of recollection were called for in the Issei interview schedule.

Virtually all the interviews with the immigrants were conducted in Japanese. The bilingual interviewer recorded responses and simultaneously translated them into English for entry on the schedule.[1] Only 16 percent of the men and women studied were classified by the interviewer as fluent in English. And the men were far more proficient in the new tongue than were the women (see Table 4.2). Twenty-two percent of the men were classified as fluent in English, but only 6 percent of the women. It is not too early to suggest that the immigrants' general inability to use English well excluded them from many kinds of contacts with the majority culture and would tend to keep them isolated in their own milieu; this was especially true of the women.

For most of the immigrants (79 percent), the trip to the U.S. mainland had been a direct one. Still, 14 percent paused in Hawaii and 7 percent tarried in other outlying places, like Mexico or Canada. Among those who had interrupted the trip, seven in ten had paused for less than a year.

ROOTS IN JAPAN

Although one might have expected that the Issei came in clusters from a few areas in Japan (one man urging his friends to follow suit), Table 4.3 reveals that they stem from virtually all over Japan. Forty-seven out of 48 prefectures (*ken*) contributed members to our Issei family sample. Although so many *ken* are represented, a few did contribute significant numbers. Hiroshima, in particular, is a popular point of origin. (The question asked was: "Where in Japan did you live the longest?") Over one-fifth of the sample is from Hiroshima. Nearly one in ten is from Wakayama, and a slightly smaller proportion, from Kumamoto. The rest of the sample is dispersed. Those from these three *ken* may have

TABLE 4.3

Respondents' Home Prefectures (*Ken*)

Prefecture	Percent of Respondents	Prefecture	Percent of Respondents
Aichi	1.3	Nagano	3.1
Akita	0.2	Nagasaki	0.3
Aomori	0.1	Nara	0.6
Chiba	0.7	Niigata	0.6
Ehime	2.4	Oita	0.1
Fukui	1.0	Okayama	6.6
Fukuoka	8.4	Okinawa	1.8
Fukushima	2.8	Osaka	0.7
Gifu	0.4	Saga	0.6
Gunma	0.8	(Saitama	0.0)
Hiroshima	21.6	Shiga	1.4
Hokkaido	0.2	Shimane	0.4
Hyogo	0.6	Shizuoka	3.1
Ibaraki	0.6	Tochigi	0.1
Ishikawa	0.4	Tokushima	0.6
Iwate	0.2	Tokyo	1.2
Kagawa	0.2	Tottori	1.8
Kagoshima	2.5	Toyama	0.9
Kanagawa	1.7	Wakayama	9.8
Kochi	2.3	Yamagata	0.2
Kumamoto	8.4	Yamaguchi	4.9
Kyoto	0.6	Yamanashi	2.1
Mie	1.2	Other	0.1
Yeheme	0.1	Total number	(906)
Miagi	1.1		
Miyazaki	0.7		

influenced others, but the decision to leave the homeland seems, for the majority, to have been an individual decision.

Unfortunately, our data do not allow us to do much more than speculate as to why some came while others stayed home.[2] We do know that 71 percent of the Issei men (including the data reported by female respondents on their deceased husbands) were not eldest sons. Given inheritance laws that then favored the eldest son, it is reasonable to suppose that an adventurous younger son might have decided to seek his fortune elsewhere since he stood to gain little at home. But we have no measure of adventuresomeness, and we did not study stay-at-homes. One further fact is of interest: Seven in ten respondents report that their own educational achievements were equal to, or greater than, those of their eldest brothers who stayed in Japan. Clearly, our respondents had the itch to sojourn, and apparently they bridled against an unfavorable system of inheritance.

The fathers of both Issei men and women were, by and large, farmers—two-thirds in either case. Nearly one in five was a manager, a proprietor, or an official. Six percent of Issei fathers were professionals, and the rest occupied positions lower down the socioeconomic ladder. The majority, then, had some potential interest in property.[3]

The Issei men themselves in Japan were largely either farmers (35 percent) or students (42 percent).[4] The Issei, both men and women, were relatively well schooled for the times. Thirty-seven percent of our respondents had completed at least nine years of formal schooling. In Chapter 5 we show that level of education in Japan has had reverberating effects upon the Nisei generation.

The respondents did not flee from Japan in the dark of night. They were, in fact, encouraged to make the journey to America. To this end, seven in ten received help, incentive, or emotional support for the sojourn. Only one in five reports that there were any objections made to the journey. And six in ten report that their families financed the trip. The journeys of many of the women were, of course, financed by their future husbands, already in America.

Contacts were always maintained with relatives in Japan (only 3 percent have had no contacts). And over half have maintained contacts with friends. Since they first came to America, a majority of the Issei queried have made at least one return trip to Japan. The tie has never been broken, but their roots are now in America.

LIFE IN AMERICA

The Issei were indeed sojourners. Fully 68 percent report that they did not intend to remain permanently in the United States when they first arrived. Among these, 54 percent planned to make enough money and then return to Japan; another 36 percent planned to return in any case. Once settled here, however, they majority entertained no notion of leaving. We asked:

"Have you ever wanted to *hikiage* (return permanently) to Japan?"

Sixty-one percent replied no. Obviously, for the many, the good features of the United States outweighed the bad. Communities formed, friendships were forged—and families sprouted.

Upon arrival in America, 58 percent of the Issei interviewed found at least one (usually only one) relative here. And of those with relatives, nearly three-fourths received help from them, of one kind or another. Only 30 percent had any friends already in America before their own arrival. Few (16 percent) report that they were aided, in getting settled, by any agencies or organizations. Although some Issei did not have to get by completely on their own, once in America, the many were left to their own ingenuity. Lacking the language would have caused many hardships.

Nearly all Issei marriages were arranged in Japan while lonely Issei men waited on these shores. Ninety-nine percent of the Issei married a Japanese, and 87 percent married Issei (the rest marrying into the Nisei generation). In their first marriages (most married only once, divorce being frowned upon), the Issei spawned large families.[5] Only 9 percent had one child, and 34 percent had two or three. Thirty-two percent had four or five offspring, while one-fourth had six or more. This was a fecund group, probably typical of other peasant-stock groups who had migrated to the United States. (Below, we see that their Nisei children have been far less prolific.) The Issei place a strong emphasis on the continuity of family life. Eight in ten stress this. Obviously, the more surviving children there were in an age before major child killers were controlled, the better the chance was that the family line would continue.

The link to Japan was maintained by a small majority (57 percent), by registering at least some of the newborn at *Koseki*, the Japanese census registry. But a third later cancelled the registration.

As we have stated, most Issei (84 percent) married only once. Fifty-one percent of these first marriages were intact at the time of the interviews. Of those no longer married, 89 percent of the unions had ended by death, 10 percent by divorce, and 1 percent by separation or desertion. Of all marriages, both intact and ended, a bare 5 percent have ended in divorce.

Proportionately few Issei made any efforts to get formal schooling in the United States—only 22 percent. It was largely the men who made the effort: 31 percent of them, as compared with a bare 6 percent of the women, got some schooling.

The plurality of Issei men (by their own reports or by those of widows) took to farming as a first job in America. The bulk of the rest were in service or other labor categories (see Table 4.4). The picture is a little different for the second job held—fewer are in service or labor categories, while the managerial category becomes larger. We eventually asked about the Issei's principal occupation in America. Table 4.4 reveals that farming still predominates (45 percent), and managerial or proprietorship jobs come second (28 percent). Only 10

TABLE 4.4

First, Second, and Principal Occupations of Issei in the United States

Category	Percent of Issei Holding Jobs in Each Category		
	First Job	Second Job	Principal Job
Professional and technical	2	1	4
Farmer	42	42	45
Manager, official, and proprietor	3	12	28
Clerical and sales	5	5	2
Craftsman, foreman	1	3	4
Operative	7	8	2
Private household, service	20	15	5
Labor (excluding farm)	20	14	10
Total number	(892)	(878)	(901)

percent have principally been manual laborers. In Chapter 5 we observe what a radical change in pursuits has occurred from the Issei to the Nisei generations. The Issei got established and provided a leg up for their children—with the help of the educational system.

The Issei's best earning years were before the Great Depression and after World War II. Their worst years were during the depression (and of course during the period of evacuation and relocation). In their prime, the Issei were doing rather well (see Table 4.5). Twenty-six percent were earning at least $12,500, and 22 percent, from $7,500 to $12,499. The other half fell below the $7,500 line. At the time of our interviews, Issei income was naturally very depressed, given their age. Thirty-six percent are surviving on less than $2,000 a year. Sixty-seven percent report that they are not now financially dependent on any of their children.

The Issei believe that success in life depends on diligence, hard work, honesty, and thrift. Few rely on luck or on taking chances. They equate economic success with comfortable living and no troubles. They largely believe they have succeeded. We asked:

"Have you achieved the kind of place in life that you wanted for yourself and your Issei family?"

Eighty-two percent said yes. One mechanism whereby the Issei assured a good start for the many was the investment group wherein resources were pooled to help the needier. Only one Issei out of 906 did not belong to some such group. Fifty-seven percent had no investments to make. Of those who did, 78 percent were members of *tanomoshi ko*, which lent pooled resources and investment

TABLE 4.5

Issei Income during Best Earning Years and at Time of Interview

Income	Percent of Issei Earning Various Incomes	
	Best Years	Now
$15,000 or more	21	6
$12,500–$14,999	5	3
$10,000–$12,499	11	3
$7,500–$9,999	11	6
$5,000–$7,499	20	14
$3,000–$4,999	17	16
$2,000–$2,999	10	16
Under $2,000	5	36
Total number	(775)	(779)

funds. The rest belonged to stock groups or credit unions. The existence of these groups goes far to explain overall Issei propsperity.[6] Mutual aid was the key to survival and prosperity.

It should be noted that the Issei report that in their work, Caucasian hostility caused little difficulty. Only 15 percent cite this as the greatest difficulty encountered. In fact, the Issei tend to discount prejudice generally—which does not necessarily mean it was absent. For example, we put this question to them:

"Aside from the World War II experience, has prejudice or discrimination ever affected your work or your career?"

Only 22 percent—occasionally, younger Issei—replied to their interviewer (usually Nisei) that prejudice or discrimination has affected them.

Again, we asked:

"Before 1940 in the United States, were there any anti-Japanese activities in your locality?"

Three-fourths say there were not.

Although prejudice is generally discounted by the Issei, nearly half of them do admit that they have been inconvenienced by laws that discriminated against the Japanese. We asked:

"Since your residence in the United States, have you been inconvenienced by any laws which discriminated against the Japanese?"

TABLE 4.6

Residence of Issei in Different Eras

Major Center	Percent of Issei Residing in Each Center					
	Before 1908	1908–24	1925–31	1932–41	1946–52	1953–Present
Los Angeles–Long Beach	8	19	27	32	27	40
Seattle	11	11	9	7	5	6
San Francisco–Oakland	16	10	7	7	6	5
Fresno	5	5	4	2	4	3
Sacramento	5	5	5	5	3	3
San Jose	4	2	2	*	2	3
Portland	*	3	3	3	2	2
San Diego	*	1	2	2	*	2
Monterey	3	3	3	*	*	2
Other Pacific	26	26	24	26	16	12
Mountain	14	11	9	10	12	7
Chicago	*	*	*	*	8	5
Other midwestern and eastern	4	3	4	6	15	11
Hawaii, Alaska	3	1	1	*	*	–
Total number	(293)	(873)	(892)	(886)	(869)	(902)

Note: The evacuation-relocation period is excluded.

* Less than 0.5 percent.

Forty-six percent say they have been so inconvenienced; specifically, 40 percent say they were affected by the alien land laws, which prohibited the Japanese-born Issei (but not their American-born children) from owning land. These laws were finally repealed in California in 1956.

The evacuation from the Pacific Coast in World War II has been the major trauma experienced by Japanese Americans, Issei and Nisei alike. All told, 87 percent of the Issei respondents were evacuated.[7] Thirteen percent were spared the experience of evacuation, and some were spared relocation because they were out of the reach of the order for evacuation of Japanese Americans living within 100 miles of the Pacific littoral. Except for a small proportion of Kibei, mostly, the vast majority of Japanese Hawaiians were spared the trauma of internment. They were left alone to live their wartime lives—and, in any case, they numbered four in ten of the Hawaiian population in 1942. Interestingly, Peru decided to show her unity with the United States by transporting some 20,000 Japanese Peruvians to the internment camps in the United States. No other U.S. ally followed suit.

Two-thirds of the Issei were interned for three years or more. And 84 percent suffered property losses as a result of such drastic dislocation. Of those who did, 80 percent claim they received some compensation (but hardly complete, in most cases) after the war.

Since their arrival, the Issei have always been largely Pacific Coast dwellers. Table 4.6 traces their habitats from the early years through the mid-1960s, excluding the World War II period. When interviewed, 23 percent of the Issei lived off the Pacific Coast. The figures are lower for earlier eras, except 1946-52, when 35 percent lived in the Mountain states or further east; this was the immediate postwar period, following upon relocation. Thereafter, a return to the coast took place.

Table 4.6 shows that from 1908 on, Los Angeles has always been (except for the war) the major place of abode for the Issei; over the years, they have become ever more concentrated in Greater Los Angeles. In the 1960s, 40 percent of them lived there. There are other, smaller, Issei centers. Sizable communities have persisted in Seattle and in San Francisco-Oakland since pre-1908 days. The same is true for the Nisei: We find that theirs, too, is largely a West Coast, especially a Los Angeles, experience. The roots of Japanese American cohesion lie largely in their relative concentration in selected areas. Still, a goodly minority are dispersed.

Chicago is an exception to the West Coast story. There were always a few Issei living there, but the relocation period saw the arrival of many more. And they have tended to stay, even after the trek back to the West, to form a cohesive community together with the Nisei and Sansei generations.

The Issei have managed to retain many patterns from the old country, but they have lost others. For example, nearly three-fourths eat Western-style food nearly every day. One-fourth report that they never eat Japanese-style food. About half say that they have celebrated Hirohito's birthday while in America. In contrast, most have participated in Japanese cultural activities in the United States. We asked:

TABLE 4.7

Education in Japan, by Religion at Time of Interview

	Percent of Issei with Education	
Religion	0–8 Years	9 or More
Traditional*	70	42
Christian	28	55
None	2	3
Total number	(597)	(236)

*Largely Buddhists.

"Have you ever demonstrated in, participated in, or observed any cultural activities which the Japanese introduced in this country?"

Only 15 percent have not taken part in any such activities. Nine out of ten Issei do read or have read Japanese newspapers in the United States, and nearly as many read magazines. They are split on American publications: 44 percent read none, while 56 percent have read them. Largely, the Issei are not, then, divorced from American culture. Only 4 percent never watch television and 32 percent watch less than one hour a day. The rest, 64 percent, watch an hour or more a day.[8] All told, the Issei would seem to have a bent toward the American culture around them. Like other Americans, they are hardly immune from exposure to the mass media. And, consequently, they presumably keep abreast of the news.

The Issei largely feel themselves to be Americanized. The final question in the Issei schedule read like this:

"This is our last question, and it is one way of summing up our whole interview. It is a very important question. Some Issei are still more Japanese than others; some have become much like Americans. Below is a line. Think of the left end of the line as standing for an Issei who has become completely American in his dress, eating habits, recreation, and all other aspects of his life. Imagine the right end of the line as standing for an Issei who has not changed his way of life at all, since coming to America. Please mark a place on this line which shows where you think you belong between these two extremes. The existing marks are intended merely to help you to estimate; you do not have to mark yourself as being on any one of the points. I would like to have you think about this question carefully before you make your decision."[9]

Fully 61 percent say they believe themselves to be more American than Japanese. Twenty-four percent put themselves in the middle. Only 15 percent rank themselves toward the pole of Japanese identity.

Religious affiliation can be used as another measure of a tendency toward Westernization. Upon arrival, only 10 percent of the Issei claimed to be Christians. At the time of the interview, 35 percent did so. It is interesting to note that only 35 percent of the Issei claim "true conversion" as a reason for the change. The rest remarked about social and familial reasons.

Conversion, incidentally, is highly related to education in Japan. As Table 4.7 shows, only 28 percent of the less educated are Christians, but 55 percent of the better educated are. Japanese education is a strong factor making for acculturation.[10] We will see in Chapter 5 that parental Japanese education has had a strong impact on the achievements of the Nisei.

The Issei use English differentially. Only 21 percent speak it with their mates, while 58 percent speak it with their Nisei children at least part of the time. Only 14 percent use any English at all with Issei friends and acquaintances. But 70 percent use it with Nisei friends, and 85 percent do so, at least part of the time, with their Sansei grandchildren. In fact, over half use it most of the time with Sansei. (We will see later how few Sansei know any Japanese.) Virtually all Issei of course use English with Caucasians when they have dealings with them.

Friendship patterns tend to be strictly limited to other Issei. Half or more of the friends of 88 percent of our respondents are other Issei. In sharp contrast to the Nisei, only 5 percent of the Issei have half or more Caucasian friends.

Although in some respects acculturated, and relatively well able to navigate in American waters, socially the Issei have kept to themselves. Having few Caucasian friends, it follows that they have visited Caucasian homes, or have been visited by Caucasians, with no great frequency. Forty-eight percent have never had a visit from a Caucasian, and 56 percent have never visited one. Still, some cross-visiting has taken place. Many in either group have seen how the other lives. But, largely, Issei visits are not with Caucasians; they are with other Issei. Fifty-four percent visit, or are visited by, other Issei at least once a month.

Issei interaction also takes place in organizational settings. Our respondents are great joiners. Eight in ten belong to at least one organization, and the majority, to two or more.[11] Organizational participation is one more factor that has made for cohesive Issei communities. In the main, the Issei have presented a unified front. We put this question to them:

"Were there strong differences in the Japanese communities where you lived that caused splits in the community?"

Nearly eight in ten denied the existence of such schisms.

Although few Issei (5 percent) say they were interested in Japanese politics before coming to the United States, fully 54 percent express an interest in

American political affairs. Even so, 61 percent never discuss politics in their homes. Ninety-seven percent believe the Nisei should go into politics.

Only 61 percent of those in our sample have received U.S. citizenship; before 1952, citizenship was, of course, precluded. Of citizens eligible and registered to vote (40 percent of the respondents), nine in ten voted in either the 1960 or the 1964 presidential election, or both. In these elections the Issei split their votes evenly between the Republicans and the Democrats.

The Issei have undergone partial acculturation to the American scene, while retaining their own distinctive ways and communal patterns. They have largely not favored assimilation through marriage by the Nisei. In fact, only 10 percent of the Nisei have broken the marriage wishes of the Issei. Sansei exogamy is startlingly high, as we show below—a condition the Issei must frown upon. Choices of marital partners for the Nisei provide a good reflection of how the Issei regard various groups and value their own racial integrity. Table 4.8 provides the story: Marriages with Japanese, especially other Nisei, are approved. They are split on marriages to Caucasians or Chinese. No other group rates very much approval. Fifty-one percent cite racist reasons for disapproval; the rest cite the preservation of group integrity and the continuity of bloodlines.

TABLE 4.8

Issei Approval of Nisei Marriage to Various Groups

Group	Percent Who Approve	Total Number
Nisei	99	900
Visiting Japanese	64	857
Recent Japanese immigrants	62	863
Caucasians	43	862
Chinese in this country	40	864
Koreans in this country	31	863
Filipinos	17	863
Mexicans	15	867
Negroes	3	893

The Issei have tried to preserve their own ways, while blending with the American scene. And they have tried to encourage the Nisei to preserve the kind of community they themselves have formed. Let us now see how closely the Nisei have followed their parents' edicts, prescriptions, and proscriptions.

NOTES

1. We recognize that a source of error is that we did not have a Japanese-language interview schedule, with interviewers recording replies verbatim.

2. Many Japanese left Japan to improve their economic opportunities. Melvin S. Brooks and Ken Kunihiro, "Education in Assimilation of Japanese: A Study in the Houston Area of Texas," *Sociology and Social Research* 27 (1952): 17.

3. In a study of Japanese Americans in the Houston, Texas, area, 17 of the Issei men surveyed came from propertied or middle-class families. Ibid. Some in our sample of farmers' sons came from richer backgrounds than others. Their fathers owned *yama*, more fertile upland holdings.

4. The Issei women in the sample were asked to report on their spouses' occupations.

5. The centrality of the Issei family as an institution providing for moral as well as biological continuity is pointed out in John Modell, "The Japanese American Family: A Perspective for Future Investigations," *Pacific Historical Review* 27 (1968): 67–81.

6. Ivan Light, *Ethnic Enterprise in America: Business and Welfare Among Chinese, Japanese, and Blacks* (Berkeley and Los Angeles: University of California Press, 1972).

7. Four percent underwent internment and three percent, voluntary evacuation.

8. We are unable to tell how many of these watch Japanese-language programs where they exist.

9. The interviewer was provided with a standard Japanese translation for this one question.

10. Melvin L. DeFleur and Chang-Soo Cho, "Assimilation of Japanese-Born Women in an American City," *Social Problems* 4, no. 3 (1957): 252.

11. Virtually no Issei have belonged to largely Caucasian organizations, either before or after the war.

5

CHARACTERISTICS OF THE NISEI

In this chapter we set forth the major parameters that describe the second-generation Japanese Americans in our sample. The chapters that follow provide elaboration. Even so, the bare parameters are of interest.

Of the Nisei offspring of the Issei, we obtained data, by one device or another (personal interviews, telephone interviews, or mail questionnaires), from 2,304—52 percent were sons and 48 percent daughters. (See Appendix B, the Nisei interview schedule.) Only 11 percent of the Nisei respondents were under 30 years old at the time of the contact, and 25 percent were between 30 and 39 years old. Thus, about a third (36 percent) of the sample constitutes the younger subgeneration. Twenty-five percent fell between 40 and 44 years old, and 25 percent, between 45 and 49, while 14 percent were 50 or older.

As explained before, priority was given to eldest sons in the interviewing phase of the Nisei part of the study. Not surprisingly, they form one-quarter of the sample. Eldest daughters, given secondary favor, comprise 13 percent. Thus, over a third of the Nisei respondents are first born. Our original hypothesis, that the first-born sons would have an advantage over younger brothers in the socio-economic climb, may not be borne out by the data. But we still gain in over-sampling them, in the sense that they would be most likely to adhere to, and to attempt to enforce, community norms among the younger Nisei and among the Sansei.

As would be expected, a very high percentage of the Nisei are married (81 percent); virtually none (1 percent) are divorced, widowed, or separated; and only 17 percent are single.[1] Some of these, of course, among the younger subgeneration, will marry or will have been married by now. Howsoever, the Nisei are a very married group. We must stress the family-centered character of the Nisei, and how it relates to the persistence of communal ties. Being married means that one is more likely to be drawn into the net. It is of note that only one Nisei of every ten married a non-Japanese American. (A comparison between the outmarried and the inmarried appears later.)

The Nisei tend to be members of fairly large broods. Only 10 percent are an only child or have only one brother or sister. Forty-six percent have two to four siblings, and over a third (37 percent) are members of sets comprised of six through nine siblings. The remaining 7 percent have nine or more siblings. clearly, the Issei favored large families. And family size is one measure we have of the degree to which social control can operate in containing the attitudes and behavior of individual family members.

The Nisei tend to have smaller families than their parents. Twenty-six percent of the married Nisei had had no children by 1967, 36 percent had had one or two, and the remaining 38 percent had given birth to three or more offspring. Otherwise put, 62 percent of the Nisei had had fewer than three children by 1967, while only 10 percent of their families of origin had been as small. The full implications of relatively small Nisei family size, in regard to social control, would be felt later among the Sansei generation.

Another indicator of family size is the number of household relatives a person has in his environs (for our purposes, the city or county). In Chapter 6, we attempt to account for variations in relational scope, and we use it to account for other phenomena as well. Suffice it to report here that an overwhelming 83 percent of the second generation have at least one nonhousehold relative living in the area, and that 15 percent have as many as 15 thereabouts. Over half (54 percent) have at least one relative outside the home and living in the same neighborhood. This clustering will be partly explained when region of the country is considered simultaneously, for Japanese Americans tend to cluster on the West Coast—especially in Los Angeles. In fact, 38 percent of the Nisei live in Greater Los Angeles, 39 percent live elsewhere in the Pacific states, and only 23 percent live to the east. We have more to say on regional distribution later in this chapter.

Although the Nisei tend to abound with relatives in the cities in which they reside, do they actually visit with them? That is to say, do shared norms have the opportunity for reinforcement through interaction with family? The answer is really not obvious when you consider how many Nisei live in giant urban complexes like Los Angeles, or the San Francisco Bay Area, or Chicago. It is easy enough to eschew contact with relations in those areas. Further, consider that virtually no Nisei live in a Japanese American ghetto, which entity barely exists. Forty-two percent live in mixed neighborhoods and 58 percent live in largely Caucasian areas. In spite of their apparent residential assimilation, seven of every ten Nisei visit with courban relatives at least once a month. Over a third (35 percent) make five or more visits. Visitations are a key mechanism whereby familial and communal norms persist and become strengthened.

We consider the occupations of the Nisei men below (and relate them to region of residence). In gross terms, it can be reported here that the Nisei are doing well, especially as compared with the total population (as shown later). One-third are in the professions or semiprofessions (mostly the former). One-fifth are administrators, managers, or proprietors; and one-seventh are in clerical or sales work. Fully two-thirds, then, have white-collar jobs. Twenty-two percent have blue-collar pursuits. There remain 280 farmers, or 13 percent. This compares with 45 percent of the Issei who were either farm owners or laborers. Most Nisei born on the farm have left it for greater rewards in the city. The chief device for upward movement generally has been education. But before revealing Nisei educational accomplishments, a few more occupational facts are in order.

Sixty-two percent of the Nisei work for others.[2] Three-fourths are satisfied with their lot. They prefer to have no other pursuit. Nine of ten of the employers of the nonself-employed are not Japanese American.

The self-employed have enjoyed success. Between 1960 and 1967, the size of their businesses had tended to increase (64 percent cited this), and business earnings had gone up 72 percent. (We do not, of course, have data on their lot during the depressed 1970s.)

Whether self-employed or not, the majority of Nisei (73 percent) work where there are no other Japanese. It is not, then, at the workplace that community norms would find opportunity for reinforcement. The tendency would be in the other direction. Fifty-six percent of the employed Nisei see their co-workers not only on the job, but off the job, socially, too. The import of these findings is spelled out in Chapter 7.

Family incomes tend to be high. Forty percent earned $10,000 or less in 1966, 47 percent earned $10,000 to $19,999, and 13 percent earned $20,000 or more. As compared with 60 percent of Japanese American families who were above the $10,000 level in 1966, 47 percent of all American families had incomes as high in 1969.[3]

Education follows the same pattern. Forty-three percent of the Nisei respondents (again including the women) are high school graduates, 30 percent have had at least some college, 14 percent are college graduates, and 13 percent have carried out postgraduate work. Fully 57 percent of the Nisei queried have thus gone beyond high school. The same holds for only 20 percent of all Americans 14 years old and over.[4] As with other ethnic groups, among the Japanese, education has been the ladder to success—economic, if not necessarily social.

It should not be inferred that the Nisei have suffered social exclusion from Caucasian circles, however. A good many pursue integration with the larger society through extracommunal social relations. When we asked our respondents to tell us the ethnicity of their two closest friends, over half (54 percent) cited at least one Caucasian; fully one-fourth (24 percent) cited two Caucasians. In terms of preservation of the community, this becomes one of our most important measures. It tells of a growing tendency toward acculturation, differentially distributed. These friendship patterns are explained partly by the ethnic composition of the neighborhood, partly by the workplace.

Another indication that communal pressures have weak spots is organizational membership. Thirty-six percent of the respondents belong to no organization at all, whatever its make-up and purpose. Of those who belong to any organization, only 43 percent are members of one that is largely Japanese American in composition. Put another way, a third of the Nisei do not assemble with anyone, Japanese American or not; among the other two-thirds, well over half tend toward mingling with Caucasians in terms of voluntary association membership. Only a minority of the sample, then, is potentially subject to communal control through this avenue.

Religious affiliation provides another clue to the integrative tendencies among the Nisei. Fifty-four percent are now of a Christian confession, while only 37 percent classify themselves under Buddhism, the traditional faith. (Nine percent are nonbelievers.) Compare this with their parents: fully 60 percent of them are Buddhists. That there are so many Christians among the Nisei does not necessarily mean that they go to church and socialize with Caucasians.[5] Unfortunately, we neglected to ask the ethnic composition of the respondents' congregations. But it is fair to assume that some, if not many, do go to churches whose members are predominantly Caucasians.

Some of our findings point toward communal control and the persistence of the community. Others indicate strong trends toward acculturation and the dissolution of the community. This is the basic conundrum we set out to resolve below. It might be well to stress the still Japaneseness of the majority of the Nisei—a condition that does not hold among their children, the Sansei. Two-thirds of the Nisei read a Japanese American newspaper at least occasionally. Six of ten speak Japanese well or fluently. Forty percent read Japanese. This reflects the fact that 80 percent of the respondents attended a Japanese-language school, an institution that did not survive the war with any vigor. (Twelve percent of the Nisei sample, incidentally, are Kibei—Nisei sent to Japan by their parents for part of their education.)

It should be mentioned also that the Nisei have no strong political bent one way or the other. Fifty-three percent say they are Democrats, 37 percent are Republicans, and 10 percent are independents. About half have a high interest in politics.

We turn now to a more detailed discussion of where the Nisei live, and how this relates to their earning a living. Residence and occupation are two of our strongest controlling measures, in relation to which other findings must be viewed.

OCCUPATIONAL DISTRIBUTION

The occupational distribution of the Nisei is remarkable. One-third of the Nisei men in our sample (and a small number of single working women) are in the professions. This compares with a national proportion of all American men 16 years old and over of 14 percent.[6] In other respects, too, the Japanese Americans under study diverge occupationally from the national data. As Table 5.1

TABLE 5.1

Occupational Distributions of Nisei Men and of All U.S. Men 16 and Older in the Experienced Civilian Labor Force in 1970

Category	Percent in Each Category	
	Nisei Men	U.S. Males in Labor Force
White-collar	65	38
Professional, technical, and kindred workers	32	14
Managers and administrators (except farm)	19	10
Sales, clerical, and kindred workers	14	14
Blue-collar	35	62
Craftsmen, operatives (including transport)	12	43
Laborers (including farm), service, and private household	10	16
Farmers and farm managers	13	3
Total number	(2,190)	(49,454,750)

Source: Data on males in U.S. in labor force are from Census Bureau, *U.S. Census of Population: 1970. Detailed Characteristics*, U.S. Summary, Final Report PC(1)-D1 (Washington, D.C.: Goverment Printing Office, 1970), table 221.

shows, 33 percent of the Japanese Americans have other white-collar pursuits (19 percent are managers and administrators, and 14 percent are in clerical or sales work). Thus, a stunning total of 65 percent of the Nisei sample do non-manual work, as compared with 38 percent of all Americans. Twenty-two percent of the Nisei do manual work (as operatives, craftsmen, and unskilled and service workers), and the remaining 13 percent are engaged in farming (mostly small operations). This compares with only 3 percent of the nation who are still farmers. In gross terms, about a third of the Nisei breadwinners (35 percent) are engaged in blue-collar labor, as compared with nearly two-thirds (62 percent) of all American men.

The 263 Nisei farmers are an interesting lot, and are treated separately here. But when gross comparisons are made among professional, other white-collar, and blue-collar workers, the farmers are included with others who work with their hands. Still, their singularity must be kept in mind: They tend to be older than other Nisei; they are less likely to have outmarried; they often visit relatives; they are largely self-employed; they are among the least educated; they are among those whose best friends are Japanese; they are most likely to belong to Japanese American organizations; they are most likely to be religiously traditional (i.e., Buddhist); they are among the most likely to speak Japanese and to read it as well. They are largely concentrated on the Pacific Coast—16 percent of them live in Los Angeles County. In short, in myriad ways the farmers are set off from their peers. But these facts do not themselves set the farmers off from the other Nisei. More notably, they are much more isolated from other Japanese Americans than are the others. Fully 73 percent live in communities where there are fewer than 10,000 other Japanese (as compared, for example, with 36 percent of the professionals in such communities); likewise, 59 percent live in areas where less than 1 percent of the population is Japanese (as compared with 22 percent of the unskilled and service workers).

The farmers' Issei fathers had relatively little education in Japan, as did their wives. And their fathers attained the least education in the United States. Like their farming sons, the fathers are the most likely to be Buddhist. And these Issei are the least facile of all with English.

It can be seen that for all their small proprietorships, there is good cause for including the Nisei farmers among blue-collar workers in some of our work.

REGIONAL RESIDENCE

We have mentioned the residential location of the farmers in the Nisei sample. It is important now to note the residence of all our Nisei respondents. Like occupation, residence becomes a critical explanatory variable in the rest of our story. By now the Nisei are spread across the 48 contiguous states (see Table 5.2). But it is striking that the vast majority reside on the Pacific Coast—nearly

TABLE 5.2

Nisei by Region of Residence

Region	Percent of Nisei Residing in Each Region
New England	*
Middle Atlantic	3
East North Central	8
West North Central	3
South Atlantic	1
East South Central	*
West South Central	1
Mountain	7
Pacific	77
Total number	(2,288)

*Less than 0.5 percent.

TABLE 5.3

Nisei Region of Residence, by Era

| | Percent of Nisei in Each Region | | | |
Era	Los Angeles	Other Pacific	Other	Total Number
1932–41	29	59	12	(2,063)
1942–45	14	27	59	(1,888)
1946–52	29	37	34	(2,161)
Current	38	39	23	(2,282)

eight of every ten. Even so, Japanese Americans do live elsewhere, and they do form communities in some of these locales.

The metropolis of Japanese Americans is Los Angeles, where 38 percent of the Nisei queried presently reside. Another 39 percent are spread elsewhere about the Pacific states. And the remaining 23 percent live to the east. The proportion of Los Angelenos is higher now than it has ever been. In Table 5.3, we see that in earlier periods, before and after the war, it was lower—especially, of course, during the relocation period. Since then, there has been a steady return to Los Angeles and a growth of the Japanese American community there. As compared to the prewar period, the Nisei Pacific Coast population outside Los Angeles has declined. Not only has Los Angeles gained, but there have been gains in midwestern and eastern areas.

Throughout the book, when region of residence is taken into account simultaneously with other variables, we distinguish among the three regions cited: Los Angeles, elsewhere on the Pacific, and further east. A more exacting view of Nisei residence can, however, be given: As indicated earlier, Japanese Americans live in places where they are fewer or greater in number (less than 10,000, or 10,000 or more) and where they form a smaller or larger proportion of the population (less than 1, or 1 or more percent of the population—the cutoff point attesting to the tiny size of the minority). In Table 5.4, the residential distribution of the Nisei is shown in four types of settings: a smaller or a larger percentage of Japanese together with smaller or larger absolute numbers. We find, where both the percentage and number are small, the greatest spread in Nisei localities. Eleven percent live in urban California, 18 percent in rural California, 11 percent in urban Oregon or Washington, 3 percent in the rural Pacific, 24 percent in the Mountain states, 25 percent in the Midwest or South, and 8 percent in the East. These thinly concentrated and widely spread small aggregations of Nisei account for 28 percent of the sample. Their lot is neces-

TABLE 5.4

Proportion and Number of Japanese Americans, by Location of Nisei

Location	Proportion of Total Population Under 1 percent		Proportion of Total Population One Percent or More	
	Fewer than 10,000	10,000 or More	Fewer than 10,000	10,000 or More
Los Angeles	—	—	—	89
San Francisco	—	42	—	—
Calif. urban	11	—	75	11
Calif. rural	18	—	23	—
Seattle	—	29	—	—
Pacific urban	11	—	—	—
Other Pacific	3	—	—	—
Mountain	24	—	2	—
Chicago	—	29	—	—
Midwest and South	25	—	—	—
East	8	—	—	—
Total number	(601) (28%)	(399) (18)	(236) (11)	(963) (43)

Source: The census data in this table were assembled by Ronnie T. Tsukashima.

sarily far different from that of the Los Angeleno, for example. And community formation is necessarily more difficult.

Where the proportion is small, but the number high, we find 18 percent of the sample. They are all residents of San Francisco (42 percent), Seattle (29 percent), or Chicago (29 percent). In this type of setting, community formation is at least possible and even likely.

In the third setting, wherein 11 percent reside, we find a relatively large proportion of Japanese Americans who are but few in number. In this setting, the conditions for community formation would be adjudged good. Seventy-five percent live in urban, and 23 percent in rural, California. Two percent are Mountain-state dwellers.

Finally, 43 percent of the Nisei live where both their numbers and proportion are high. In this setting, the conditions for community formation would be excellent. Nearly nine of ten live in Los Angeles. The remaining 11 percent dwell in other California urban settings (e.g., Fresno, San Diego).

Given their numbers and locations, then, one may say that the potential for functioning and cohesive communities is good to excellent among 72 percent of the Nisei sample. And perhaps the others, for all their small numbers and proportions, have reason, too, to band together.

Neighborhood

Given their paucity in numbers, Japanese American ghettoes have not been the rule. Living in mixed neighborhoods, or even in largely Caucasian ones, has more often been the case, even in the early years. There has in fact been a steady increase in the proportion of Nisei who reside among their Caucasian countrymen (see Table 5.5). We witness a gradual decline in the proportion of Nisei who

TABLE 5.5

Ethnicity of Nisei Neighborhoods, by Era

Year	Percent of Nisei Living in Each of Three Types of Ethnic Neighborhoods			Total Number
	Japanese	Mixed	Caucasian	
1915	30	33	37	(183)
1920	22	38	39	(566)
1925	21	41	39	(1,151)
1930	19	43	38	(1,550)
1935	19	43	38	(1,801)
1940	17	45	38	(1,952)
1945	13	36	51	(1,882)
1950	9	44	47	(2,214)
1955	6	44	50	(2,243)
1960	5	43	52	(2,261)
1965	4	41	55	(2,279)

live in largely Japanese neighborhoods (from 30 percent in 1915 to a bare 4 percent in 1965), a fairly constant proportion in mixed neighborhoods (roughly four of ten), and a steady increase of those living in largely Caucasian environs (from 37 percent in 1915 to 55 percent in 1965). The Nisei have increasingly had a choice of residential areas, and they have increasingly taken the opportunity of mingling with majority-culture fellow Americans. We suspect, for one thing, that as they have risen socioeconomically, they have tended to go where the better schools and safer surroundings are. That is, they have not moved next door to Caucasians to mingle with them, but have moved, instead, to housing in areas commensurate with their living standards. The mingling would come later.

Occupation and Residence Are Related

Occupation and residence are the two overarching factors that help explain variations in our data. With some consistency, they are introduced as controls in that which follows. But the two themselves are related. In Table 5.6, it is seen that there are proportionately more professionals east of the Pacific than on the coast. We find that 44 percent of the easterners are in the professions, as compared with less than three of ten elsewhere. Another highlight is the disproportionate concentration of farmers on the Pacific outside Los Angeles. In other respects, differences are not remarkable, except for a somewhat heavier concentration of blue-collar workers in Los Angeles. Whatever, social position and location work separately and together to explain much of our data.

TABLE 5.6

Relationship between Nisei Occupation and Region of Residence

Category	Percent of Nisei in Each Category		
	Los Angeles	Other Pacific	Other
Professionals	28	28	44
Managers and proprietors	21	18	17
Clerical and sales	16	14	11
Operatives and craftsmen	13	10	14
Unskilled and service	17	8	5
Farmers	5	22	9
Total number	(818)	(856)	(516)

COMPARISON OF THE ISSEI AND NISEI

There is no better way to demonstrate the strides second-generation Japanese Americans have made than to compare them with their parents. Having sprung from relatively lowly origins, the Nisei have come far socioeconomically.[7]

As pointed out in Chapter 4, it is not that the Issei were a totally destitute and unschooled lot—far from it. About a third of the men had completed nine or more years of school in Japan, a good record for the times. But over half of their offspring have gone beyond high school. This is no mean record—even in later times, in a more advanced system. Issei encouragement could not have been lacking in regard to education.

TABLE 5.7

Comparison of Occupations of Nisei Men and Principal
Occupations of Issei Men

	Percent of Men in Each Category	
Category	Nisei	Issei
White-collar	65	35
Professional, technical, and kindred workers	32	5
Managers and administrators (except farm)	19	28
Sales, clerical, and kindred workers	14	2
Blue-collar	35	65
Craftsmen, operatives (including transport)	12	5
Laborers—service and private household[a]	10	15
Farmers and farm managers[b]	13	45
Total number	(2,190)	(902)

[a] Nisei farm laborers are in this category.
[b] The category includes Issei farm laborers.

It should be repeated that many Issei were eager, once on these shores, to improve their minds, and perhaps their prospects, through the device of formal education. About one-fourth of the men made the effort to obtain at least some schooling in the United States.

Occupationally, the Nisei have turned the tables on the Issei. Whereas only 35 percent of the Issei men have a white-collar pursuit as a principal occupation, as already reported, fully 65 percent of the Nisei follow such lines of work (see Table 5.7). Most obviously, the ranks of Japanese American farmers and farm laborers have been sharply reduced. The farmers' children have tended to go to town; and, with their educational advances, they gain white-collar jobs.

Along with the move up, the Nisei evidence other differences from the Issei. Proficient in the language and able to navigate (at least after the war) in Caucasian society, the Nisei have been exposed to tendencies toward integration with the larger society (as fully discussed in Chapter 7). A full 54 percent of them number at least one Caucasian among their two closest friends. More to the point, a large proportion of Nisei have made the partially symbolic move of embracing Christianity. When interviewed, fully two-thirds of the Issei said they clung to traditional Japanese faiths. As reported above, only 37 percent of the Nisei classify themselves as Buddhists. Again, there has been a turnabout.

The effects of Issei characteristics upon the Nisei cannot be gauged by looking at comparative statistics. In order to gauge these effects, we must present intergenerational data showing the relationship between Issei of different kinds and the characteristics of their children. To this task we now turn.

Intergenerational Relationships

To a degree, individual (and, we suspect, familial) Nisei fates were already sealed before the Issei set sail from Japan.[8] As we have observed, the Issei men (and women) who made the journey were not all of a piece. They differed in background, in talents, in reasons for sojourning—and we see below that they differed, too, in their orientation to the new land, in their willingness to become part of it, and not just a part in it. These differences among them have had discernible effects upon the outlooks, preoccupations, and accomplishments of their American-born children, the Nisei.

At the turn of the century, mass public education was spreading rapidly in Japan. Most of our sample had had at least a few years of formal schooling before departure. We have divided the men, for analytic purposes, into two groups: those who had received fewer than nine years of schooling, and those who had achieved nine or more years.[9]

Table 5.8 shows that the greater the schooling an Issei man had in Japan, the more likely it is that his children have become college educated. Among Issei with less schooling, 23 percent of the offspring (male and female alike) are at least college graduates. In comparison, 35 percent of the children of the better-schooled Issei have such a level of attainment. The difference may not seem great, but further findings reveal that the original educational disparity among

TABLE 5.8

Relationship between Issei Men's Educational Achievement in Japan and Educational Achievement of the Nisei

	Issei Education	
Nisei Educational Attainment	0-8 Years	9 or More Years
High school graduate or less	47	33
Some college	30	32
College graduate and higher	23	35
Total number	(1,474)	(715)

Note: Women respondents were asked to report on their spouses' education. Thus, virtually all male Issei are included in the table.

the Issei has persistent and consistent effects. The better schooled could plainly give their children some advantages—and present them with a perhaps broader horizon.

The children of the better-schooled Issei tend to differ from their peers in several respects. Economically, they fare better, for one thing. Sixty-five percent of the Nisei sons of better-educated Issei earned over $10,000 in 1966, compared with 57 percent of the sons of the less educated. Thirty-nine percent of the sons of the better-educated Issei find themselves in the professions, compared with 29 percent of sons of the less educated.

Greater education of fathers in Japan seems to have made for relatively more acculturative tendencies among the Nisei. Perhaps the better-educated Issei were surer of their decision to migrate, and related to their progeny the conditions under which they might best be part of the landscape. For two instances, witness that children of the better educated are more likely to have at least one close Caucasian friend, and that they are more likely to live in Caucasion neighborhoods than their less-advantaged peers.

But the most remarkable finding relates to religion. The conversion from a traditional Japanese religion to Christianity can be variously viewed: as a true act of faith and as a symbolic action designed to make the convert more like, or less different from, his majority-group neighbors. Whichever the interpretation, the offspring of Issei with more schooling and of those with less schooling in Japan have a quite contrasting display of religious confessions (see Table 5.9). Whereas only 49 percent of the latter count themselves Christian, 65 percent of the former do so.

A final item with regard to education in Japan: A third of the children of better-schooled Issei live off the Pacific Coast, compared with a fifth of the children of the less schooled. The better-educated Issei, with more tools and, certainly, courage, were more likely to set out for the heartland and less likely to cling to the Pacific littoral.

TABLE 5.9

Relationship between Education in Japan of Issei Males and Nisei Religious Affiliation

	Issei Education	
Nisei Religion	0–8 Years	9 or More Years
Traditional	42	24
Christian	49	65
None	9	11
Total number	(1,431)	(690)

TABLE 5.10

Relationship between Issei Men's Educational Achievement in the United States and Educational Achievement of the Nisei

	Issei Education in the U.S.	
Nisei Educational Achievement	None	Some
High School graduate	47	28
Some college	29	36
College graduate or higher	24	36
Total number	(1,664)	(516)

Note: In this table again, wives' reports on their husbands' education are included with the responses of men interviewed.

Fortunately, we have more direct measures of Issei proclivities or disinclinations to proceed with acculturation on the American scene, and to influence their children in a like direction. One is the pursuit of formal education in the United States, taken as a sign that the man wanted to forge ahead here quicker than did his reluctant mates. About a fourth of the Issei men (and a smaller proportion of the women) did get at least some schooling in the United States. The impact for the Nisei is obvious. As Table 5.10 reveals, 36 percent of the children of the American-schooled Issei are at least college graduates; 24 percent of the others have gone as far.

The advantage for the Nisei of Issei U.S. schooling shows up in other ways. Forty-one percent of the children of the American schooled are in the professions, compared with 29 percent of the children of the unschooled.

American schooling, while giving the Nisei a boost, also tended to move them away from Japanese culture. The offspring of the schooled are less likely to have attended a prewar Japanese-language school, are less likely to belong to Japanese American organizations, and are less likely to be able to speak more than a little Japanese.

The findings, just related, for the indicator of a tendency toward acculturation, American schooling of the Issei, hold equally well for another indicator: proficiency in English. About half the Issei men are counted as proficient, compared with only one-quarter of the Issei women. The children of the proficient men are more likely than those of the nonproficient to be in the professions, to be better educated, to have Caucasian friends, to have eschewed language school; and are less likely to speak Japanese. If the extent of Issei contacts with Caucasians is considered, we emerge with the same findings: Issei oriented toward the majority culture tended to produce sons and daughters with the same bent.

Whatever their orientation toward American society, the Issei had to make a living—and perhaps this brute requirement accounts for the culturally inward or outward pose they adopted. In making a living, they provided the basis for their children's chances perhaps as much as did the larger economic scene. We see, in Table 5.11, that higher-status Issei are more likely than lower-status ones to have professional sons and sons-in-law.[10] In general, the move has been out of the farming and laboring ranks. Previously, we showed that some two-thirds of the Nisei are in white-collar ranks, having sprung from farmers and laborers.

TABLE 5.11

Relationship between Most Recent Issei Occupation and Nisei Occupation

Nisei Category	Issei Category		
	Professional and White-Collar	Farm Owners and Managers	Blue-Collar
Professional and White-Collar	77	62	67
Farm	5	19	6
Blue-Collar	18	19	26
Total number	(173)	(908)	(735)

Note: Nisei include both sons and sons-in-law.

Now that we have mentioned sons-in-law, it might be interesting to broach the matter of marital mobility among the Nisei. Within the stratification system of the Issei, there has been a good degree of Nisei marriage contracted upward— for example, the farmer's daughter marrying the doctor's son. This is entirely reasonable given the relatively small pool of high-status Issei that existed. The son or daughter of a well-off Issei might have had to look down the class scale for a mate. We find that fewer than half of the Nisei have married at their own level and that among them upward mobility through marriage has been somewhat more frequent than downward mobility.

We do not believe that class differences have been all that important among Japanese Americans. Marital mobility has, then, presented little difficulty. But if class has been of little import, family is of extreme importance. We proceed in Chapter 6 to discuss the primacy of the Japanese American family— only to have to reconcile it later with counterfamilial, acculturative tendencies in the Nisei and Sansei generations.

NOTES

1. Japanese Americans of the second generation are less likely to be single than are their countrymen. For the U.S. population as a whole, 14 years old and over, 28.6 percent of the men are single (never married), and 22.6 percent of the women. Bureau of the Census, *United States Census of Population: 1970, Detailed Characteristics,* United States Summary, Final Report PC(1)-D1 (Washington, D.C.: Government Printing Office, 1970), table 203, pp. 1-640–41.

2. The import of this datum is spelled out in Edna M. Bonacich and John Modell, *The Economic Basis of Ethnic Solidarity: A Study of Japanese Americans* (Berkeley and Los Angeles: University of California Press, 1980).

3. *U.S. Census, 1970,* table 250, p. 1-873.

4. Ibid., table 199, p. 1-627.

5. Leonard D. Cain, Jr. "Japanese-American Protestants: Acculturation and Assimilation," *Review of Religious Research* 3, no. 3 (1962): 113–21.

6. *U.S. Census, 1970,* table 221.

7. We have already remarked about the unusual age disparity between the two generations—a disparity that has made for tensions and conflicts. See Daisuke Kitagawa, "The Japanese-American Community: A Profile," in Staten W. Webster, *Knowing and Understanding the Socially Disadvantaged Ethnic Minority Groups* (Scranton, Pa.: Intext Educational Publishers, 1972), pp. 408–11. See also Bill Hosokawa, *Nisei: The Quiet Americans* (New York: William Morrow and Co., 1969), pp. 179–89.

8. In Chapter 3 we described how the Nisei data are woven together in sibling sets of various sizes. Unfortunately, these data could not be exploited for this volume. We can thus only guess that Nisei siblings may tend to share, say, equivalent levels of socioeconomic or educational achievement. But the story, to be told later, is much more complicated. The routes of girls and boys certainly have differed. Some sons may have had advantages over others, or greater ability, or drive for achievement. Surely, we will find some downward- as well as upward-mobile Issei offspring.

9. Male education is gotten by adding male respondents' reports on themselves to female respondents' reports on their husbands.

10. Daughters were asked about their husbands' occupation.

6

NISEI IMMERSION IN THE JAPANESE AMERICAN COMMUNITY

In this chapter we examine a set of centripetal forces that tend to bond the Nisei to the core of the Japanese American community. We argue that the family, with its attendant ties, is the centerpiece for having secured Nisei attachment to Japanese cultural values and to Japanese American associations.[1] In support of our argument, we first treat social relationships. Specifically, we examine the degree of contact Nisei have with other family members, and how this affects their relation to the environing Japanese American community. Next, we explore certain values, transmitted by the family, that contribute to a sense of Japanese identity and thereby produce affinity with the Japanese American community.

An ethnic community is made up families linked together by interaction that reinforces central values and norms. The stronger the family bonds, the stronger will be the communal structure. What kind of family do the Japanese Americans typically have? Do we find the nuclear family typical of Anglo America; or are elements still preserved from the traditional extended family? The latter condition still holds for the majority of first- and second-generation Japanese Americans.

We trace the evolutionary changes the Japanese American family is presently undergoing. Questions like this are posed: Are the better-educated Nisei less likely to visit with their relatives than are their less-educated peers? Similarly, what of the impact of work upon the maintenance of community bonds within the Japanese American community? We would suspect, for example, that the higher-placed Nisei would be affiliated less with their community than would those Nisei who have not been as upwardly mobile, for many of the former have had to, or have chosen to, move away from their local communities, either socially or geographically, to pursue their careers.[2]

How do the younger Nisei differ from the older? Since the younger generally have a higher level of educational achievement, this in turn has implications for their way of life. Their education allows for greater mobility, both occupationally and residentially. Are they torn away from the ethnic community? Are community ties disrupted? Do they indicate the future of the Japanese American community in terms of its maintenance or dissolution?

We begin our study of the Nisei family by examining three areas: the structure of the Japanese American family in terms of size, number of children, and related variables; Nisei affiliations and interaction with relatives; and the impact of Nisei outmarriage—a phenomenon affecting only 10 percent of the Nisei—upon ethnic-group solidarity.[3]

THE STRUCTURE OF THE JAPANESE AMERICAN FAMILY

Based on our data, we have reasoned that the size of the family from which the Nisei respondents come would in turn be related to different sets of attitudes and behavior. For example, families the Nisei respondents spring from range from only-child families to some with 12 or more members. The modal number of children the Issei reared is five. If we add two to each sibling-set size, we have an indication of the size of the family in which the Nisei were reared, and of the concomitant impact of socialization and social control within each family. In Table 6.1, the distribution of family size is displayed.

It has been reported that Japanese Americans have one of the lowest rates of divorce of any group—fewer than 2 percent of those ever married.[4] Similarly, Table 6.2 reveals that in the present sample, only 1 percent of those ever married are divorced. Unfortunately, we did not actually ask our respondents whether or not they had ever been divorced, but simply their current marital status. Regardless of this omission, we can assume that their divorce rate is relatively low.

The reasons for high marital stability among the Nisei are many. Issei and Nisei marriages are held together by the same influences and pressures that hold white families together—peer-group pressure, shame, protection of the children. What is different for the Japanese American family is the greater degree of peer and communal pressures. The Japanese Americans share a generalized wish not to bring shame on the family—or on the community; divorce may be defined as a shameful act. Thus, social pressures and values—along with the self-consciousness of this small minority who come from a strong, extended family structure—work toward marital stability.

The Nisei have produced small families relative to the Issei. Three of four of our Nisei respondents have one or more offspring. One-quarter have two, and 38 percent have produced three or more Sansei. Fewer than one of four were childless when we interviewed them.

TABLE 6.1

Distribution of Issei Offspring

Number of Nisei Children	Percent of Families
One	2
Two	8
Three	13
Four	15
Five	17
Six	15
Seven	10
Eight	8
Nine	4
Ten	4
Eleven	1
Twelve	1
Thirteen	0
Fourteen	1
Fifteen	*
Sixteen	*
Total number	(2,284)

*Less than 0.5 percent.

There is further proof of the high value Nisei place upon familism. When we asked them about the residential proximity of their relatives, we learned that more than eight of ten live within the same city or county as one or more of their relatives live in (see Table 6.3). Of these, 30 percent live near close relatives—their parents (5 percent), siblings (5 percent), or both (20 percent). Besides the common pattern found, that Nisei tend to live near their closest relatives, we find that another third of our respondents (36 percent) live near other relatives—to wit, grandparents, aunts, uncles, and cousins. The latter figure further indicates the degree of familism among Japanese Americans. They choose to live not only among their close family members, but within easy reach of more distant relatives as well. Do the Nisei choose the company of their relatives for the sake of ethnic survival, or are there other factors that help explain this residential pattern? Later, we propose some answers to the question.

Indeed, the Nisei also tend to stay close to collateral relatives. As we noted above, 83 percent of our sample live in the same city or county as other relatives live in. Fewer than two of ten are isolated from easy access to kin. To make the point stronger, over half of the Nisei sample live within the same community as at least five of their relatives.

TABLE 6.2

Marital Status of the Nisei Sample

Status	Percent of Nisei
Single	16
Married	81
Divorced	1
Separated	*
Widowed	1
Total number	(2,302)

*Less than 0.5 percent.

When we asked the Nisei about their neighbors, we learned (see Table 6.3) that a majority of the Nisei (53 percent) live in the immediate neighborhood of one or more of their relatives. True, the bulk of these are parents (11 percent) siblings (5 percent), or both (16 percent). Still, 8 percent live solely among other relatives, and 15 percent live among a combination of parents, siblings, and other relatives.

We find another proximity indicator of the level of Japanese American familism: that nearly one of four of the Nisei have a non-nuclear-family member living within their household. As we would expect, the bulk of these are the Nisei's aging parents, the Issei. Four percent represent relatives other than the Nisei's parents. The non-nuclear-family relatives are distributed as follows: 10 percent have one relative in the household and 14 percent have two or more.

Why, then, do many Nisei tend to live near relatives? Surely, it is not because they are compelled to by restrictive covenants. An important reason is their desire to conceive of their nighborhood and community as a home. There is, amongst Japanese Americans, the tendency to convert into primary-group relations (intimate, face-to-face relations) those dealings that, for Caucasians, would be classified as secondary-group relations (formal and impersonal contacts).[5] The Nisei have retained, to a degree, the Japanese value of extending primary-group relations into their neighborhoods and community.

VISITING PATTERNS

We find that Nisei who make frequent visits to relatives see their neighborhood as a real home. In Table 6.4, we find that 77 percent of the Nisei who make ten or more monthly visits to relatives consider their neighborhood as a real home, in contrast to 43 percent who make no visits to relatives. Nisei who make the most frequent visits to relatives are also the most immersed in their immediate community. Visiting enhances a cultural commitment to values and

TABLE 6.3

Nisei Ethnic-Community Affiliation

Affiliation with Community	Percent of Respondents
Number of relatives residing in same city or county as respondent	
0	17
1–4	32
5–14	35
15+	15
N	(2,259)
Number of relatives residing in respondent's neighborhood	
0	46
1–2	23
3–6	20
7+	10
N	(2,195)
Number of relatives residing in respondent's household	
0	76
1	10
2	7
3+	7
N	(1,173)

Note: Relatives referred to are non-nuclear-family members.

TABLE 6.4

Monthly Visits with Relatives, by Whether Neighborhood Is Seen as a Real Home or Just a Place

Reaction to Neighborhood	Visits with Relatives				
	None	1 or 2	3 or 4	5 to 9	10 or More
Really home	43	54	69	75	77
Just a place	57	46	31	25	23
Total number	(174)	(413)	(478)	(488)	(461)

TABLE 6.5

Visits with Relatives, by Nisei Age

Age	Percent Who Pay Many Visits
Under 30	33
Total number	(194)
30–39	38
Total number	(435)
40–49	34
Total number	(943)
50 and older	38
Total number	(265)

TABLE 6.6

Visits with Relatives, by Nisei Education

Education	Percent Who Pay Many Visits
High school graduate or less	37
Total number	(774)
Some college	41
Total number	(572)
College graduate	27
Total number	(244)
Postgraduate	25
Total number	(249)

artifacts Japanese—and this occurs no matter what the ethnic makeup of the neighborhood.[6] Exchanges of visits would serve to reinforce both ethnic bonds and familial ties.

Let us explore further. If we find the younger Nisei are the less likely to associate with kin, two possible inferences can be drawn. First, the younger definitely are moving away from the ethnic community, owing to the inevitable consequences of the economic climb, including movement (social and geographic) away from less successful peers that typically goes hand in hand with absorption into the larger society. Alternatively, the young, however successful, have not yet pulled away from their community. As they mature, it could be expected that the better educated among them would gradually develop extra-communal ties drawing them out of the familial net.[7] (Age and education aside, it should be noted that sex makes absolutely no difference in visiting patterns: Nisei men and women visit at the same rate.)

The data reveal, first, that age and education are indeed highly related. The younger the respondent, the more likely he or she is to have attained a higher level of education. Whereas 36 percent of the Nisei under 30 years old have at least graduated from college, the same holds for but one-fifth of the men and women 50 years old or older. Secondly, and surprisingly, age is not related to our measure of family and community solidarity—visiting relatives. The youngest are just as likely to pay visits as the oldest (see Table 6.5). Education, however, does make a difference: The better educated visit less than the less educated (see Table 6.6).

TABLE 6.7

Visits with Relatives, by Age and Education

Age	Percent Who Pay Many Visits			
	High School Graduates or Less	Some College	College Graduates	Post-graduates
Under 30	31	37	20	37
Total number	(26)	(97)	(40)	(30)
30–39	36	46	32	32
Total number	(137)	(147)	(82)	(68)
40–49	37	40	24	19
Total number	(455)	(267)	(95)	(125)
50 and older	41	40	30	24
Total number	(155)	(58)	(27)	(25)

In Table 6.7, we look at the joint relationship between age and education and visiting patterns. Looking across columns, we find that generally, the younger (under 40 years old) visit at about the same rate regardless of education. Among the older, however, the rate of visiting with relatives falls off sharply among the better educated. It is seen that younger, less-educated Nisei visit less than the older of the same educational level. Among postgraduates, however, the younger visit more than the older. The least likely to pay visits to relatives are the older, better-educated Nisei.

These findings would indicate, first, that high educational attainment draws Nisei away from the Japanese American community, but that it has a delayed effect. The younger educated tend still to be tied to the community; the older have apparently developed competing ties in the larger world. The eventual impact of high educational attainment must be viewed as being corrosive of bonds within the ethnic community.

Community Interaction and Affiliation

Does the opportunity for affiliation (e.g., the sheer presence of relatives in the same neighborhood, city, or county) actually result in interaction? That is, does the opportunity for communal participation translate itself into actual association with relatives and other ethnic brethren?

TABLE 6.8

Number of Monthly Visits with Relatives, by Number of Relatives in City or County, and Number of Relatives in Neighborhood

	Percent Paying Monthly Visits to Relatives			
Item	None	1–4	5+	Total Number
Number of relatives in the city or county				
None	100	0	0	(383)
1–4	19	49	31	(602)
5–14	11	45	44	(724)
15 or more	5	33	62	(326)
Number of relatives in the same neighborhood				
None	47	33	31	(951)
1–2	15	45	40	(439)
3–6	14	35	50	(383)
7 or more	4	30	66	(205)

Among Nisei who do have relatives in the same metropolitan area (city or county), fewer than a third (29 percent) choose not to pay them regular visits. At the other end of the continuum, over one-third visit, or are visited by, relatives five or more times a month. This finding underscores the fact that the mere presence of relatives in the same city or county does not automatically lead to intensive visiting patterns. In the second generation, at least, the heat of kinship ties may have begun to abate. For a minority, then, opportunity does not necessarily make for close interaction. Almost 600 Nisei in the sample score as unaffiliated with, or perhaps even estranged from, their kin and, inferentially, from their community. Are they outcasts or willing converts to another way of life? Is their action purposeful or does it irrevocably follow from functional adaptation to new ways of life? The simple opportunity for interaction does not activate everyone.

The opportunity for visiting is strongly related to the actual visiting of the Nisei relatives. Whereas almost one-fifth of our sample have no relatives living within the same city or county, the remainder live among one or more relatives. Almost one of six of the Nisei live among 15 or more of their kin.

The presence of relatives is strongly related to visits with them. The more relatives one has living within the same city or county, the more likely he is to make visits. For example, of those who have comparatively few relatives (one to four), three of ten Nisei visit five or more times a month. Of those with many relatives (15 or more), fully six of ten visit that often. Clearly, then, the Nisei do tend to seize the opportunity to maintain and strengthen their ethnic affiliation through frequent visitations with their ethnic kin, when the opportunity is there.

Table 6.8 reports the extent of visiting that occurs among the Nisei when they live in the same city or county, and when they live in the same neighborhood as their kin. Again, the data reveal that the Nisei take the opportunity to visit. Of those who live in the same neighborhood with few relatives (one or two), four of ten visit them with frequency—that is, five or more times per month. Similarly, of those who live within a neighborhood where they have seven or more relatives, almost seven of ten visit that frequently.

Interestingly, we note that the Nisei do not simply visit out of convenience, due to the sheer proximity of relatives. This is also revealed in Table 6.8. Of those Nisei who have no relatives living within the same neighborhood, a majority (54 percent) still visit relatives elsewhere in the city or county one or more times per month. And one of five visits as frequently as five or more times per month.

We may conclude that regardless of the artificial barriers of time and space as indicated by residential proximity, the Nisei appear both to perceive an obligation to, and to have a desire to, intermingle with their ethnic kin. And, as we have noted, this may have a profound and long-lasting impact upon the maintenance of a sense of communality. There are ample occasions for the many to bolster their ethnic identity even while they perforce operate in the Anglo-dominated world.

TABLE 6.9

Visiting Patterns According to Region of the United States in
Which Nisei Presently Reside

Present Residence	Percent Who Pay Many Visits to Relatives
New England	0
Total number	(13)
Mid-Atlantic	13
Total number	(48)
East North Central	24
Total number	(164)
West North Central	27
Total number	(49)
South Atlantic	9
Total number	(32)
East South Central	0
Total number	(1)
West South Central	38
Total number	(16)
Mountain	30
Total number	(139)
Pacific	39
Total number	(1,571)
Alaska	0
Total number	(2)

Visiting Patterns according to Region of the United States

The number of visits paid to relatives varies according to the density of the Japanese American population in a given region of the United States. We find that most of the visitations with relatives occur in the Pacific area. There, 39 percent of the Nisei say they make frequent visits to their relatives. In contrast, in the New England states none of our respondents make frequent visits (see Table 6.9). Hence, the size of the Japanese American population in any given area is an important determinant of immersion in the Japanese American community.

An ethnic community can only prosper when it is dense enough to make for continued reinforcement of norms. When ethnic-group members are thinly dispersed in an alien setting, these occasions plainly do not and cannot arise. When a Japanese American from California moves to the East, he or she may miss the easy familiarity experienced with ethnic peers in so ethnic a center as Los Angeles. Periodic visits home, letters, and phone calls may help maintain ethnic identity. For the native Nisei New Englander (a rare bird, in any case), the situation is different. He or she has never known, or been involved in, the community, and is likely to be ignorant of its norms and sanctions. Head them West, however, and they may undergo a striking conversion when, for the first time, they strike up acquaintances with an abundance of ethnic peers.

Types of Relatives the Nisei Visit

Whom, specifically, do the Nisei visit? Do they visit only their aging parents out of familial obligation? If so, the social meaning of their visiting—as an indicator of ethnic solidarity—is undermined. But if they visit more distant family relatives, we may reason that there is a desire to intermingle with their own kind. There would take place a reinforcement of group norms. This quality of social relationships takes on import as a socializing function of the young and, further, it serves as an agency of continuing socialization for the adult Nisei.

Our data reveal that of those who visit, about one-third visit their aging parents and their own brothers and sisters exclusively. Initially, we would characterize these as Nisei who pay calls out of a sense of obligation, as opposed to a real desire to intermingle with their kin generally. We find, however, that the remaining two-thirds of our sample visit a combination of parents, siblings, and more distant relatives. More than one of every ten Nisei exclusively visit relatives other than their parents and siblings.

Both the extent and the quality of the Nisei ethnic affiliation suggest that there is a considerable opportunity for ethnic socialization and reinforcement within the Nisei generation. Visiting doubtless has some impact upon the Sansei, too.

Spouse Ethnicity and Family Visiting

We now take up the matter of exogamy in regard to family visiting. It should be noted that only one Nisei of ten has married outside the ethnic fold. Even so, the exogamous make for an interesting story and a telling comparison with the others. As Table 6.10 reveals, outmarriage is strongly related to the propensity for maintaining family ties through visiting one's relatives. The endogamous are about twice as likely as the exogamous to visit often (five or more times a month).

One of the most telling indicators of the degree of amalgamation of one ethnic group with another is the extent of outmarriage from the immigrant to the host society.[8] Our interest is to determine the extent to which outmarriage provides a good indicator of the disruption of social ties and the severing of affiliation with the Japanese American community. The Japanese Americans have traditionally discouraged outmarriage. This has perhaps been, in part, a strategy of survival, given their small numbers. In part, low rates of exogamy have been rooted in Japanese feelings of propriety. And, perhaps more important, Japanese have placed a high value on continuing the family line.

TABLE 6.10

Number of Monthly Visits with Relatives, by Ethnicity of Spouse

| Spouse Ethnicity | Percent Paying Monthly Visits | | | |
	None	1–4	5+	N
Japanese American	25	36	39	(1,453)
Non-Japanese American	49	31	20	(163)

Although the outmarriage rate for the immigrant Issei was less than 1 percent, it increased among their Nisei children to approximately one of ten.[9] In turn, it is increasing even more rapidly among the grandchildren, the Sansei. If the rate of outmarriage should escalate rapidly, Japanese Americans, given a generation or two, could well disappear as a distinct ethnic group—unless the offspring of intermarried couples consciously choose to maintain distinctiveness and solve their identity problems in a Japanese American direction.

If we find that educational attainment is positively related to outmarriage, the community has cause for concern. Given the substantial gains in education, income, and occupational status that the Nisei and, in turn, the Sansei are making, this would lead us to predict an accelerating rate of outmarriage among younger Nisei, and especially among the Sansei and Yonsei (the generation next in line, now just appearing as babies on the mainland).

Age and Spouse Ethnicity

We find that age is inversely related to outmarriage (see Table 6.11). That is, the younger the Nisei, the more likely he or she is to marry a non-Japanese American. More than one of five of our youngest Nisei have outmarried, as opposed to one of 20 of their older-generation mates. This finding is consistent with the view that the younger Nisei tend to be less traditional, and of higher socioeconomic status, than the older Nisei. Owing to their relatively high socioeconomic status, they are more often thrust into the larger Anglo society for both career fulfillment and unpredetermined mate selection.

Sex and Spouse Ethnicity

The outmarriage rate, we reasoned, ought to be quite different for men and women. We based our thinking upon evidence that Nisei women tend to be more traditional, in terms of religion, language, and Japanese culture generally, than the men. As in other cases contingent upon this view of Nisei women, however, the findings do not support the expectation. Table 6.11 reveals essentially no relation between sex and outmarriage. Thus, we can state that regardless of

TABLE 6.11

Age, Sex, and Education, by Ethnicity of Spouse

| | Percent of Nisei, by Ethnicity of Spouse | | |
Variable	Japanese American	Non-Japanese American	N
Age			
Under 30	81	19	(85)
30–39	87	13	(364)
40–49	94	6	(867)
50 and older	95	5	(221)
Sex			
Male	89	11	(902)
Female	91	9	(862)
Education			
High school graduate or less	94	6	(797)
Some college	91	9	(511)
College graduate	87	13	(234)
Postgraduate	78	22	(221)

sex, one of ten Nisei has outmarried. Throughout, we find that Nisei men and women are remarkably alike in outlook, attitudes, and behavior.

Education and Spouse Ethnicity

We expected education to be the most reliable predictor of rate of out-marriage. Table 6.11 also reveals a moderate, positive association between these two variables. The higher the Nisei's education, the greater the likelihood that his or her marriage would have been exogamous. Whereas only one of 20 Nisei at the lowest rungs of the educational ladder outmarry, one of every five Nisei at the highest (postgraduate) educational step has chosen a non-Japanese mate. We suspect that this is partly a result of attendance at largely white college campuses for four or more years, with the concomitant internalization of new values and attitudes and the forming of new bonds, during that period of resocialization.[10]

We have seen that the highly educated Nisei, as compared with their lesser-educated peers, have lessened their ties with their ethnic communities to the greatest extent, and in some cases have cut off interaction altogether. They are much less likely to visit their relatives, choose a Japanese organization as their favorite one, or name a Japanese American as their closest friend, and are less likely to marry within their own ethnic group.

JAPANESE VALUES AND AMERICAN VALUES

This discussion is not to predict the eventual dissolution of the Japanese American community in coming generations. The community will certainly be transformed, however, in ways that are hard to predict. In spite of a lessening of ties with the Japanese American community, the Nisei have received from their parents the imprint of the traditional Japanese ethical system. In this section we examine how the Nisei have retained an orientation to the Japanese American community by way of values that they have been given by their Issei parents. These cultural variables, in conjunction with our focus on interaction, help to explain Nisei behavior. Socialization and child rearing in the Japanese American family take into account minority-group position and power, and the continuation of important elements of Japanese culture. Those values, norms, and actions most likely to endure are those of the Japanese culture that intersect with the relative power position of the Japanese in the United States. Many Japanese American behavior patterns have been tagged by the majority group in such a way that they have become stereotypes of the Japanese Americans. These include the keeping of a low profile, conformity, loyalty, persevering and careful work habits, good citizenship, high educational achievement, group orientation, and a high sense of family obligation.

The Nisei are significantly acculturated into the values of white American society, as shown by their high achievements in education, occupational attainment, and better-than-average incomes. These socioeconomic achievements push the Nisei into the white society, while at the same time providing them with an anchor in the Japanese American community—where the source of these achievements is to be found in familially derived values so compatible with American life.[11]

In establishing a measure to determine the major factor providing for a continuing Nisei adherence to the values of the Japanese American community, we look to sources that are rooted in the family. As we have observed in their visiting patterns, the Nisei tend to be strongly attached to the family. And it is from the family that Japanese Americans acquire their basic values and norms. That the family is important to the Nisei is evident in one question put to them. We asked our respondents whether they agree or disagree that "the best man is the one who puts his family above everything." Fully two-thirds agree with the statement. We posed another question that also indicates a high level of family primacy among the Nisei: whether, "when it comes to spending time, family demands come first." Nearly nine of every ten men and women queried agree that family demands take priority. The Nisei were introduced, by the immigrant family setting, into the traditional Japanese ethical system, wherein the central value is duty, a term interchangeable with social obligation or social responsibility.[12] The very foundation of the Japanese American family is the ethical system built upon collective obligations. Individual members are made to feel an impelling sense of duty in fulfilling their responsibilities to the family and to the community.

In order to determine the degree to which traditional Japanese values have been inculcated in the Nisei, we now examine Nisei attitudes toward their parents and toward their children. Have they indeed internalized Japanese values, and do they desire to pass them on to the next generation? We specify components of a measure of adherence to the values of the Japanese American community, report the distribution of Nisei along a value index, and then discuss the correlates of differential adherence.

Two Components of an Index of Adherence to Japanese American Values

In our instrument, there are two independent indicators of Nisei ties to the Japanese American community, based on adherence to familial values. Each indicator separates respondents into those who adhere more, and those who adhere less, to the values of the Japanese American community. We then establish two bivariate relations, in the belief that the two components measure the same variable: adherence to family-derived, communal values. The family values are ambition and obligation to family.

Ambition

We asked the Nisei to respond to two statements that relate to ambition: "The best man is the one who puts his family above everything"; and, "The most important qualities of a real man are determination and driving ambition." The responses were precoded into agree-disagree categories.

TABLE 6.12

Responses to Statement That the Best Man Places the Family above All, by Responses to Statement that Important Qualities of a Real Man Are Drive and Ambition

| Important Qualities of a Real Man Are Drive and Ambition | Best Man Puts Family above All | | | |
	Agree	Disagree	Total	Number
Agree	42%	11%	52%	(1,067)
Disagree	26	21	48	(975)
Total	68	32	100	
Number	(1,382)	(660)	(2,042)	

TABLE 6.13

Scores Assigned to Family Ties, Where 1 = Agreement That
Ambition Is the Mark of a Real Man, And Agreement That the
Best Man Puts Family Above All

Important Qualities of a Real Man Are Drive and Ambition	Best Man Puts Family above All	
	Agree	Disagree
Agree	1	0
Disagree	0	0

In Table 6.12, we cross-tabulate responses regarding the most important qualities of a real man, by those regarding characteristics of the best man. Then, in Table 6.13, we show the scoring procedures used to ascertain the proportion who agree that ambition is the mark of a real man, and that the best man is the one who puts his family above all.

Table 6.12 indicates that 42 percent of the Nisei who agree that the best man is the one who puts family first also agree that the most important qualities of a real man are determination and driving ambition. In contrast, 21 percent of the Nisei who disagree that the best man is the one who puts family above all also disagree that the most important qualities of a real man are determination and driving ambition. These findings indicate that the plurality of the Nisei both put family first, and see drive and ambition as the qualities of a real man. Achievement for the Nisei includes not solely a desire for personal satisfaction, but also an effort to bring honor to the family and, derivatively, to the Japanese American community. Success also acts as a recompense for the efforts the Issei made in rearing and educating their children.[13] To insure that the relationship between these two variables—family primacy and ambition—has not occurred by accident, we introduced control variables. Our findings indicated the original paired relationship is not significantly affected by income, occupation, or education—or by sex, for that matter.

As shown in Table 6.13, the respondents are scored in a subindex based upon how they conceive of the mark of a real man and of the family-primacy measure. A point (1) is given if they agree that the mark of a real man is ambition, and if they also agree that the best man puts family above all.

Family Obligation

Another indicator of strong continuing ties with traditional Japanese values, and hence increased relatedness to the Japanese American community, is the attitude that the primary obligation of parents is the furtherance of the advancement of their children in America.

Both the family and community exert influence on the individual Nisei, and both are intertwined. Each person is seen, and sees himself or herself, as a representative of his or her family in community relations. Individual family solidarity makes for collective solidarity in the Japanese American community.[14] As indicators of this component, we asked the Nisei to respond to two statements: "The best man is the one who puts his family above everything"; and, "The most important thing for a parent to do is to help his children get further ahead in the world than he did." Respondents again could agree or disagree with either statement.

TABLE 6.14

Responses to Statement That the Best Man Puts Family above All, by Responses to Statement That the Most Important Thing for a Parent To Do Is To Help His Children Get Further Ahead in the World

| Parents Help Children Get Ahead | Best Man Puts Family Above All | | | |
	Agree	Disagree	Total	Number
Agree	48%	12%	60%	(1,234)
Disagree	20	20	40	(808)
	68	32	100	
	(1,382)	(660)	(2,042)	

Table 6.14 shows that of our Nisei respondents, 48 percent agree that the best man is the one who puts family above all and, similarly, agree that the best thing for a parent to do is to help a child get ahead. In contrast, 20 percent of the Nisei disagree that the best man is the one who puts the family above all and, likewise, disagree that the best thing for a parent to do is to help children get ahead. Thus, the plurality of Nisei who put family above all also emphasize helping their children get ahead.

Christie Kiefer, in his perceptive ethnographic study of Japanese Americans in San Francisco, notes that the Nisei do not see their way of life as an attempt to conform to white pressures or demands, but as the satisfaction of their obligations to parents, society, and children.[15] Implicit in this attitude are prescriptive values of hard work and the desire to bring credit to the Japanese American community in the eyes of white society. This orientation focuses on the family as a collective where the success of one member is seen as success for all. The worth of the person to his or her group in Japanese culture is measured,

TABLE 6.15

Intercorrelations among the Value-Index Components

	Gamma Correlation Coefficients	
Component	Ambition	Family Obligation
Ambition	1.00	.91
Family obligation	.91	1.00

to a fair extent, by what he or she contributes toward the group's goals; "self-worth and group-worth tend toward an explicit unity."[16]

Intercorrelations among Index Components

Using Gamma coefficients, we discover that the two value-index components intercorrelate with one another to a high degree. (The coefficients are reported in Table 6.15.) Indeed, obligation to family and ambition intercorrelate well at the +.91 level. This association indicates that a personal drive such as achievement motivation is, among the Nisei, also a sign of value congruence within their family and their close circle of neighbors who are ethnic mates. Evidently, the Nisei are responding to a value demand to fulfill an obligation to the family and to the ethnic community, by providing honor to them both in the personal success they achieve.[17]

The Index of Adherence to Japanese American Values

Combining the two values components, ambition and the obligation to family, we emerge with the index of adherence to Japanese American values. Scores range from 0 (low adherence) to 2 (high). In the rest of this chapter, we divide the value-adherence index into high scorers (those with scores of 1 or 2, or 54 percent of the Nisei sample) and low scorers (those with scores of 0, or 46 percent). We consider Nisei who subscribe to at least two of three components to be highly adherent to Japanese American values. As shown here, 46 percent of the Nisei sample adhere less, a reflection of their greater adherence to countervalues in the white American society that surrounds them:

Adherence	Score	Percent of Nisei
High	2	35
	1	19
Low	0	46
Total number		(2,042)

TABLE 6.16

Value-Adherence Index, by Age, Outmarriage, Neighborhood Composition, Education, and Region of Residence

Variable	Percent Who Score High (1, 2) on Adherence Index	Total Number
Age		
Under 30	47	(215)
30–39	50	(494)
40–49	54	(1,043)
50 or more	68	(283)
Outmarriage		
Spouse is Japanese American	57	(1,414)
Spouse is non-Japanese American	46	(126)
Neighborhood composition		
Mostly Japanese	69	(77)
Mixed	60	(776)
Mostly non-Japanese	50	(1,180)
Education		
High school graduate or less	68	(872)
Some College	52	(623)
College graduate	39	(275)
Postgraduate	30	(269)
Region of Residence		
Los Angeles	56	(765)
Other Pacific	57	(783)
Other	48	(483)

Correlates of Value Adherence

Table 6.16 reveals that Nisei who subscribe to Japanese American values differ from those who do not. First, the younger the respondent, the less he or she is drawn into the value nexus. Whereas only 47 percent of the Nisei under 30 score high on value adherence, 68 percent of the oldest, those 50 years old or older, do so. The older clearly adhere more to Japanese-derived values.

Table 6.16 also shows that the Nisei who have outmarried score lower than the endogamous—46 as against 57 percent. This difference is not as great as we had expected. It would seem to mean that although outmarried Nisei may have tended to achieve associational ties with the family and community, as measured by visiting patterns, they have not been so easily able to shed the values learned in the ethnic family and community.

TABLE 6.17

Scores on Value-Adherence Index, by Region of Residence and Education

Region	Percent Who Score High (1, 2) on Adherence to Japanese American Values			
	High School Graduates or Less	Some College	College Graduates	Post-graduates
Los Angeles	69	52	47	31
Total number	(328)	(258)	(90)	(87)
Other Pacific	70	55	36	35
Total number	(356)	(231)	(101)	(94)
Other	64	49	36	23
Total number	(185)	(132)	(80)	(86)

Nisei who reside, by choice or by circumstance, in Caucasian neighborhoods (58 percent of the sample) are the least likely to score high on the value measure: 50 percent of them tend to adhere to Japanese values, as compared with 69 percent of those who live in largely Japanese neighborhoods (a bare 4 percent of the sample).

Education makes the real difference. The data in Table 6.16 indicate that the better the education of the Nisei, the less likely they are to adhere to Japanese values. Only 30 percent of those who have gone beyond college score high, in contrast to fully 68 percent of those who have just completed high school (or less). Once again, we observe that educational achievement draws the Nisei away from the ethnic community—here not only from associational patterns, but also from its core values. The educated evidently adhere to the values of the larger society.

In Chapter 7, we reencounter the same pattern of relationships with education—which, along with region of residence, are our two strongest explanatory variables. The all-important fact of regional residence needs now to be considered. Los Angeles Nisei, 38 percent of our sample, and others on the Pacific Coast adhere more to Japanese values than do Nisei to the east. We find (see Table 6.17) that education explains more of the variation in value adherence than does residence. Wherever they are, the less schooled are more likely to adhere to Japanese-derived values than are the more schooled. Region does become very important, however, in interpreting the associational patterns discussed in Chapter 7.

Surprisingly, adherence to ethnic values and adherence to ethnically oriented behavior (as measured by visiting patterns) are not intercorrelated (see Table 6.18). Those who frequently visit relatives are just about as likely as those who visit less (or not at all) to score high on the value-adherence index (47 as against 44 percent).

Let us look at the data another way in Table 6.19. There, we observe that only 20 percent of our respondents score in an ethnic-communal direction on both measures: They visit relatives frequently and tend to adhere to Japanese American values. This fifth would comprise those Nisei who stand at the center of the Japanese American community. At the other extreme, 31 percent neither visit relatives with any frequency, if at all, nor subscribe to the core values we have tapped. This third would represent those Nisei who have either drawn away from, or were never part of, the community, either in terms of association or of values. Another 15 percent visit a lot but do not subscribe to communal values. These may represent men and women who are on the verge of moving away from the community, who perhaps take the dominant society as a positive reference group in which they aspire to membership. The final third do not visit, and thereby do without the reinforcement of norms that this would entail, but they do subscribe to the core values of the subculture. This third represent, we believe, the point toward which the majority of Nisei, and of Sansei, are heading: They will be integrated into the larger society (economically, socially, residentially), but will continue to retain key elements of the Japanese American subculture that serve to set them apart.

Whatever the interpretation of Table 6.19, it is clear that there is considerable variation among the Nisei in their closeness to, or distance from, the center of the Japanese American community. Some have stayed at the core, more are on the periphery; others have left the fold altogether. We now turn to forces that have led a majority of Nisei to become integrated into the American mainstream, regardless of contrary forces.

TABLE 6.18

Visiting with Relatives, by Index of Adherence to Japanese American Values

Value-Adherence Score	Monthly Visits With Relatives	
	None, Few	Some, Many
Low (0)	47%	44%
High (1, 2)	53	56
Total number	(1,190)	(652)

TABLE 6.19

Visiting with Relatives, by Index of Adherence to Japanese American Values as Indicator of Proximity to Japanese American Community

Value-Adherence Score	Monthly Visits With Relatives	
	None, Few	Some, Many
Low (0)	31%	15%
High (1, 2)	34	20
Total number		(1,842)

NOTES

1. Kitano and Kikumura argue that Japanese Americans have a distinct cultural tradition that continues to have a strong impact on family life. They note: "In combination, the impact of discrimination, persecution, and devotion to group cohesiveness has produced a family life style that remains distinctly Japanese." Hary H. L. Kitano and Akemi Kikumura, "The Japanese American Family," in Charles H. Mindel and Robert W. Habenstein, eds., *Ethnic Families in America: Patterns and Variations* (New York: Elsevier Scientific Publishing Co., 1976), pp. 41–60.

2. Kitano and Kikumura report, however, on the holding power of the ethnic community, the family, and home state (especially California) that tends to inhibit migration to "some of the larger Eastern centers in which opportunities in certain fields may be more plentiful." Ibid., p. 48.

3. On intermarriage, see ibid., pp. 50–51; and Akemi Kikumura and Harry H. L. Kitano, "Interracial Marriage: A Picture of the Japanese Americans," *Journal of Social Issues* 29, no. 2 (1973): 67–81.

4. Harry H. L. Kitano reports that the Issei have shown a divorce rate of only 1.6 percent. *Japanese Americans: The Evolution of a Subculture* (Englewood Cliffs, N.J.: Prentice-Hall, 1969), p. 156.

5. Shotaro Frank Miyamoto, *Social Solidarity Among the Japanese in Seattle*, Publications in the Social Sciences, vol. II, no. 2 (Seattle: University of Washington, 1939), pp. 57–130.

6. The majority of our respondents live in largely Caucasian neighborhoods. We cannot agree with Nakane, who notes that neighbors are more important than relatives as a point of normative reference in the American context. If neighbors *are* more important, for the bulk of the Nisei, this would have an acculturative effect. Chie Nakane, *Japanese Society* (Berkeley: McCutchan, 1970).

7. Some would say that this very success is due to characteristics of the Japanese American family; and that, further, the Japanese American has merely risen to a middleman-minority position. Harry H. L. Kitano, "Japanese Americans: A Middleman Minority?" *Pacific Historical Review* 43, no. 4 (1974): 500–19.

8. Milton M. Gordon, *Assimilation in American Life: The Role of Race, Religion, and National Origins* (New York: Oxford University Press, 1964).

9. Since the western states had laws against such marriages, e.g., California, up to November 1948, the marriages would have had to be performed in states without such laws,

or they would have had to be initiated after court decisions declared such laws unconstitutional.

10. It depends, however, on the campus context. There are sufficient Sansei at UCLA for them to shut themselves off from outgroup influences. At smaller schools, or even at larger ones where they are few in number, this is not possible.

11. William Caudill, "Japanese-American Personality and Acculturation," *Genetic Psychology Monographs* 45 (1952): 3–102; William Caudill and George DeVos, "Achievement, Culture and Personality: The Case of Japanese Americans," *American Anthropologist* 58 (1956): 1102–26.

12. Miyamoto, *Social Solidarity*, p. 60.

13. See Kenji Ima, "Japanese Americans: The Making of 'Good' People," in Anthony Gary Dworkin and Rosalind J. Dworkin, eds., *The Minority Report: An Introduction to Racial, Ethnic, and Gender Relations* (New York: Praeger, 1976), pp. 254–96; Kitano, *Japanese Americans* (1969).

14. Christie W. Kiefer, *Changing Cultures, Changing Lives: An Ethnographic Study of Three Generations of Japanese Americans* (San Francisco: Jossey-Bass Publishers, 1974).

15. Ibid., p. 77.

16. Ibid., p. 200.

17. Audrey James Schwartz, "The Culturally Advantaged: A Study of Japanese-American Pupils," in Edgar G. Epps, ed., *Race Relations: Current Perspectives* (Cambridge, Mass.: Winthrop Publishers, 1973), pp. 147–50.

7

INTEGRATION INTO AMERICAN SOCIETY

In the preceding chapter, we have discussed the degree to which, and the ways in which, the Nisei are tied to their family and immersed in the Japanese American community. As a leading indicator of behavioral immersion, we have used this item:

> "About how many times in the past month have you visited with or been visited by relatives living in (city/county)—apart from those living in the same household as you?"

It is important to note that 18 percent of the Nisei sample have no relatives nearby. They are, in effect, isolated from familial contacts and, therefore, from many kinds of communal ties. Among the majority who do have relatives nearby, only 11 percent fail to exchange at least monthly visits with them. To that extent, we may say that the Nisei, given the occasion, tend to maintain at least minimal contact with—and thus to be subject to the social control of—family and the community. It can be concluded that there are strong forces at work that serve to sustain Japanese American family life, and to maintain Japanese communities wherever there are sufficient numbers to make a community possible (in Los Angeles, certainly; in the Northeast, highly doubtful).

But what of forces that tend to pull the community apart, to separate the individual from his ethnic counterparts, and to enmesh him in the larger society? Our data show, among the Nisei, strong trends toward integration into the larger scene that run counter to the concept of a solidary community. In this chapter we discuss the components of the measure of integration; report the distribution of the Nisei along an index of integration; discuss the correlates of differential integration; and then create a typology that combines the index with immersion in Japanese American communal life. A comparative profile of four types is finally presented: the monocultural Japanese American, the American, the bicultural, and the culturally disengaged. Finally, we speculate on the implications for the continuance of a distinctly Japanese American way of life, given the amount of flight from the community. In the next chapter, the issue of flight is further considered in regard to members of the Sansei generation.

FOUR COMPONENTS OF AN INDEX OF INTEGRATION

In our instrument, there are four workable measures of Nisei bonds with non-Japanese Americans (by and large, Caucasians). These are organizational memberships, off-the-job socializing with coworkers, neighborly relations, and friendship patterns.[1] Let us lay out the components and their distributions one by one.

Organizational Memberships

We asked two questions that bear upon the issue at hand. First, we asked:

"About how many groups or organizations do you belong to? I mean groups which have a more or less regular membership and meet more or less regularly. In the count, please don't include the church you belong to; we'll come back to that later."[2]

The replies were precoded in the following fashion: none (no groups), none, one, two, three, four or five, six to nine, 10 to 24, and 25 or more. We also asked:

"(Does that group have mostly Japanese American members?) (Of these groups, how many have mostly Japanese American members?)"

In Table 7.1, we cross-tabulate the total number of organizations respondents belong to, by the number that are largely Japanese American in membership. Then, in Table 7.2, we demonstrate the scoring procedures used to determine the proportion who belong to non-Japanese American associations.

Before looking at Table 7.1, it must be noted that 37 percent of the Nisei belong to no organization, ethnic or otherwise; they exclude themselves from participation in formal associations altogether. In this respect and in that proportion, they are not unlike Americans at large.[3] The table itself shows that of the joiners, a surprising number belong not to, or not only to, Japanese American organizations, but to nonethnic groups instead, or as well. Take, for example, the men and women who belong to only one organization. Forty-two percent of them belong to a non-Japanese American group. As another example, consider

TABLE 7.1

Percentage of Organizational Members Who Belong to Japanese American Groups

	Number of Groups That Are Japanese American								
Total Number of Groups Respondents Belong to	0	1	2	3	4, 5	6–9	10–24	25+	Number of Nisei
1	42	58	—	—	—	—	—	—	(480)
2	28	44	28	—	—	—	—	—	(411)
3	28	35	21	16	—	—	—	—	(256)
4 or 5	27	34	17	11	11	—	—	—	(162)
6 to 9	22	31	16	16	5	10	—	—	(58)
10–24	26	26	21	11	5	—	11	1	(19)
25 or more*	(1)	(0)	(0)	(0)	(0)	(0)	(1)	(3)	(5)

*Too few respondents to percentage.

TABLE 7.2

Scores Assigned to Organizational Ties, Where 1 = Affiliation with a Non-Japanese Group, and 0 = No Such Ties

Total Number of Groups Respondents Belong To	Number of Groups That Are Japanese American							
	0	1	2	3	4, 5	6–9	10–24	25+
0	0	—	—	—	—	—	—	—
1	1	0	—	—	—	—	—	—
2	1	1	0	—	—	—	—	—
3	1	1	1	0	—	—	—	—
4, 5	1	1	1	1	0*	—	—	—
6–9	1	1	1	1	1	0*	—	—
10–24	1	1	1	1	1	1	0*	—
25+	1	1	1	1	1	1	1	0*

*It is possible, in regard to this figure, that a respondent could belong to a nonethnic association. We have, however, assigned them to the all-Japanese American category. Twenty-seven respondents present this confusion.

those who have joined four or five associations. Twenty-seven percent belong only to extracommunal groups, while another 62 percent belong to at least one non-Japanese organization.[4]

All told, 67 percent of the joiners belong to at least one non-Japanese American organization; 33 percent of them, only to nonethnic groups.

In Table 7.2, respondents, including the nonjoiners, are scored according to whether or not they belong to any nonethnic associations. A point (1) is awarded if they do; 0 is given if they do not. Component scores for this part of the eventual index of integration, as for the other three, can range only from 0 (Nisei belong to no nonethnic organizations) to 1 (they belong to at least one outgroup). For this component, over four of every ten Nisei (42 percent) do have ties to an organization that is not primarily Japanese American. In terms of formal organizations, then, the degree of integration into the larger society is relatively high. We find the same phenomenon for the other three components of the integration index.

Off-the-job Socializing with Coworkers

It is a fact of contemporary economic life, among Japanese Americans, that fully 71 percent of the Nisei work with no ethnic counterparts (46 percent) or hardly any (25 percent). We put this question to them:

"About what proportion of the people you/your husband see(s) regularly at work on your/his present job are Japanese Americans— nearly all, about three-quarters, about half, about a quarter, almost none, or none at all?"

Working with non-Japanese is one thing. Engaging in sociable relations with them is another. We also asked:

"Now, about the people you/your husband see(s) at work—do you/does he meet them off the job often, sometimes, or almost never?"

In Table 7.3, we cross-tabulate these two items in order to arrive at the scoring of the integration-index component shown in Table 7.4.

Table 7.3 shows, first, that the Nisei are more likely to associate with coworkers after work if the latter are Japanese American. Where there are no other Japanese Americans at work, 55 percent see colleagues off the job often or sometimes; where about three-quarters are ethnic peers, 81 percent see them after work as frequently. But, second, a large proportion of Nisei who work with non-Japanese Americans do associate with them after work. About half who work with no other Japanese Americans, or hardly any of them, do see non-ethnic coworkers after work to some extent.

TABLE 7.3

Ethnic Composition of Respondents' (or Spouses') Coworkers, by Off-the-Job Socializing

Proportion of Japanese Americans at Workplace*	Percent Who Socialize Off the Job			
	Often	Some-times	Almost Never	Number of Nisei
None	11	44	45	(552)
Almost none	12	37	51	(1,047)
About 1/4	16	47	37	(292)
About 1/2	19	53	28	(134)
About 3/4	26	55	19	(76)
Nearly all	27	51	22	(85)

*Ten respondents report that they meet no one at work.

TABLE 7.4

Scores Assigned to Off-the-Job Ties, Where 1 = Association with Non-Japanese Americans, and 0 = No Such Associations

Proportion of Japanese Americans at Workplace	Respondents Socialize Off the Job		
	Often	Some-times	Almost Never
None	1	1	0
Almost none	1	1	0
About 1/4	0	0	0
About 1/2	0	0	0
About 3/4	0	0	0
Nearly all	0	0	0

In Table 7.4, we score the work component in preparation for the integration index. Only Nisei who work exclusively or mostly with non-Japanese Americans, and who see them off the job often or sometimes, receive a point. All others get a 0. On this component, 37 percent of the Nisei score toward integration with outsiders

Neighborly Relations

Only 4 percent of the Nisei report living in predominantly Japanese American neighborhoods. Thirty-seven percent reside in mixed areas; and the rest, 59 percent, live in non-Japanese American environs. There is, thus, opportunity aplenty for the majority of Nisei to socialize with outgroup neighbors.

Apart from asking, "Would you say that this neighborhood is made up mostly of Japanese Americans, mostly non-Japanese, or is it mixed?," we also inquired:

"About how many of your neighbors, including relatives, are you on visiting terms with?"

It would have been better had we asked separately about visits with non-Japanese Americans, but we believe we can still salvage this index component in a sensible fashion.

In Table 7.5, we show the relationship between ethnicity of neighborhood and number of neighborly visits. Then, in Table 7.6, as before, we report on our scoring procedures for this integration component.

The Nisei are neighborly folk. Whatever the composition of their environs, about seven of every ten are on visiting terms with three or more neighbors. Put another way, residents in nonethnic neighborhoods exchange visits with neighbors just as much as the minority who are still in ethnic enclaves. In terms of scoring for the integration-index construction, we have only given a point to Nisei, living in mostly non-Japanese American neighborhoods, who are on visiting terms with at least three neighbors. We reasoned that those who visit with only one or two neighbors just might be making exchanges of visits with relatives also resident there. All other respondents receive a 0 score. On this third index component, 40 percent of the respondents score toward integration with nonethnic neighbors.

Ethnicity of Friends

The final component of the integration index is the ethnicity of the Nisei's two closest friends. Here, indeed, we encounter a pure volitional item. One can choose to join an organization that is nonethnic for a variety of reasons, including political ones, and willy-nilly be thrown into the company of nonethnic fellow members. One works usually where one can, and one may choose to see nonethnic coworkers off the job. With the breaking down of any existing

TABLE 7.5

Relationship between Ethnicity of Neighborhood and Neighborly Visits

Neighborhood	Number of Neighbors Nisei Are on Visiting Terms with (in percent)					Number of Nisei
	None	1-2	3-4	5-9	10+	
Mostly Japanese Americans	6%	17	23	34	20	(86)
Mixed	8%	20	25	24	23	(867)
Mostly non-Japanese American	9%	22	23	23	23	(1,328)

TABLE 7.6

Scores Assigned to Neighborly Visits, Where 1 = Association with Non-Japanese Americans, and 0 = No Such Associations

Neighborhood	Number of Neighbors Nisei Are on Visiting Terms With				
	None	1-2	3-4	5-9	10+
Japanese American	0	0	0	0	0
Mixed	0	0	0	0	0
Non-Japanese American	0	0	1	1	1

Japanese American ghettoes, attendant upon gains in education and income among the Nisei, as well as the lessening of discrimination in housing, Nisei have tended to disperse into nonethnic communities where it seems quite natural that many of them associate with their new, usually Caucasian neighbors in common pursuits or just plain socializing. But friendship is another matter: This is purely a question of free choice. We asked:

> "Now let's talk about the people who are presently closest friends outside your immediate family—I mean people whom you see most often or feel closest to. . . . Is he/she an Issei, a Nisei, a Sansei, a Caucasian, or of another background?"

We find that fully 54 percent of the Nisei respondents number at least one non-Japanese American among their closest friends. This is perhaps the strongest and most compelling of the integration-index components, and gives independent proof that a substantial proportion of the Nisei look outside Japanese American confines for the closest of nonfamilial ties. Respondents who have at least one closest friend who is a non-Japanese American receive a score of 1. The others get a 0.

Intercorrelations among Index Components

Using gamma coefficients, we discover that the four integration-index components intercorrelate with one another to an acceptable (and respectable) degree. The gammas are reported in Table 7.7.

TABLE 7.7

Intercorrelations among the Four Integration-Index Components

Component	Gamma Coefficients Shown			
	Neighborhood Ties	Work Ties	Organizational Ties	Friendships
Neighborhood ties	1.00	+.30	+.45	+.39
Work ties	X	1.00	+.33	+.37
Organizational ties	X	X	1.000	+.39
Friendships	X	X	X	1.000

The highest correlation ($\gamma = +.45$) is between organizational and neighborhood associations. Perhaps Nisei join nonethnic organizations as a result of previously established neighborly relations. Or perhaps they meet outsiders in organizations and move to their neighborhoods?

The weakest association (γ = +.30) is between work and neighborhood. But this is not surprising. Most Americans tend to segregate their occupationally related lives from their home life. Still, the correlation is there.

The Index of Integration

Combining the four components of integration into the nonethnic society —organizational affiliations, off-the-job associations with coworkers, neighborly visits, and friendship choices—we emerge with the index of integration. Scores range from 0 (low integration) to 4 (high). Here is the distribution.[5]

Integration	Score	Percent of Nisei
High	4	10
	3	20
	2	25
	1	27
Low	0	18
Total number		(1,988)

In the remainder of this chapter, we dichotomize the index into high scorers (scores of 2, 3, and 4, or 55 percent of scores) and low scorers (scores of 0 and 1, or 45 percent). This means that we consider as relatively integrated Nisei those who score toward integration on at least two of the four components. It should be noted that only 18 percent score at the 0 end of the index. These are those who are totally cut off (by our measures) from social relations with the nonethnic society. At the other extreme, one Nisei of every ten appears to be totally integrated. We now discuss some correlates of integration.

SOME CORRELATES OF INTEGRATION INTO THE LARGER AMERICAN SOCIETY

Let us start off with major independent variables that do not correlate with degree of integration into the wider society. First, there is no difference between men and women in their index scores. A little over half of either sex score relatively high. Second, with two significant exceptions, age makes no difference. Except for Nisei under 30 years old and 60 or older, over half the Nisei, of all ages, score high on integration (see Table 7.8).

How can we explain the curvilinear relationship between age and integration? To take the oldest group first (there are only 20 Nisei 60 years old or older in the sample), it can be said that they came of age before tendencies toward

TABLE 7.8

Relationship between Age of Nisei and Scores
on Index of Integration

Age	Percentage Who Score Relatively High (2-4)
Under 30	42
Total number	(202)
30–34	55
Total number	(172)
35–39	58
Total number	(302)
40–44	58
Total number	(506)
45–49	56
Total number	(500)
50–59	54
Total number	(25)
60 or older	35
Total number	(20)

associations with the nonethnic community came into sway. Accordingly, only 35 percent of them score high on the index. The youngest group, under 30 years old, present a different story. They have not yet had the chance to form the kinds of nonethnic bonds that characterize their elders. Some were still at school when interviewed. They would not yet have joined organizations, settled into jobs, or started families that would involve them with non-Japanese Americans. Thus, only 42 percent of the youngest Nisei score high on integration.

To bolster the story, it should be related that integration is related to marital status: 48 percent of the (still) single, as compared with 57 percent of the married, score high on the index. The single (largely young) have yet to establish ties outside the community, but it seems inevitable that they will.

If neither sex nor age is strikingly correlated with integration, practically every other variable of significance is. We now take up these variables: anticipatory socialization, religion, income, occupation, education, and residence.

Anticipatory Socialization

There is evidence that the Issei prepared their Nisei offspring to accept or even seek out relations with non-Japanese Americans. We asked:

"While you were growing up, would you say that your parents wanted you to take an active part with Caucasians in their activities, or to stick pretty much with Japanese Americans?"

Only 34 percent of the Nisei report that their parents wanted them to confine their social lives to ethnic peers. Six of ten whose parents wanted them to take an active part with Caucasians, or who were indifferent about it, score high on integration. Only 43 percent of the Nisei whose parents urged them to stay with their own group score high.

We also asked:

> "Do you (would you) want your own children to take an active part with Caucasians in their activities, or to stick pretty much with Japanese Americans?"

A startling 93 percent of the Nisei want their Sansei offspring to take part with Caucasians. Presumably, they encourage them to do so. Fifty-seven percent of the Nisei who want the Sansei to mingle with the outgroup score high on integration. Of the minority of Nisei who do not, only 22 percent have relatively high scores.

As we have reported already, only a small proportion of Nisei, about one of ten, have gone so far, in associating with Caucasians, as to marry them. If the parents wanted them to mix, they were also highly successful in enforcing a ban on Nisei exogamy. (Until 1948, Nisei in California legally could not marry Caucasians.) But among those who did outmarry, fully 83 percent score extremely high on the integration index. The exogamous have clearly left Japanese American confines. It remains to be seen what the far more exogamous Sansei will do.

Integration does have its price. There is evidence that the most highly integrated Nisei feel some remorse about the gradual wearing away of Japanese American communal bonds in favor of their melting into the larger pot. We put this question to them:

> "Would you say that generally the Nisei are just about right [in regard to being Americanized]?"

Three-quarters of the respondents believe the Nisei are just about right. But here are the index scores: 52 percent of the Nisei who say that their generation is just about right score high on integration; 58 percent who say their peers are not American enough score high, while 66 percent of those who believe the Nisei are too American have high scores. This latter group of 100 respondents are the most telling. Apparently, they are reporting that although they have been successful in mixing socially with Caucasians, there is cause for regret—something has been lost. There are echoes of this sentiment in the Sansei data reported in the next chapter. Their rate of outmarriage is quite high; their educational achievements are phenomenal; they tend toward Caucasian friends—and yet, while only 2 percent report fluency in Japanese, nine of ten Sansei would like to speak it better. Among Nisei and Sansei alike, there are strong anti-communal forces at work. But there are countervailing tendencies that reveal that some would not like entirely to lose their identity. Can the latter overcome the massive forces of the former—entwined as they are in Japanese American involvement in the mainstream of American educational and occupation trends?

Perhaps at least the Nisei still feel the tugs of past discrimination, and the attendant need to seek their own and to reestablish ties with their own kind. This question was put to the Nisei:

> "How much do you think that being a Japanese American has hindered your (or your husband's) advancement—not at all, only a little, somewhat, or very much?"

Fifty-seven percent report that Nisei advancement has not been hindered at all. And 17 respondents even say being Japanese American has actually helped. The rest report at least some blockage. With regard to integration, consider the extremes: 82 percent of those who say being Japanese American has helped score high on the index; only 33 percent who say it has hindered them very much score high (only 67 respondents). Those who have been hurt keep on their own. But their better-treated fellows must know of what others have suffered—and what, in an uncertain world (with memories of the war), could happen again.

Religion

We neglected to ask Nisei Christians about the ethnic composition of their congregations. But religion is highly correlated with integration, nonetheless. Fifty-four percent of the Nisei are Christians, and 62 percent of the Christians score high on integration. Thirty-seven percent maintain traditional faiths (mostly Buddhism), and only 44 percent of them score high on integration. The rest claim no religion, and 54 percent of these score toward the integrative end. But of course, religious affiliation is highly related to other major variables, especially to education and occupation; the higher either of these two, the more likely the Nisei is a Christian.

Income, Education, and Occupation

Whichever the socioeconomic measure, we find a regular relationship with integration. Table 7.9 shows that income, education, and occupation are positively and strongly related to integration scores—the higher the variable, the higher the score. Take income: 42 percent of the lowest earning group score high on the index, as compared with 65 percent of the highest earning group. The correlation with education is even more striking: 34 percent of the Nisei who have not completed high school score high, as against 82 percent of the men and women who have done at least some graduate work. Likewise with occupation: 73 percent of the professionals have high index scores, as compared with only four of ten of the unskilled; gardeners have the lowest figure, as only 33 percent of them score high. We take these findings to mean that as the Nisei have moved

TABLE 7.9

Scores on the Index of Integration, by Income, Education, and Occupation (Percent Who Score High — 2-4)

Income		Education		Occupation	
Under $7,500	42	Less than high school graduate	34	Professionals	73
Total number	(348)	Total number	(94)	Total number	(476)
$7,500–9,999	52	High school graduate	48	Semiprofessionals	62
Total number	(401)	Total number	(733)	Total number	(164)
$10,000–14,999	55	Some college	52	Proprietors	54
Total number	(665)	Total number	(601)	Total number	(365)
$15,000–19,999	64	College graduate	61	Farm owners, managers	52
Total number	(272)	Total number	(284)	Total number	(221)
$20,000–29,999	68	Postgraduate	82	Clerical and sales	44
Total number	(166)	Total number	(272)	Total number	(262)
$30,000 or more	65			Operatives	49
Total number	(88)			Total number	(242)
				Unskilled laborers	40
				Total number	(63)
				Gardeners	33
				Total number	(147)

90

up the socioeconomic ladder, they have moved out of, or have been pulled out of, the close confines of the ethnic community. Success has meant the weakening of community bonds, even for physicians and dentists, who presumably service, in part, Japanese Americans. Of the 41 in our sample, 78 percent score high on integration. They presumably neither live in the community (what remains of it geographically) nor socialize very much with their ethnic peers. Rather, they limit themselves if at all to patient contacts. In contrast, the poorly educated gardeners still cluster together residentially. Their relations with Caucasians are economic ones only. They do not mix socially with their customers.

Education and Interest in Politics

One correlate of Nisei integration into social relations with Caucasians is a heightened interest in politics. We asked:

"Generally speaking, how much interest would you say you have in politics—a great deal, a fair amount, only a little, or no interest at all?"

Only 8 percent report great interest; 48 percent report a fair amount; 39 percent, a little; and 5 percent, no interest at all. But interest in politics and integration scores are highly correlated (see Table 7.10). Seventy-one percent expressing great interest score high, as compared with only 31 percent who have no interest.

Interest in politics is, of course, highly correlated with education (see Table 7.11). Fully 74 percent who have done graduate work say they have a great or fair amount of interest; only 23 percent who have not completed high school express so much interest. But education does not account for all of the

TABLE 7.10

Scores on Index of Integration, by Interest in Politics

Interest in Politics	Percent Who Score High (2-4)
Great	71
Total number	(167)
A fair amount	60
Total number	(953)
Little	47
Total number	(767)
No interest	31
Total number	(99)

TABLE 7.11

Interest in Politics, by Education

Education	Percent Who Have a Great or Fair Amount of Interest
Less than high school graduate	23
Total number	(94)
High school graduate	50
Total number	(732)
Some college	56
Total number	(601)
College graduate	68
Total number	(284)
Postgraduate	74
Total number	(271)

variation on index scores at different levels of political interest. Some of the best educated express little interest, and some of the least educated have great interest. Is it, then, education or involvement in the political scene that accounts for high index scores. The answer appears in Table 7.12.

And the answer is that both education and political interest are related to high index scores. Reading down the columns of Table 7.12, we observe the familiar finding that integration scores rise with educational attainment, regardless of interest in politics. But reading across the rows of the table, it can be seen that at each educational level, Nisei with an interest in politics score higher on integration than those who have little or no interest.

We interpret these findings thus: Greater education draws the Nisei into the integrative net. It impels the Nisei toward deeper associations with Caucasians. But political interest, at any educational level, has the same impact. Having a concern for the larger, extraethnic scene, the interested seek out ideologically compatible associates and ignore the more insular atmosphere of the closely knit sector of the Japanese American community. Political interest, then, attests to an involvement in the nation, not the subnation. Its consequence is to draw Nisei, at any educational level, away from ethnic peers, and to turn them toward other kinds of brethren.

We have seen so far that socioeconomic variables like education, occupation, and income are highly correlated with differential integration into the informal structure of the larger, environing Caucasian society.[6] And we have observed that an indicator of more formal societal integration, political interest, is correlated directly and positively with informal integration, regardless of educational attainment. Thus, informal integration among the Nisei can derive from

TABLE 7.12

Scores on Integration Index, by Education and Political Interest

Education	Percent Who Score High on Integration Index	
	Great, Fair Political Interest	Little, None
Less than high school graduate	39	29
Total number	(38)	(58)
High school graduate	53	43
Total number	(356)	(376)
Some college	59	43
Total number	(334)	(267)
At least college graduate	74	64
Total number	(394)	(161)

two sources: from their reaching a relatively high level in the socioeconomic order, which puts them into close contact with Caucasians out of choice or inevitability; and from ideological commitment, which probably leads them to seek out associations with Caucasians, who are more likely to be politically active than peers in the close confines of the ethnic community.

Residence

We have not, however, reported one set of findings that places the foregoing into necessary relief. It will be recalled from Chapter 5 that the Nisei are concentrated on the West Coast, especially in Los Angeles. To repeat the distribution, 38 percent of the Nisei queried live in Greater Los Angeles, the metropolis of Japanese America. Another 39 percent live elsewhere in the Pacific states. And the remaining 23 percent live to the east.

We now find that current residence is highly correlated with scores on the index of integration. As Table 7.13 shows, fully 84 percent of the Nisei living in the Northeast are relatively integrated. And 90 percent who dwell elsewhere in the East, in the Midwest, or South, score high—except for the contingent in Chicago; there, only 62 percent receive high scores on the index. In the Mountain states, 70 percent, and in the Pacific states, outside of Los Angeles, six to seven of every ten, are relatively integrated. But in Los Angeles, a bare 37 percent receive relatively high scores. We conclude that concentration makes for less integration, and that dispersion makes for more. Only in Los Angeles, with its large Japanese American population, can the Nisei avoid close social contacts with Caucasians. Elsewhere, even in Seattle or San Francisco, their upwardly mobile ranks have become too spread out to preserve a full-blown sense of

TABLE 7.13

Scores on the Index of Inegration, by Present Residence

Region	Percent Who Score High (2–4)	Total Number
Northeast	84	(64)
Chicago	62	(104)
Other Midwest, South	90	(168)
Mountain	73	(140)
Seattle	56	(103)
San Francisco, Oakland	59	(140)
Los Angeles	37	(739)
Other Pacific	56	(619)

community among the many. The Japanese sections have merely become quaint tourist attractions to which Nisei may go, like any others. Japanese in Los Angeles, even with their Little Tokyo, do not require a locus—nor does one exist, for them or any group. The relatively sizable Japanese American population may be as dispersed as elsewhere, but they make use of the freeways and telephone to stay in easy contact with each other. If there remains solidarity in a Japanese American community, it can only persist in Los Angeles.

Chicago proves the point. There has been a small, but hardly negligible, Japanese American group there especially since the war. In spite of integration among their peers in the Midwest and East, Nisei Chicagoans are somewhat more likely to avoid Caucasian social contacts (although the majority of them do not).

What is surprising are the high rates of integration in Seattle and in San Francisco.[7] These are cities in which Japanese Americans have been settled for years. And their numbers are not negligible. But, while not negligible, they have apparently not been large enough, as in Los Angeles, to turn back the tides of behavioral integration. Those in Seattle and San Francisco tend to go the way of the rest of the nation, toward intimate social mixing with Caucasian fellow citizens.

Education, Political Interest, Residence, and Integration

Given the strong findings with regard to present residence, we need to ask whether those relating to socioeconomic status and political interest still hold in regard to integration.

Let educational attainment stand for socioeconomic status. We first find that education is related to residence (see Table 7.14). (The relationship between occupation and region of residence has already been reported in Table 5.6. There, we found a much higher proportion of professionals in the East than on

TABLE 7.14

Region of Residence, by Educational Level

| | Percent in Region | | |
Level	Los Angeles	Other Pacific	Other
Postgraduate	11	13	19
College graduate	12	14	18
Some college	34	29	26
High school graduate	38	39	33
Less than high school graduate	5	5	3
Total number	(736)	(754)	(476)

the Pacific.) Los Angelenos tend to have achieved less education than their peers elsewhere. Only 23 percent of Los Angeles Nisei are at least college graduates, compared with 27 percent of those elsewhere on the Pacific, while 37 percent of the easterners are as educated.

The question arises as to whether Los Angelenos are less integrated because they are less educated; or whether education makes no difference. Put another way, regardless of education, do Los Angeles Nisei tend to be less integrated than their ethnic peers elsewhere, or does education make a difference even in Los Angeles?

The answer appears in Table 7.15. Both things are true. Looking at the rows of the table, we see that education matters even in Los Angeles. But observing the columns, it is evident that Los Angeles matters seemingly more than education. The best educated in Los Angeles are, in fact, less integrated than lesser-educated Nisei living elsewhere. For example, only 44 percent of the Los Angeles Nisei with college degrees score high on integration, compared with 72 percent of those in the East holding only high school diplomas.

Living in Los Angeles, then, does have a powerful effect on the pattern of social relations even among the educated. In this Japanese American metropolis, protection is provided against alien ties, whatever the socioeconomic level. In places where the Japanese American population is less dense, i.e., everywhere else, the Nisei bend toward associations with Caucasians, no doubt because they do not have much choice. Sufficient numbers of Japanese Americans are just not available, even for the less educated (but to a lesser degree), for the Nisei to construct a social life wholly within the confines of an ethnic community. The community, both geographically and sociologically defined, does not have a chance to form.

TABLE 7.15

Scores on the Index of Integration, by Present Residence and Education

	Percent Who Score High (2-4) on the Index		
Residence	Less than High School Graduate	High School Graduate	At Least Some College
Los Angeles	21	29	44
Total number	(34)	(278)	(424)
Other Pacific	40	52	62
Total number	(43)	(290)	(419)
Other	57	72	83
Total number	(14)	(159)	(302)

It might also be said that eastern Nisei, so many of whom are well educated, got that way because they were taking flight from the close confines of ethnic communities such as that existing most notably in Los Angeles. They perhaps wanted to succeed in the larger world, removed from what they perceive as the claustrophobia of the old ethnic community. Unfortunately, our data do not allow us to trace the motivations of migrants. It is enough to say that integration into the larger society proceeds apace where the density of the Japanese American population is low. Except for the peculiar case of Los Angeles (and the plurality of Nisei live there), our respondents tend toward social as well as economic integration into the engulfing Caucasian world. Whether or not they truly prefer their situation is a question we cannot answer.

As with the relationship between education and integration, so, too, with that between political interest and integration: Residence, once controlled, appears to be the stronger factor. Table 7.16 shows that although there is still a direct relationship between level of political interest and scores on the index of integration, the interested Los Angelenos are less integrated than the less interested in the East. In fact, the easterners score largely high on social integration with Caucasians, regardless of their level of political interest. In Los Angeles, political concern, unlike elsewhere, is not very likely to translate itself into association with ideological peers outside the ethnic community. Elsewhere on the Pacific, this process appears to be at work.

Residence, Age, and Integration

The question might be raised as to whether the age of our respondents plays a part in explaining differential integration. On the one hand, one might speculate that the younger Nisei are more likely than the older to seek out

TABLE 7.16

Scores on the Index of Integration, by Present Residence and Political Interest

	Percent Who Score High (2-4) on the Index	
Residence	Great, Some Political Interest	Little, None
Los Angeles	45	39
Total number	(387)	(351)
Other Pacific	64	47
Total number	(419)	(335)
Other	79	76
Total number	(302)	(173)

associations with Caucasians. They do tend to be better educated, and hence more mobile. On the other hand, a case can be made for the older, who have had more time to form such associations. The youngest Nisei, those under 40, are indeed the most integrated—fully 83 percent of them score high on the index. But the oldest group, those 50 and older, are more integrated than those in their forties.

The finding might be explained in this fashion: The youngest came of age well after World War II, when discriminating barriers had largely crumbled. The oldest attained maturity before the war, and had learned how to form ties with Caucasians—but perhaps of a different texture from those formed by the youngest. The men and women in their forties, however, were just coming of age when the catastrophe of relocation struck. We may be observing here the traces of hostility and resentment built up against the larger society during that dreadful period. A 45-year-old in the mid-1960s was, after all, an adult of 21 in 1942—with all his hopes and plans destroyed, for the period, perhaps an endless period.

But how does residence fit in? The Los Angeles Nisei tend to be younger than the others. Forty-one percent of them are under 40, compared with 35 percent living elsewhere on the Pacific, and only 29 percent of the easterners. Are the youngest in Los Angeles heavily involved in social relations with Caucasians, or does Los Angeles itself exert the effect we have already encountered?

Table 7.17 reveals that residence virtually obliterates the relationship between age and integration. Los Angeles Nisei tend to score low, regardless of age. At the other extreme, the easterners tend to score high, although the oldest score not quite as high as the younger.

TABLE 7.17

Scores on the Index of Integration, by Present Residence and Age

Residence	Percent Who Score High (2–4) on the Index		
	Under 40	40–49	50 and Older
Los Angeles	38	38	34
Total number	(303)	(330)	(102)
Other Pacific	54	58	61
Total number	(260)	(389)	(104)
Other	79	80	69
Total number	(138)	(276)	(62)

We must also reason that our discussion of the curvilinear relationship between age and integration was perhaps artifactual. Once residence is controlled for, it disappears. We conclude that the trauma of relocation did not differentially affect any age group to the point that it has affected the ties they have formed with the environing Caucasian world.

A Methodological Note on the Index

It will be recalled that we approached our Nisei respondents in different ways: 33 percent were confronted with personal interviews, 63 percent returned self-administered mail questionnaires, and 4 percent were interviewed over the telephone. One might imagine that those subjected to personal interviews by Caucasian interviewers would be more eager to speak of, even to enhance, their associations with Caucasians. In contrast, in the privacy of their homes, respondents filling out the questionnaire would feel less pressure to please and possibly shade replies.[8]

Our data reveal little of this type of effect, either among men or among women (see Table 7.18). We do find some tendency for those interviewed by telephone (only 70 respondents) to achieve higher index scores than the others— but they were interviewed by phone only because they live in remote areas where the National Opinion Research Center does not usually interview. And the less chance there is of a Japanese American population, as we have seen, the higher the integration scores.

TABLE 7.18

Scores on the Index of Integration, by Sex and Type of
Approach to Respondent

Sex	Percent Who Score High (2-4) on the Index		
	Interview	Mail	Telephone
Men	53	57	70
Total number	(565)	(452)	(59)
Women	51	54	64
Total number	(166)	(734)	(11)

A TYPOLOGY OF NISEI SOCIAL RELATIONS

Thus far, we have seen that the Nisei are differentially involved both with other Japanese Americans (using monthly visits with relatives close-by as the indicator) and in social relations with members of the larger society. How are the two factors correlated? Do we find that the more intensive the one kind of involvement, the less the other, or what? Table 7.19 reveals that there is little relationship between the one variable and the other. Frequent visitors are only somewhat less likely to score relatively high on integration (50 as against 57 percent).

TABLE 7.19

Monthly Visits with Relatives, by Scores on the Index
of Integration

Degree of Integration	0-4 Visits	5 or More
Low scores (0, 1)	43%	50%
High scores (2-4)	57	50
Total number	(1,169)	(638)

TABLE 7.20

A Typology of Social Relations: Visits and Integration

	Visits	
Integration	Few (0–4)	Many (5 or more)
Low (0, 1)	1. Disengaged = 28%	2. Monocultural Japanese Americans = 17%
High (2–4)	3. Monocultural "Americans" = 37%	4. Bicultural = 18%
		(1,807)

To bring coherence to this result, we have constructed a typology that distinguishes among four types of Nisei (see Table 7.20).

Type one includes respondents who neither visit with relatives much (if at all) nor have intensive ties with non-Japanese Americans. We label them the disengaged—involved deeply in neither cultural realm. They are 28 percent of the sample.

Type two includes the monocultural Japanese Americans. Highly involved in their community, they are fairly shut off from contacts with the larger society. They constitute only 17 percent of the sample.

Type three includes what we call monocultural "Americans"—that 37 percent of the Nisei (the plurality) who score high in integration, but low on visits with relatives.

Type four, the final 18 percent of the sample, includes the bicultural, with a foot in either camp. It should be stressed that fully 55 percent of the respondents are labeled "American" or bicultural. To this extent, the Nisei have largely left the confines of the monolithic subcommunity and entered the mainstream. The Sansei, it will be seen, extend the trend. It now remains to distinguish among the types.

Comparisons among the Four Types

In Table 7.21, we distinguish among the four types of Nisei by a series of demographic characteristics. In the table, by comparing the disengaged and the monocultural Japanese Americans, we see that Nisei groups differ little from each other, if at all. A distinction between them becomes unnecessary. We may actually consider both types to be monocultural Japanese Americans as measured by their low degree of association with white Americans, regardless of how much or little they associate with one another.

Between the monocultural Japanese Americans and the other types, there are both striking similarities and even more striking (though not unexpected) differences. For one thing, there are no differences among the four types according to sex, age, or marital status. And the divorce rate is astonishingly low among Nisei of all types. Once married, Nisei stay married. And this is true even among the "American" group, nearly one of five of whom, in contrast to the other types, have outmarried.

Apart from their greater proclivity toward exogamy, those of the "American" type, high on associations with Caucasians and low on visits with relatives, differ markedly from their fellows. They tend to be wealthier, better educated; they are more likely to be Christians, are far less likely to live in Los Angeles, typically live in a Caucasian neighborhood, and are far more likely than the others to have a professional or other white-collar occupation. The bicultural tend to resemble the "Americans," but less so. They truly have a foot in either camp.

It is of interest to note in Table 7.21 that the types do not differ in political-party identification. Over half of each type call themselves Republicans. Nonvoting is at a reported minimum, too, regardless of type. If their reports are correct, the Nisei turn out at the polls in record numbers.

Political interest, however, is variable. The Japanese American types are much less likely than the more integrated to report a high level of interest in politics. Furthermore, they are less likely to be opinion leaders. We asked:

"During the last few months, has anyone outside your family asked you for advice about politics or public affairs?"

One-fifth of the "Americans" report having been asked for political advice, compared with only 9 percent of the disengaged. Given the better education of the "Americans," and their wider associations, this is not surprising. To the outer world, perhaps even in Los Angeles, they are the real Japanese Americans. Perhaps they are considered, and consider themselves, qualified to speak for the community—a community of which they have become only peripheral members. Enmeshed with Caucasians, and seldom involved with ethnic peers, they are nonetheless Japanese Americans and regarded as such. To know what Japanese Americans think, to whom else but the integrated would Caucasians turn? The Japanese Americans are hidden from view in a social sense. Thus, the better educated, the wealthier, the Christians, those with Caucasian ties, serve to speak for the community. They may, however, be totally ignorant about what members of the core of that still viable community are thinking. But, then, can it really matter? The "Americans" are already nearly one of four of the Nisei, and the bicultural, another fifth. Over half the Nisei, the integrated Nisei, represent Japanese America to the outer world. To the extent that they demonstrate to

TABLE 7.21

Demographic Comparisons among Four Types of Nisei

Demographic Item	All	Disengaged	Japanese American	"American"	Bicultural
Percent male	54	54	53	55	54
Total number	(1,987)	(502)	(317)	(667)	(321)
Percent single	15	16	14	14	6
Total number	(1,987)	(502)	(317)	(667)	(321)
Percent divorced	1	2	1	1	1
Total number	(1,987)	(502)	(317)	(667)	(321)
Percent under 40	39	35	40	35	33
Total number	(1,983)	(501)	(316)	(666)	(320)
Percent outmarried	10	6	5	18	7
Total number	(1,556)	(379)	(221)	(531)	(283)
Percent with income of $15,000 or more	27	21	20	33	32
Total number	(1,941)	(489)	(308)	(656)	(310)
Percent with at least some college education	58	50	52	68	59
Total number	(1,984)	(500)	(313)	(667)	(321)
Percent Christian	53	49	42	65	54
Total number	(1,980)	(488)	(309)	(647)	(312)
Percent Republican	54	55	57	52	52
Total number	(1,859)	(461)	(292)	(628)	(305)

	Total	4	3	1	2
Percent who do not vote	2	4	3	1	2
Total number	(1,966)	(496)	(212)	(659)	(320)
Percent interested in politics	56	49	43	66	60
Total number	(1,986)	(502)	(317)	(665)	(321)
Percent who were asked for political advice	15	9	13	21	14
Total number	(1,980)	(498)	(317)	(665)	(320)
Percent living in Los Angeles	38	51	56	23	31
Total number	(1,789)	(493)	(317)	(659)	(320)
Percent living in a non-Japanese neighborhood (1965)	40	37	30	78	68
Total number	(1,977)	(501)	(316)	(662)	(319)
Percent in white-collar occupations	52	42	43	64	55
Total number	(1,940)	(481)	(309)	(656)	(318)
Percent who took great interest in interviews	65	57	60	71	69
Total number	(799)	(223)	(141)	(258)	(156)

that outer world that "we" are no different from "you," they break down barriers of prejudice and discrimination. It is problematical as to the degree to which they ease the lot of the poorer, less-educated Nisei who typically cling together in the metropolitan jungle of Los Angeles. The bifurcation of the Nisei generation is, of course, transitory. Virtually all Nisei, integrated and non-integrated alike, will give the Sansei a college education. And that attainment will radically alter the face of Japanese America, as the data in Chapter 8 show.

It is interesting to note that among the interviewed, the "Americans" showed the greatest interest in the proceedings. Since they are the most experienced in dealing with Caucasians, they would tend to have greater rapport with the Caucasian interviewers and the subject matter under study. Even so, nine of ten Nisei interviewed were cooperative regardless of type.

Apart from demographic and political differences, the "Americans" differ in other ways from those still locked into the subculture of Japanese America. Some of these differences are revealed in Table 7.22. About six Nisei of every ten, of all types, believe that Caucasians would be disturbed if an offspring of theirs married a Japanese American. The Japanese Americans are far less disturbed about this, and show no strong predilection for endogamy. Although half of those of the Japanese American type would be disturbed at an outmarriage, fewer than one of three of the "Americans" express concern. Thus, not only are the "Americans" more likely to be exogamous themselves; they would seem to encourage it—or, at least, not actively discourage it—in their children.

And yet, even the "Americans" do not want their children to utterly forget their heritage. They were asked:

> "Do you think your children ought to know how to speak Japanese?"

Fully nine of ten Nisei, even 81 percent of the "Americans," reply yes. The "Americans" also tend to keep in touch, albeit to a slightly lesser degree, with the goings-on in the Japanese American formal community. Seventy-two percent of them, compared with 90 percent of those of the Japanese American type, report reading a Japanese American newspaper. Nearly half who do, of all types, do so regularly.

In some attitudinal ways, the types are virtually alike. Only four of ten agree that "I can usually shrug my shoulders at misfortune." Fully nine of ten agree that "when it comes to spending time, family demands come first." Nine of ten disagree that "when a man is born, the degree of success he is going to have is already in the cards, so he might just as well accept it and not fight against it." Seven of ten concur that "Americans put too much stress on occupational success." About one of three concurs that "the family often asks too much of a person." To this extent, there is agreement among the Nisei.

On two other items, however, there is less concurrence. First, we asked whether or not the respondents agree or disagree with this statement:

TABLE 7.22

Attitudinal Comparisons among Four Types of Nisei

Attitudinal Item	All	Disengaged	Japanese American	"American"	Bicultural
Percent who would be disturbed if son married Caucasian girl	40	50	46	28	39
Total number	(1,925)	(488)	(304)	(647)	(312)
Percent who would be disturbed if daughter married Caucasian boy	40	49	47	29	39
Total number	(1,926)	(484)	(307)	(648)	(314)
Percent who believe children should know how to speak Japanese	87	88	93	81	92
Total number	(1,979)	(500)	(317)	(661)	(320)
Percent who believe parent should help child get further ahead than he did	59	68	65	50	60
Total number	(1,973)	(499)	(314)	(662)	(317)

"The most important thing for a parent to do is to help his children get further ahead in the world than he did."

Sixty-five percent of those of the Japanese American types agree with the statement, compared with 50 percent of the "Americans." The explanation is not very hard to find: The latter have, by and large, gotten as far ahead as they beleve it is possible for any Japanese American to get. Thirty-seven percent of them are professionals, and only 14 percent of the Japanese Americans. If the children of the "Americans" get as far ahead as they have gotten, they will presumably be happy; whereas, the others, starting lower, have high aspirations for their offspring.

Not only do the "Americans" differ in attitudes from the others; they also differ in social background. As Table 7.23 shows, the "Americans" have had a different set of experiences from the others—and want the same for their children. We asked a question noted before:

"While you were growing up, would you say that your parents wanted you to take an active part with Caucasians in their activities, or to stick pretty much with Japanese Americans?"

Whereas only 24 percent of those of the Japanese American type state that their parents wanted them to mix with Caucasians, 44 percent of the "Americans" report the same. Clearly, the latter had undergone anticipatory socialization, encouraged by their parents, that bent them toward ties with Caucasians.

The large majority of Nisei of all types, however, want their own children to take an active part with Caucasians. Sixty-nine percent of the Japanese Americans say this, and 80 percent of the "Americans." Thus, even among the relatively unintegrated, the tendency is to hope for integration in the Sansei generation. The Nisei want the Sansei to be more integrated into the larger society than they have been able to be—while not altogether losing their distinct heritage and identity.

One more set of data gives us insight into the process that separates the types. The Nisei were asked about the ethnic composition of their grade-school and high-school friends. As Table 7.23 shows, even in grade school, the more integrated were more likely to have had mostly non-Japanese American friends although overall, only one of three had such friends). The gap widened in high school. About one-fifth of the less integrated had mostly non-Japanese American friends, while one-third of the more integrated did. We presume that the opportunity for making Caucasian friends would have been less in grade school, since a larger proportion of the student body would have been Oriental. In high schools, although we have no data on the types of high schools they attended, the proportion of Japanese Americans would have been smaller, and the student body larger. Some Nisei, who were to carry through the pattern, elected to stay together and avoid extraethnic contacts. Others, who perhaps had higher aspirations socioeconomically, sought out ties with Caucasians that would continue

TABLE 7.23

Social-Background Comparisons among Four Types of Nisei

Item	All	Disengaged	Japanese Americans	"American"	Bilcultural
Percent whose parents wanted them to take an active part with Caucasians	37	30	24	44	41
Total number	(1,922)	(485)	(308)	(649)	(308)
Percent who want children to take active part with Caucasians	75	70	69	80	74
Total number	(1,949)	(488)	(312)	(654)	(318)
Percent whose grade school friends were mostly non-Japanese Americans	34	27	30	36	41
Total number	(1,942)	(479)	(309)	(659)	(314)
Percent whose high school friends were mostly non-Japanese Americans	29	23	19	34	33
Total number	(1,930)	(476)	(306)	(653)	(315)

into adult life and be functional for their careers. The patterns of integration or nonintegration were, then, being set in the adolescent years. Those who turned in upon themselves are also the less successful; those who looked outward were more likely to go upward. It remains to be seen how the next generation has conducted itself. It need hardly be forecast here that we shall find even greater tendencies toward integration among the Sansei.

NOTES

1. Another possibility, interaction with non-Japanese Americans at church, is impossible to determine since we neglected to ask Christians for the ethnic composition of their congregations.

2. This is the interviewer version. For the mail questionnaires, the item was modified appropriately.

3. We may be a nation of joiners, but a significant proportion of the population do not so associate. In a study of Los Angeles Jewry we found that about four of ten belong to nothing—not even to the synagogue. See Gene N. Levine et al., "Affiliations of Los Angeles Jewry: A Sample of the Metropolitan Area," *Jewish Sociology and Social Research* 2, no. 1 (1975): 4–9.

4. Our categories 4 or 5, 6 to 9, 10 to 24, and 25 and above present a problem. In our scoring, it will become clear that we have always gone in the Japanese American direction. If, for example, a respondent belongs to four or five groups, and states that four or five are Japanese American, we have considered all of them to be Japanese American.

5. To be included in the index, respondents must have replied on all four components. By this rule, we lose 14 percent of them. The total N for the index is therefore 1,988.

6. This means Japanese Americans increasingly take the value orientation of the larger society. William Caudhill, "Japanese-American Personality and Acculturation," *Genetic Psychology Monographs* 45 (1952): 3–102; William Caudhill and George DeVos, "Achievement Culture and Personality: The Case of Japanese Americans," *American Anthropologist* 58 (1956): 1102–26.

7. For an ethnographer's view of the Japanese American community in San Francisco, see Christie W. Kiefer, *Changing Cultures, Changing Lives: An Ethnographic Study of Three Generations of Japanese Americans* (San Francisco: Jossey-Bass Publishers, 1974). Kiefer studied 30 families in depth.

8. The matter of response bias in our data has been treated in Darrel Montero, "A Study of Social Desirability Response Bias: The Mail Questionnaire, the Face-to-Face Interview, and the Telephone Interview Compared" (Paper presented at the 1974 Meetings of the American Sociological Association, Montreal, 1974).

8

THE THIRD GENERATION

The Sansei generation, offspring of the Nisei, reflects trends already apparent among their elders. If the Nisei were becoming integrated into American society, as we have seen in the previous chapter, the pace is quickened among the Sansei. Our findings do not reveal any sharp break between the generations. (A copy of our mail questionnaire sent to Sansei appears as Appendix C.) Rather, the Sansei tend to be like the Nisei—only more so. As we report later, they are considerably more exogamous (or are likely to be), they are on their way to becoming even more highly educated and professionalized, and they have even wider and deeper associations with the Caucasian world than the second generation had. Still, on some key value items, the Sansei differ hardly at all from the Nisei. Nor on other, broader matters do they have differing apperceptions and judgments. And when it comes to preserving the shards of an eroding Japanese American culture, the Sansei are virtually unanimous in wishing for its continuance.[1] Whether or not, with so many mixed marriages occurring, the Sansei will be able to exemplify Hansen's Law of Return is, however, subject to doubt. (According to Hansen, "What the second generation has forgotten, the third generation will try to remember.")

We shall have to conclude that the forces that already have served to erode a sense of community among the Nisei work even stronger among the Sansei. The latter are even less able than the former to resist the attractions and pulls of the larger society. Nor were they apparently groomed to resist them. At the same time, the pulls from within Japanese America, whose boundaries are by now so ill defined, become ever weaker and less compelling.

In this chapter, we first take up the overshadowing question of Sansei out-marriage, so critical an issue with respect to their integration into the larger scene. Next, a set of comparisons along a number of lines—social, psychological, and economic—between the Nisei and Sansei generations is reported. Finally, intergenerational data are presented in order to discern whether certain types of Nisei (and of Issei, too) have spawned certain types of Sansei. For example, do the offspring of the more integrated Nisei, as defined in Chapter 7, tend also to be more integrated into the larger American society themselves? Or has some indication of a counterreaction set in? The thrust of this chapter is to be able to foretell the survival or disappearance of Japanese Americans as a distinct sub-culture.

OUTMARRIAGE

The Sansei queried in 1967 were a young lot. It will be recalled that we asked their parents to list all their children. We sent questionnaires, however, only to those then 18 years old or older.[2] We thus have tapped the older Sansei. Even so, 42 percent were not yet 21 at the time of the fieldwork, and 77 percent were under 25 years old. Not surprisingly, seven of ten of the young men and women (53 percent of the sample of 802 are female) were still single in 1967. Of those who had married by the same year, 40 percent had wed non-Japanese Americans (mostly Caucasians).[3] The figure can be compared to the bare 10 percent of the preceding generation who had sought mates outside the fold. Although there is no difference in outmarriage rates between the sexes, age does matter: Two-thirds of those under 21 (N = 15) had outmarried, compared with 30 percent of those 25 or older (N = 132). Only five Sansei were, at the time, divorced, separated, or widowed. Like their parents, the Sansei seem to form stable unions.

The tendency toward exogamy becomes greater when other data are considered. In 1967 we asked the unmarried Sansei respondents whether they were engaged, going steady, dating casually, or not dating. Slightly over a third were engaged or going steady. In turn, we inquired about the ethnic background of the steady or the fiancé. Fully 55 percent reported that he or she was a non-Japanese. The question arises as to whether or not marriage plans were actually carried out. Fortunately, we have data to this point.

In 1972, another mail questionnaire was sent to the original Sansei respondents. Together with a special series of questions on ethnic and other identities, many of the 1967 questions were repeated.[4] Six of ten of the Sansei respondents returned the second questionnaire.

The 1972 data show that of the single Sansei in 1967, 36 percent had wed by 1972. (Three new divorces and one separation were recorded over the time span.) A striking 55 percent of the recently married had chosen non-Japanese American partners, the majority being Caucasians (72 percent). Overall, by 1972 the generational outmarriage rate had risen from 40 to 44 percent as the new unions formed.

Unfortunately, our data do not allow us to relate age at marriage to ethnicity of spouse. We suspect that the earlier the Sansei marry, the more likely they are to form an exogamous union—and this is because the Nisei have encouraged the Sansei to form associations with Caucasians as early as grade school. Marrying young, the Sansei draw from a pool of acquaintances that is predominantly Caucasian. Close friendships among the Sansei tend to be formed with Caucasians more often than with other Japanese Americans. This inference can be drawn from the results of the questions on engagement and dating status, and on the ethnic characteristics of fiancés and steadies.

The younger are discernibly less likely to have wed than the older. For example, in 1967, 96 percent of the under-21-year-olds were still single, compared with 68 percent of the 21-to-24-year-olds, but only 27 percent of those 25 or older.

Marital intentions appear largely to be carried out. Nine of ten of the engaged in 1967 were married in 1972, as were 57 percent of those originally going steady. And we have observed that outmarriages were commonplace— which leaves the intentions and ties of the yet-to-be-married, who tend to be younger.

In 1972, the single Sansei engaged or going steady were also asked about the ethnicity of their prospective mates. Sixty-seven percent were involved with non-Japanese Americans (eight of ten of them being Caucasians). We have no reason to doubt that for the majority of these Sansei, marriage plans will also be carried out. When they are, the overall exogamy rate for that portion of the Sansei generation sampled should top the 50 percent mark.

And this leaves the younger subgeneration, whom we have not surveyed. If we project our data—that is, if trends noted continue—the overall exogamy rate for the total Sansei generation should encompass a clear majority, perhaps six of every ten.

The proclivity of Sansei of either sex to be just as likely to marry outside the community as to marry within it presents Japanese Americans with the most serious questions about their ability to survive as an autonomous group. There are, of course, some hopeful signs. For example, the Sansei under study show the keenest sympathy for Japanese culture and a wish to know more. In many respects, we observe they do not differ from the Nisei generation on a variety of subculturally related items. (On other items, of course, they differ markedly.) How are the children of mixed unions brought up—as Japanese Americans or as soon-to-be members of the dominant culture? There are no data on the subject. But it may be that the Sansei who form mixed unions also have the intent of acquainting their offspring with the fundamentals of Japanese American culture—in which, however, they themselves are not overly well versed. Disclaimers aside, the high rate of Sansei exogamy, seemingly irreversible as one generation succeeds the other, does not augur well for the survival of the

Japanese American subculture as we have known it in its Nisei manifestation.[5] Still, for the observer, there can be no doubt that at least some Sansei are highly conscious of their Japanese American identity—even militant about it. This may augur an increasing return to roots. The path of the younger Sansei, within an increasingly ethnically conscious ethos, will have to be watched, as will that of the Yonsei—who, on the mainland, are largely still infants or children.

Prejudice: Perceived and Actual

The high rate of outmarriage that we have found among the Sansei must also mean that prejudices against Japanese Americans may well have eroded. Do Japanese Americans perceive more prejudice than actually exists, or do they have a realistic picture of the degree to which they have been accepted—even to the point of having their offspring accepted as mates by the dominant Caucasian community? We asked some questions in this regard not only of the Nisei and Sansei respondents, but also of a sample of all adult Californians, in 1967. In June and in September of 1967 we purchased portions of the Field California Polls in order to determine the actual degree of anti-Japanese prejudice in the larger populace, in the state wherein so many Japanese Americans live, as related to the degree of prejudice Japanese Americans perceive.

We put these questions to the Nisei, the Sansei, and a cross section of Californians alike:

> "Do you suppose most Caucasians in America would be disturbed if a Japanese American girl married a son of theirs?" "Do you suppose that most Caucasians in America would be disturbed if a Japanese American boy married a daughter of theirs?"

Table 8.1 shows that Japanese Americans, of either generation, are fairly accurate in their appraisal of the mixed-marriage situation. A slight majority perceive that Caucasians would be disturbed in the first situation (a Japanese American bride with a Caucasian bridegroom), and a larger majority see a greater sensitivity when it comes to the prospect of Caucasians having Japanese American sons-in-law. Their perceptions are verified by the California sample, who perceive about the same amount of prejudice.

We went on to ask the Nisei and the Californians (but not the Sansei) another pair of questions. To the Nisei:

> "Do you suppose that *you* would be disturbed if a son/daughter of yours married a Caucasian (girl/boy)?"

To the California sample:

> "Do you think that *you* would be disturbed if a son/daughter of yours married a Japanese American (girl/boy)?"

TABLE 8.1

Mixed-Marriage Items: Comparison of Nisei, Sansei, and Californians

	Percent Who Say Yes		
Item	Nisei	Sansei	California Cross Section
Believe Caucasians Would Be Disturbed If			
Japanese American girl married son	58	52	52
Total	(2,193)	(783)	(880)
Japanese American boy married daughter	62	67	59[a]
Total	(2,177)	(778)	(887)
Respondent Would Be Disturbed If			
Son made a mixed marriage	41	N.A.	39
Total	(2,213)		(879)
Daughter made a mixed marriage	41	N.A.	44[b]
Total	(2,216)		(870)

[a]We report the June 1967 result in the table. This item was asked again of another California cross section in September 1967. Sixty-three percent said yes then (N = 845).
[b]In September, 49 percent said they would be disturbed (N = 913).

These results also appear in Table 8.1, and the findings are clear. First, only four Nisei of every ten would be disturbed by such mixed unions. Second, and even more surprising, only about the same proportion of the preponderantly Caucasian respondents in California would likewise be distressed. In other words, both the Japanese American community and members of the larger community perceive a higher degree of prejudice toward Japanese Americans than actually exists. As our data show, when it comes to actually forming mixed unions, the Sansei have not encountered much resistance.

Californians express a good deal of familiarity with the Japanese American community. About half of them say they have lived in neighborhoods where there were Japanese American families. Seventy-six percent remark that they have had a Japanese American acquaintance, and 44 percent say that they have had a good friend who is a Japanese American. It is small wonder that prewar hostilities have been replaced by postwar amity, to the point where even that most intimate association, marriage, with Japanese Americans is accepted by over half of the cross-sectional California sample.

NISEI AND SANSEI SIMILARITIES AND DIFFERENCES

In some respects, the Sansei are very like the Nisei, while in other ways, they are markedly different. We have already taken up one point of dissimilarity: the Nisei disinclination to form mixed marital unions (born, no doubt, from the temper of the times, the illegal status of such unions in some states, and their more limited associations with Caucasians in the nubile years) and the Sansei's marked proclivity for them. Of course, the latter process has taken place only because the Nisei have laid the groundwork for Sansei actions. Stated another way, if the Sansei increasingly lean toward outmarriage, it is only because the Nisei have prepared the way through upward social mobility, and through concomitant broader and deeper associations with Caucasians. They have, in effect, provided the Sansei with the social setting in which mixed unions would prosper. The move to the suburbs (recall that six of ten Nisei live in Caucasian neighborhoods), friendships with Caucasians, amicable competition in school—the entire sharing of a like childhood and youth— have all worked to make the Sansei feel very much at home in the larger Caucasian society.

TABLE 8.2

Ethnic Character of Grade-School and High-School Friendships: Nisei Compared with Sansei

	Percent Who Say That Most of Friends Were Non-Japanese Americans	
School	Nisei	Sansei
Grade	34	64
Total number	(2,244)	(799)
High	29	54
Total number	(2,226)	(800)

Consider these findings: We asked both the Nisei and the Sansei about the ethnic character of their close friends in grade school and in high school—whether they were mostly Japanese Americans, non-Japanese Americans, or about an equal number of both. As Table 8.2 shows, in grade school, only a third of the Nisei, but nearly two-thirds of the Sansei, had mostly outgroup friends. Likewise, in high school: 29 percent of the Nisei and 54 percent of the Sansei report having mostly non-Japanese American friends. We account for the lower proportions in high school in this fashion: In mixed neighborhoods, Japanese Americans would find relatively few ethnic peers with whom to associate. In the context of larger high schools, it is relatively easier for like to seek out like, and for them to isolate themselves in ethnic cliques.

The data presented reveal clearly that the Nisei move into non-Japanese neighborhoods, as already reported, has had the inevitable result of placing their children in the close company of Caucasians. Socialized to interact with Caucasians, it should be no surprise that the outmarriage rate has climbed among the Sansei—especially so when we consider that the majority of Nisei do not object to outmarriages, as reported earlier.

The Nisei have also been far more encouraging than were the Issei about their offspring associating with Caucasians. We asked:

"While you were growing up, would you say that your parents wanted you to take an active part with Caucasians in their activities, or to stick pretty much with Japanese Americans?"

Table 8.3 reveals that the Nisei report that the Issei tended to be a restrictive and an exclusive group. Only 37 percent of the Nisei say that their parents wanted them to take an active part with Caucasians in their activities. In contrast, 58 percent of the Sansei report parental encouragement in forming Caucasian contacts.

TABLE 8.3

Parental Wishes Regarding Children's Ethnic Associations: Nisei Compared with Sansei

Item	Percent Who Say Their Parents Wanted Them to Take an Active Part with Caucasians and Percent Who Want Their Own Children To Do So	
	Nisei	Sansei
Parents wanted them to take an active part with Caucasians	37	58
Total	(2,208)	(792)
Want own children to take an active part	75	80
Total	(2,245)	(794)

Table 8.3 also shows that the large majority of Nisei and Sansei alike want their children to associate with Caucasians. The question was:

> "Would you want your own children to take an active part with Caucasians in their activities, or to stick pretty much with Japanese Americans?"

It is now further apparent that, first, the Nisei have groomed their children to associate closely with Caucasians; and, second, that the Sansei will intensify the process among their own children. It is worth speculating whether or not the children of mixed marriages will be especially encouraged to seek out their associations in the larger Caucasian world, and whether or not they will follow the direction given to them. On the one hand, we could forecast that such offspring would be especially susceptible to parental pressures pushing them in the direction of Caucasian associations. On the other hand, being a child of a Japanese-Caucasian union may present special problems of identity that could be solved by moving back into the Japanese American sphere. It remains for later study, once the Yonsei generation has matured, to gauge the social and psychological consequences mixed marriages have engendered. Still, data presented at the conclusion of this chapter give us some insight into the consequences of mixed marriages, as we compare Sansei who are offspring of such Nisei unions with those who are not.

It should not be assumed that all Nisei are oblivious to the problems that mixed marriages might create both for mates and for their children. The majority of the Nisei, of course, deny that their parents have tried to influence them when it comes to marriage. Only 31 percent say their parents did. The prospect of mixed marriages in the Nisei generation was not very great, however. The Issei had little experience with it. But 42 percent of the Sansei confess to parental influence concerning marriage. And what did these parents urge them to do—or not to do? Whereas only 32 percent of the pressured Nisei report that their parents urged them to marry within their own race, fully 65 percent of the similarly pressured Sansei report such urging.

It might be said that the question of Sansei outmarriage has polarized the Nisei generation. A majority do not object to it. But a substantial minority apparently do so in strenuous terms. The split on the issue is, of course, related to Nisei integration into the Caucasian community. As we report later, children of relatively more integrated Nisei are far more likely to have outmarried, or to be contemplating such an action, than the children of the less integrated. Nisei orientation is hardly ignored by the Sansei.

The Sansei generation tends also to be split on the issue of intermarriage. We asked:

> "Some people are talking about Sansei marrying Caucasians. How important a question do you think this is for the Sansei? Very important, rather important, rather unimportant, or very unimportant?"

Only 22 percent of the sample rate the issue as "very" important. Another third judge it to be "rather" important. Nearly half of the Sansei, however, place little or no importance on the subject. The more integrated the Sansei are, the less likely they are to perceive this issue as important.

We went on to put another question to the Sansei respondents:

"Speaking just for yourself now, do you think that on the whole, the effect of Sansei marrying Caucasians is good for the Japanese Americans, bad for them; or do you think this will make little difference one way or the other?"

Significantly, only 10 percent of the respondents perceive intermarriage to be bad for Japanese Americans, while 16 percent say it would have positive effects. The large majority, three of every four, do not see that outmarriage would make any difference one way or the other. We take this to mean that most Sansei do not actually perceive a distinct and separate Japanese American subculture that would be threatened by the phenomenon of outmarriage. The process of integration into the mainstream of American society has gone too far among them for them to react negatively to what other groups (Jews, for example) think of as a pernicious threat to group boundaries. As a generation, the majority of the Sansei have come to accept their assimilation into the larger society.

Curiously, however, they seem to accept the trend with some reluctance— and perhaps misgivings. We asked:

"In your opinion, should minority groups in America try to preserve something of the culture of their own group, or should they blend their culture into the mainstream of American life?"

Two-thirds of the respondents vote for cultural pluralism in which distinctive group identities, presumably including their own, would be preserved. Again, we might ponder the fate of the children of Sansei mixed marriages. Will the Japanese American partner attempt to socialize them into Japanese America, or will the heritage of the Yonsei be lost?

That the Sansei do tend toward integration into the larger culture is indicated by their friendship patterns. Unfortunately, we are unable to construct an index of integration parallel to that for the Nisei, since so many Sansei are not yet settled into jobs but are completing their education. Nor do we have data on neighborly visiting patterns. Further, the large majority of Sansei are not yet of an age when they can become members of formal organizations. (Whereas 36 percent of the Nisei belong to no organizations, 68 percent of the Sansei belong to no nonschool organizations.)

Like the Nisei, the Sansei were asked for the ethnicity of their two closest friends. It will be recalled that 54 percent of the Nisei count, among their closest friends, one or two non-Japanese Americans (who are virtually all Caucasians). The process is exaggerated for the Sansei: Fully 74 percent of them number at least one non-Japanese American among their closest friends. We return later to correlates of their friendship patterns, as an indicator of integration into the larger society. We want here to make the point that even though, as measured by outmarriage and friendship patterns, the Sansei appear to bend toward absorption in the larger society, on some items they voice sentiments that make them supporters of the preservation of Japanese American culture.

We have already seen that a majority vote for cultural pluralism. We also discover that while only 12 percent (as compared with 61 percent of the Nisei) can speak Japanese, nine out of every ten wish that they could speak it better. And another nine of ten believe they ought to know more about Japanese culture.

These findings indicate a contradiction in the outlook of Japanese American youths. They have largely been accepted by Caucasians as equals, even as marriage partners, but they realize that they are still different in aspect and in outlook. Situated between two worlds, like the classical marginal man, they are fully a part of neither. How they resolve the conflict, either individually or collectively, will in large measure determine the fate of the Japanese American community, and its ability to endure as a distinct entity.[6]

Occupation

If the Sansei differ from the Nisei in rates of exogamy, and in extragroup friendship patterns, they do so only because they tend to be acting out of the social conditions the Nisei have largely set for them. In other ways, too, the Sansei appear to be following paths laid for them by the preceding generation. This is nowhere more apparent than in the occupational accomplishments and plans of the Sansei. It will be recalled that 65 percent of the Nisei men (and single women) occupy white-collar positions; and that one-third are classified as professional, technical, or kindred workers.

We asked the Sansei:

"What occupation would you *most like* to make your life work—the work you hope to be doing throughout your career?"

Given their youth, only 23 percent of the Sansei sample had finished with school by 1967. Fifty-six percent were students at the time, and the rest were planning to reenter school.

In Table 8.4, we compare the principal occupations of Issei and Nisei men with the desired occupations of Sansei men and women. Looking at the table, we observe that only 5 percent of the Issei were professionals, and a third of the Nisei are. But about three-quarters of the Sansei, men and women alike, hope to

TABLE 8.4

Principal Occupations of Issei and Nisei Men, Compared with Desired Occupations of Sansei Men and Women

Category	Issei Men	Nisei Men	Sansei Men	Sansei Women
			Percent of Respondents	
White-collar	35	65	87	90
Professional, technical, and kindred workers	5	32	77	73
Managers and administrators (except farm)	28	19	8	5
Sales, clerical, and kindred workers	2	14	2	12
Blue-collar	65	35	13	10
Craftsmen and operatives (including transport)	5	12	9	3
Laborers; service and private-household workers[a]	15	10	2	7
Farmers and farm managers[b]	45	13	2	-[c]
Total number	(902)	(2,190)	(370)	(307)[d]

[a]Includes Nisei farm laborers.
[b]Includes Issei farm laborers.
[c]Less than 0.5 percent.
[d]Excludes 53 women who desire to become housewives.

119

become professionals. Nine of ten contemplate white-collar jobs. (We have not considered Sansei women who plan to be housewives—only 15 percent of the female sample. Thus, most Sansei women hope to enter the labor market, primarily as professionals—teachers, nurses, and social welfare workers.)

We went on to ask the Sansei about the likelihood that they would in fact be doing their desired work. Sixty-four percent are either certain, or believe it likely, that they will achieve their aims. And 80 percent hope for an above-average level of achievement therein. To those who stated that they have only an even chance of doing their desired work, or are unlikely to be doing it, we put the question of what they realistically expect to be doing. It should be noted that only 18 percent of the men, but 40 percent of the women, are pessimistic about being able to do their desired life's work. Of the unsure, six of ten of the women realistically expect to be housewives. Of the men with professional aspirations, six of ten anticipate being in a less-skilled position. Surprisingly, of the men with nonprofessional aspirations, 47 percent realistically expect to be doing more-skilled work, and only 29 percent less-skilled, than they originally intended doing. The same pattern holds among nonprofessional women who expect to be in the labor market: One-fourth realistically anticipate more-skilled work than they desire and only 11 percent, less-skilled.

There is an indication that at least some Sansei see themselves as doing what their parents urged them to do, rather than following a self-selected course.

Although only 28 percent of the Sansei report that their parents want a specific occupation for them, of those who do report parental pressure, nearly nine of ten say they are expected to be professionals. There is thus a hint in the data that not all the Sansei are content with the high level of occupational achievement that is expected of them.

Although about half the Sansei were still students in 1967, the others (even if planning to return to school) had already entered the labor market. Table 8.5 shows the level of jobs in which they were engaged at the time. Half were already professionals; altogether, over three-fourths were in white-collar ranks. This is already a higher level of achievement than displayed by the Nisei generation. Whereas 38 percent of the Nisei are self-employed, only 13 percent of the Sansei expect to be so. Of those employed in 1967, only 8 percent were self-employed. The Sansei, in large numbers, then, either expect to be or are salaried men and women. Thus, their occupations—as engineers, architects, and technicians, or as social workers and teachers, for example—would tend to take them out of the close world of the Japanese American community and into the larger, more bureaucratically organized world.

The Sansei have relatively high aspirations as to income. Although three-fourths of them were earning less than $7,500 a year in 1967 (so many were students), 34 percent expect to be earning $20,000 a year or more at the peak of their careers. This compares with only 13 percent of the Nisei who were earning as much when approached in 1966–67.

TABLE 8.5

Types of Jobs Held by Sansei in Labor Market in 1967

Job	Percent of Sansei
White-collar	78
Professional	52
Managerial	8
Clerical	13
Sales	5
Blue-collar	19
Crafts	8
Operatives	6
Service	4
Labor	1
Farm owner	3
Total number	(360)

Given their educational attainments and prospects, the Sansei do indeed seem destined for higher accomplishments in occupation and income than shown by the Nisei. Let us look only at the amount of education achieved by the Sansei in 1967. Already 88 percent had had at least some college training (25 percent had already finished college, or gone further). In contrast, only 57 percent of the Nisei, whose education was completed, had had at least some college training when approached. No doubt, the Sansei generation will, when mature, have an astonishing level of educational accomplishment. And this prospect is sufficient to draw more and more of them out of the confines of the Japanese American community and into mainstream America. For, as we have seen, region of residence aside, nothing leads Japanese Americans out of the ethnic community, as classically defined, more than does high educational attainment.

Just as the Sansei tend to have Caucasian friends in grade and in high school, they continue these associations in college and out—and thereby reinforce their ties to the Caucasian world. They do so, of course, with some Nisei disapproval. For example, 52 percent of the Nisei believe the Sansei to be "too American"; only 36 percent of the Sansei take that view (and this is related to their differential integration).

Regarding adult associations, we asked a number of questions on organizational membership. As we reported earlier, with regard to nonschool organizations, two-thirds of the Sansei do not belong to any. Should they belong, they are just as likely to have joined a non-Japanese American group as a Japanese one. And when asked which of the organizations they belong to, they devote the

TABLE 8.6

College-Group Memberships and Ethnic Composition

Group	Percent Who Belong to Groups	Percent of Groups with Primarily Japanese American Members
Political, or student government	38	
Total	(604)	
Fraternities or sororities	21	
Total	(607)	
Informal circles	40	
Total	(596)	
Other	47	
Total	(603)	

most time to, seven of ten mention a nonethni⟨
members are not largely oriented to intracomn
Nisei, for that matter.)

On the college scene, we asked the Sans⟨
number of different types of groups, and abo
groups. Table 8.6 sums up the findings. We s⟨
not belong to any groups in college—not even to informal circles. When they do, they are likely to eschew groups (if they can be formed) that are largely Japanese American. True, among the members of informal circles, 43 percent cluster with ethnic peers. We suspect that this takes place on large campuses, like UCLA, that have a significant number of Sansei students. Given the chance, Sansei students may well seek out each other's company—especially if they have come from remote areas containing few Japanese Americans. But given the chance or not, it is still true that three-fourths of them number at least one Caucasian among their two closest friends.

The Sansei are a sanguine lot. Nearly eight of ten do not believe that being a Japanese American has hindered their advancement at all—although a significant proportion (66 percent) believe that it did hinder their parents' advancement at least a little. Although they tend to blame the Caucasian community for hostility to the Issei, they have surprising views on the World War II relocation. Thirty-three percent actually favor the government's action, 19 percent have mixed feelings, while 48 percent have unfavorable ones. (Incidentally, according to the Field Poll of September 1967, 87 percent of Californians are familiar with what was done to the Japanese Americans in World War II, and of those who are, 48 percent favor the government's action.) Further, the Sansei tend to agree with the Nisei on one point: About eight of ten of each generation believe that leaders who acted to make the episode orderly and comfortable used a better approach than those who protested.

Patently, the Sansei, like the Nisei, do not believe that the Japanese Americans can rightfully complain about their condition. Only 18 percent of the older and 15 percent of the younger generation say this. Moreover, they agree that blacks especially, but Mexican Americans and Puerto Ricans, too, do have grounds for complaints.

Regarding the black population's plight, the Nisei, the Sansei, and the general California public have the same advice: Blacks should get more education, work harder, and improve their attitude. The California public was somewhat more sensitive to the riot situation than were Japanese Americans. In contrast to the California public, and no doubt related to their own successful struggle, Japanese Americans are far more optimistic about how long it will take for blacks to achieve their goals. Two-thirds of the Nisei and Sansei alike believe this will come about within a generation. Only four of every ten of the Californians are as optimistic. Strangely, however, in an open-ended question, virtually no Sansei relate the black struggle to the Japanese American success. Nor in 1967 were the large majority of Sansei in favor of the black-power movement. Obviously, they believe that advancement is won by individual achievement rather than by collective efforts.[7] In this sense, the Sansei could be described as a conservative group who probably would have disfavored affirmative-action programs in 1967, although we have no data on the point. Changes over the past decade could, however, have been considerable—especially among the more militant Sansei whose views of disadvantaged minorities, among whom they number themselves, could have sifted down to the rank and file.

We do not mean to imply that the Sansei are prejudiced toward blacks. Virtually all (95 percent) say they would sell their house to a black if their neighbors didn't disapprove. If, however, neighbors disapproved, only 66 percent would still sell. (Eighty-three percent of Californians would sell if nighbors did not disapprove; 50 percent, if there were disapproval.) Eighty-six percent of the Sansei themselves would not disapprove if a neighbor wanted to sell his house to a black.

Californians are in a tricky position when it comes to neighbors' sentiments. Although a majority would sell to a black, with neighborhood approval, they do not see this approval as very likely to be forthcoming. We asked, on the Field Poll: "Do you think that in this neighborhood, most of your neighbors would disapprove of your selling to a Negro?" Sixty-nine percent say yes.

Japanese Americans are viewed far more favorably. Ninety-six percent of the California sample say they would sell to one. If neighbors disapproved, 74 percent would still sell. Further, the large majority of the sample do not believe that their neighbors would disapprove selling to a Japanese American: 84 percent say that they would not. Japanese Americans are, in fact, highly approved by the Californians. They are viewed as follows:

Characteristic	Percent Who Cite Characteristic
Hard working	82
Thrifty	50
Honest	48
Clever	35
Clannish	23
Grasping	3
Sneaky	3
Poor	2
Lazy	1

This is clearly a favorable image of the minority as of the mid-1960s.

Like members of other immigrant groups, the Sansei are not very knowledgeable about the conditions of their immigrant forebears. Only 24 percent report being very close to the Issei. (Language problems, of course, present themselves.) Only 48 percent know the prefectures in Japan from which their grandparents came. And a bare 12 percent report that they are very familiar with the experiences their grandparents underwent. Apparently, the old stories of trials and tribulations undoubtedly told the Nisei have not been passed on—or else the Sansei are not interested in hearing them.

We have stated that in many ways, the Nisei and Sansei resemble each other, with some significant differences. One point of difference is in religion: Although a little over half of either generation are Christians, there are fewer members of traditional religious groups, like Buddhists, among the Sansei. Instead, intergenerationally, the proportion of nonbelievers has grown from 9 to 20 percent. The Sansei are also less likely to believe in the importance of religion.

The Sansei evidence about the same degree of political interest as the Nisei (about half of either generation are interested). But they are less likely to read Japanese American newspapers regularly or occasionally: 64 percent of the Nisei as against 46 percent of the Sansei. In terms of location, the generations, for now, find themselves similarly situated: About a third of the Sansei were in Los Angeles in 1967, a fifth were in the East, and the rest elsewhere on the Pacific.

On another significant point, we find a difference between the generations. Regarding Japanese values, both Nisei and Sansei were asked whether or not their parents stressed (1) not bringing shame to the family, (2) making returns for all kindnesses, and (3) not bringing dishonor to the Japanese American community. On the first two items, eight of ten of both Nisei and Sansei say their parents stressed this. On the third item, 81 percent of the Nisei report that the Issei stressed not bringing dishonor to the community, but only 58 percent of the Sansei report this. We can only surmise that this is some evidence for the proposition that Nisei have been as likely to promote Sansei achievement by laying emphasis on individual achievement in the classic American sense as they have been to pass on the traditional Japanese meaning of the collectivist obligation to get ahead. The finding also attests to a duality among the Sansei generation—oriented, on the one hand, to their ethnic roots, and on the other, to the larger competitive world in which the majority of them are immersed.

IMMERSION IN THE JAPANESE AMERICAN COMMUNITY

We make use of a single indicator to describe the differential degrees to which our Sansei respondents are immersed in the Japanese American community: the frequency of monthly visits to nonhousehold relatives. The Sansei are split, about equally, three ways on the question. A little under a third (31 percent) make no visits to relatives at all; a little over a third (37 percent) average one to four visits a month; and about a third (32 percent) make five or more visits a month. In attempting to account for differential involvement in Japanese American communal life, we usually make a distinction below between nonvisitors and visitors—that is to say, between those who putatively divorce themselves entirely from the normative constraints of nonhousehold relatives, and those who are, at least to some degree, exposed to the values of ethnic peers.

It is important to note at the outset that there is little difference in regard to visiting patterns according to sex or age. Sansei women are only slightly more likely to be visitors than the men. Likewise, the older are only somewhat more likely to be visitors than the younger. For example, 68 percent of those under 21 years old are visitors, compared with 75 percent of those 25 or older.

The age difference is, of course, related to marital status: Married couples are more likely to visit relatives than are their more footloose single peers. But, as Table 8.7 shows, we must also take into account the countervailing force of outmarriage. Eighty-six percent of the inmarried pay monthly visits, compared with 65 percent of the single, but only 60 percent of the exogamous. Like single status, exogamy, then, tends to reduce the Sansei's communal ties. Table 8.7 also reveals that those who tend toward exogamy (those dating or going steady with non-Japanese Americans) are less likely to visit than those who intend to marry within the fold. A further datum: 60 percent of those who believe out-marriage has good effects on the Japanese American community are visitors, compared with 76 percent of those who believe it has bad effects. Still further: Now contrasting nonvisitors and visitors, we find that the former would be less disturbed than the visitors would be if a Japanese American youth of either sex outmarried. Visiting relatives definitely reinforces norms making for endogamy. For example, only 57 percent of the Sansei who never visit relatives would be disturbed if a Japanese American girl married a Caucasian; 74 percent who visit five or more times a month would be so disturbed.

Immersion in the Japanese American community, then, is inversely related to tendencies toward assimilation, as measured by exogamy or exogamous tendencies. It is also related to a number of other variables that help clarify the

TABLE 8.7

Frequency of Visits with Relatives, by Sansei Marital Status and Tendency toward Exogamy

Variable	Percent Who Visit One or More Times per Month
Marital status	
Single	65
Total number	(541)
Inmarried	86
Total number	(138)
Outmarried	60
Total number	(96)
Those who are engaged to or going steady with:	
Japanese American	70
Total number	(86)
Non-Japanese American	60
Total number	(102)

differences between Sansei who tend to be exposed to community values and those who are relatively unexposed. Take the occupational choices of the Sansei (see Table 8.8). Those who intend to become professionals, especially free or technical, are less likely to be visitors than their peers who choose less lofty pursuits. Actually, this may be a case of anticipatory socialization: The professionals expect to deal with Caucasians in their work more than do the others; and, accordingly, may begin, early on, to reduce community contacts. In contrast, lower white- and blue-collar workers anticipate more active involvement with fellow Japanese Americans, both on and off the job, and so maintain communal ties.

Occupation is, of course, highly related to education. Table 8.9 shows the relationship between the educational level already obtained by the Sansei in 1967 and their visiting patterns. As expected, the less the education a Sansei has achieved, the greater the degree of his or her community immersion, as indicated by visiting patterns. For example, 75 percent of those who were high school graduates or less, at the time of fieldwork, visit relatives at least once a month, compared with only 58 percent of those who have gone beyond college in their training.

At the college level, we also find that the fewer organizations a Sansei belongs to, the more likely he or she is to be immersed in the community. This is a good instance of the avoidance of cross pressures. By staying out of

Caucasian-dominated extracurricular collegiate pursuits, those who visit relatives are relatively less exposed than the nonvisitors to any anticommunal pulls.

Regarding noncollegiate social organizations, there is no difference in visiting patterns between the nonmembers and the members. But the latter were also asked about the ethnic composition of their favorite organizations; here, we find that 85 percent of those who mention largely Japanese American organizations are visitors, compared with 65 percent of those who choose noncommunal associations. Communal associations reinforce the norms of the Japanese American culture; extracommunal associations subvert them.

The tendency of Sansei with certain occupational intentions to have reduced rates of visiting is further shown in Table 8.10, wherein the major at the first college they attended is taken into account. Those destined to enter the humanities, engineering, or the sciences—fields in which they would be dealing largely with the Caucasian world—are less likely to be immersed in the Japanese

TABLE 8.8

Frequency of Visits with Relatives, by Sansei Desired Occupation

Desired Category	Percent Who Visit One or More Times per Month
Natural and social sciences	66
Total number	(59)
Humanities	33
Total number	(13)
Free professions	55
Total number	(53)
Technical professions	54
Total number	(57)
Nursing, teaching, social work	69
Total number	(201)
Accountants	93
Total number	(15)
Other professions	69
Total number	(108)
Other white-collar	73
Total number	(93)
Blue-collar	75
Total number	(53)
Farm owner	4
Total number	(8)
Housewife	75
Total number	(53)

TABLE 8.9

Frequency of Visits with Relatives, by Respondents' Education

Education	Percent Who Visit One or More Times per Month
High school graduate or less	75
Total number	(93)
Some college	69
Total number	(497)
College graduate	69
Total number	(95)
Postgraduate	58
Total number	(95)

American community than are Sansei who intend to enter the free professions (e.g., medicine, law), business, or the semiprofessions (e.g., pharmacy, optometry, social work)—fields which would be more likely to put them in touch professionally with the Japanese American community.

The point that some Sansei have been socialized toward immersion, while others have been bent toward integration, is apparent in other data. The Sansei were asked about their youthful friendship patterns in grade school and in high school. In either setting, the more Japanese American friends a child had, the more intensive were his or her visiting patterns upon reaching adulthood (see Table 8.11). For example, fully 83 percent of the respondents who had mostly Japanese American friends in high school can now be classified as visitors, compared with 61 percent of those who had mostly Caucasian friends. Much to the point, the groundwork that was laid in childhood and youth determines their degree of community involvement as young adults.

There is further evidence that Sansei have been differentially socialized into the Japanese American community. We asked three questions dealing with relations with grandparents: how close they were to their Issei grandparents; whether or not they know the prefecture from which the grandparent they knew best had derived; and how familiar they are with the experiences of their Japanese grandparents in getting settled in the United States. We find (see Table 8.12) that the closer the Sansei have been with the grandparent they have known best, the more likely they are to be visitors; that those who know the prefecture of origin are more likely to be visitors than those who do not; and that the more familiar they are with the conditions of their grandparents' settling, the more likely they are, too, to be visitors. Obviously, grandparental influence, or its lack, has had an effect on the degree to which the Sansei are immersed in the Japanese American community. We might conjecture that one of the reasons for

TABLE 8.10

Frequency of Visits with Relatives, by Major at First
College Attended

Major	Percent Who Visit One or More Times per Month
Trades	73
Total number	(98)
Humanities	64
Total number	(187)
Engineering	62
Total number	(76)
Sciences	60
Total number	(97)
Professions	70
Total number	(10)
Business	77
Total number	(48)
Semiprofessions	73
Total number	(60)

TABLE 8.11

Frequency of Visits with Relatives, by Youthful Friendship Patterns
of the Sansei

Ethnicity of Friends	Percent Who Visit One or More Times per Month
Grade school	
Mostly Japanese American	82
Total number	(114)
Mixed	73
Total number	(161)
Mostly non-Japanese American	64
Total number	(502)
High school	
Mostly Japanese American	83
Total number	(157)
Mixed	73
Total number	(195)
Mostly non-Japanese American	61
Total number	(426)

TABLE 8.12

Frequency of Visits with Relatives, by Closeness of Relations with Grandparents, Knowledge of Prefectural Origin, and Familiarity with Grandparents' Settling in United States

Variable	Percent Who Visit One or More Times a Month
Closeness of relations	
Very close	76
Total number	(184)
Rather close	71
Total number	(320)
Not close, or distant	60
Total number	(272)
Knowledge of Prefecture	
Yes	75
Total number	(356)
No	64
Total number	(397)
Familiarity with settling	
Very familiar	71
Total number	(94)
Somewhat familiar	71
Total number	(373)
Mainly unfamiliar	65
Total number	(309)

a relatively low rate of immersion has been the conditions set by many Nisei parents, willingly or unwillingly, that have served to divorce so many Sansei from an intimate acquaintance with their history and origins—which only the grandparents could forcefully provide. Indeed, consider that 40 percent of the Sansei are mainly unfamiliar with their grandparents' trials in getting settled in this country.

Even so, we have found that a majority of the Sansei believe that minority groups should try to preserve something of the culture of their own group, rather than blending into the mainstream of American life. This belief, however, is strongly related to visiting patterns with relatives. The less the Sansei visit, the less likely they are to believe that minority groups should retain their distinctive character (see Table 8.13). The nonvisitors are almost as likely as not to remark that blending into the mainstream would be a good thing.

Two ways of blending into the mainstream are, of course, to give up Buddhism for Christianity, or to confess no religious belief at all. We already

TABLE 8.13

Frequency of Visits with Relatives, by Belief about Whether
Minorities Should Preserve Own Culture or
Blend into Mainstream

What Minority Should Do	Percent Who Make Various Numbers of Visits per Month		
	None	1–4	5 or More
Preserve own culture	57	62	74
Blend into mainstream	43	38	26
Total number	(238)	(286)	(243)

TABLE 8.14

Frequency of Visits with Relatives, by Sansei Religion

Religion	Percent Who Visit One or More Times a Month
Traditional	79
Total number	(194)
Christian	66
Total number	(428)
Nonbelievers	62
Total number	(154)

have reported that the Sansei are more likely to take the latter route than the Nisei. We note now that nonbelievers are less likely than either Buddhists or Christians (especially the former) to be subject to communal control. Table 8.14 shows that while 79 percent who confess a traditional religion are visitors, only 62 percent of the nonbelievers are. Upon the latter, the communally reinforcing constraints of the religious congregation are clearly unable to operate. But the rate of visiting is also relatively low among Christians. This is because so many of them belong to mixed congregations (although we lack data on the ethnic composition of Christian congregants).

Apart from religious affiliation, or lack of it, there is a further significant variable that is highly correlated with visiting patterns: interest in politics. Just as we found that interest in politics made a difference among the Nisei, the same pattern emerges among the Sansei. The greater the degree of interest, the less likely the Sansei are to be immersed in the ethnic community. The community, then, for those within its purlieu, tends to be self-contained and, in many ways, cut off from the mainstream of American life. Politics for them appears to be out of bounds. The community, at least its uneroded core, is turned in upon itself—even for the Sansei who have remained immersed, or who, better still, have been socialized into immersion, within it.

The consequences of immersion appear again when one considers reading habits. Nearly nine of ten Sansei who read Japanese American newspapers regularly (only a minority do) are visitors, compared with only 61 percent of those who hardly ever read them. The papers, of course, are a means of tying the community, far-flung as it is, together. They serve to keep its members informed about common problems, pursuits, and the comings and goings of ethnic peers. Again, only a minority of the Sansei are part of this network.

As we already made apparent regarding the Nisei, residence makes a difference. Where Japanese Americans congregate, one finds stronger communal bonds. This works equally well among the Sansei. We find that 80 percent of the Los Angelenos in our sample are visitors, compared with 71 percent of those who live elsewhere on the Pacific, and only 51 percent of the others. Clearly, Sansei immersion in a Japanese community is most likely to occur where sizable, and viable, Japanese communities exist. Los Angeles, the metropolis of Japanese America, provides the greatest chance for it—and the community controls there are, by definition, the strongest even for the third generation.

It is in strong Japanese American communities that the Sansei are subject the most to the exercise of communal norms, as evidenced by visiting patterns. And perhaps there they receive the most intensive training in Japanese American culture. We asked them, in fact, how much training they had had. Although few received extensive training, 86 percent of those who did visit relatives. At the other extreme, of those who received no training, only 59 percent are visitors.

Thus far, we have been discussing the forces that draw the Sansei into the net of the Japanese American community. We now take up the forces, from the other direction, that act to draw them away from the normative sanctions of their ethnic peers.

FORCES MAKING FOR INTEGRATION INTO THE LARGER SOCIETY

Just as we have found bonds keeping the Nisei generation within the Japanese American community, and even more potent pulls from without, bending them toward participation in the larger Caucasian society that environs them, so we encounter the same phenomenon among the Sansei—only more so. As a measure of integration into the larger society, we are unable to construct an index parallel to that used for the Nisei in Chapter 7. The majority of the Sansei are students; thus, work-related associations cannot be used. The many

TABLE 8.15

Ethnicity of Best Friends, by Marital Status and Ethnicity of Spouse

Variable	Percent with One or Two Friends Who Are Caucasians
Marital status	
Single	76
Total number	(553)
Married	70
Total number	(226)
Spouse's ethnicity	
Japanese American	58
Total number	(137)
Non-Japanese American	89
Total number	(89)
Of those engaged or going steady, would-be mate or date is:	
Japanese American	53
Total number	(87)
Non-Japanese American	95
Total number	(105)

single, living with parents; so neither can neighborly contacts be taken into account. The large majority are too young to belong to any formal organizations outside of school; this rules out the ethnic composition of organizations as part of an index. We are left with a solitary indicator of integration: the ethnicity of a Sansei's two closest friends.

It will be recalled that fully three-quarters of the Sansei count at least one non-Japanese American among their closest friends. As with visiting patterns, so it is with friendship choices: that neither age nor sex makes a difference. Marital status and ethnicity of spouse, of course, do (see Table 8.15). The single are slightly more likely to have Caucasian friends; among the married, the exogamous are far more likely to have formed such friendships than the endogamous. Further, among the single who are engaged or going steady, only 53 percent with a prospective Japanese American mate have at least one Caucasian friend, while virtually all (95 percent) going with or affianced to a non-Japanese American do. Exogamy, and tendencies toward it, either make for greater integration into the larger society or are the result of such tendencies already established.

Socializing experiences also play a solid part in explaining differential Sansei integration. The more non-Japanese American friends the Sansei had in grade school and in high school, the more likely they are to number at least one

TABLE 8.16

Ethnicity of Two Closest Friends, by Friendship Patterns in Grade School and in High School

Variable	Percent with One or Two Friends Who Are Caucasians
Friends in grade school	
Mostly Japanese American	48
Total number	(116)
Equal number of both	70
Total number	(164)
Mostly non-Japanese American	81
Total number	(501)
Friends in high school	
Mostly Japanese American	40
Total number	(159)
Equal numbers of both	66
Total number	(196)
Mostly non-Japanese American	90
Total number	(427)

Caucasian among their two closest friends (see Table 8.16). For example, only 40 percent of those who had mostly Japanese American friends in high school have, at least, one Caucasian friend now, compared with fully 90 percent of those whose friends were nonethnic peers.

There is, of course, a strong regional difference. In Los Angeles, 60 percent of the Sansei have at least one Caucasian friend; elsewhere on the coast, 76 percent do; to the east, 92 percent tend toward integration as measured by friendship choices.

We find a lack of correlation between education and friendship choices. In Table 8.17, we show whether or not this lack holds in the three regions. We find that it does. Whatever the region of residence, the least-educated Sansei in 1967 were as likely as the most educated to choose non-Japanese American friends.

The results concerning education and friendship choices are indeed not what we expected. We anticipated that the more education a Sansei had obtained, the more likely he or she would be to have Caucasian friends. Part of the lack of a difference may be explained by the fact that so many Sansei were, at the time, still completing their schooling. But then, current students were only somewhat more likely than those finished with school to score toward integration—77 as against 64 percent. A more likely explanation lies in the democratization of life among the Sansei. Even the least educated have the opportunity to circulate among Caucasians, and will do so, even in Los Angeles.

Education does not differentiate them when it comes to choosing friends. Whatever their educational level may be, and wherever they reside, the majority of Sansei tend to choose Caucasian friends.

When they do not choose students as friends, the majority of Sansei men, regardless of their desired occupational level, tend toward selecting professional people. Table 8.18 reports the desired occupations of Sansei men and women according to their best friend's occupation. We observe that those with professional aspirations tend, more than the others, toward student friends. The majority of the men select professional friends, whatever their own desired occupational level may be. The women, however, tend to seek out friends at a compatible level. Thus, Sansei men, at least, wish to circulate among professional people even if they hold blue-collar jobs themselves. The Sansei's milieu tends to be a middle-class one, whatever his desired status may be. This may help explain the phenomenon reported above regarding a lack of difference between educational level and ethnicity of friends: the fact that the Sansei are democratic, though middle class, in identification and orientation.

As would be expected, there is a difference between religious affiliation and choice of friends. Sixty-one percent of the Buddhists, 77 percent of the Christians, and 81 percent who profess no religion are integration oriented. One might say that the more secular among the Sansei are also those who have strayed the farthest from the Japanese American community. This finding is stronger than regional effect (see Table 8.19). For example, in Los Angeles the 48 percent who adhere to traditional faiths like Buddhism have at least one non-Japanese American friend, while seven of every ten of those who profess no

TABLE 8.17

Ethnicity of Two Closest Friends, by Region of Residence and Education

| Education | Percent in Each Region with One or Two Friends Who Are Caucasian | | |
	Los Angeles	Other Pacific	Other
High School	67	78	95
Total number	(29)	(37)	(19)
Some college	56	79	89
Total number	(168)	(226)	(61)
College graduate	70	55	95
Total number	(40)	(33)	(21)
Postgraduate	61	75	96
Total number	(31)	(36)	(25)

TABLE 8.18

Sansei Men's and Women's Desired Occupations, by Occupation of Best Friend

Friend's Occupation	Men			Women			
	Professional	Other White-Collar	Blue-Collar[a]	Professional	Other White-Collar	Blue-Collar[b]	Housewife
All friends' pursuits							
Professional	27%	33%	43%	25%	15%	4%	9%
Other white-collar	6	5	7	14	39	33	15
Blue-collar and farm owner	4	15	17	3	4	19	1
Student	63	46	33	59	41	44	5
Housewife	–	–	–	–	–	–	69
Total number	(258)	(39)	(30)	(220)	(46)	(27)	(85)
Pursuits excluding student and housewife							
Professional	72	62	65	60	26	7	36
Other white-collar	17	10	10	33	67	60	59
Blue-collar and farm owner	11	28	25	7	7	33	5
Total number	(97)	(21)	(20)	(90)	(27)	(15)	(22)

[a] Includes nine farm owners.
[b] Includes two farm owners.

TABLE 8.19

Region of Residence and Religious Affiliation, by Ethnicity
of Two Closest Friends

Religion	Percent in Each Region with One or Two Friends Who Are Caucasian		
	Los Angeles	Other Pacific	Other
Traditional	48	65	79
Total number	(58)	(121)	(14)
Christian	60	81	93
Total number	(150)	(150)	(118)
No affiliation	71	85	91
Total number	(58)	(61)	(32)

religious affiliation have one. Reading across in Table 8.19, however, we find
that the region of residence does have a relationship to friendship choices. Whatever the Sansei's religious confession, or lack of it, they are more likely to be
integrated into the larger society as they move away from Los Angeles.

There is a major political difference between Sansei who have Caucasian
friends and those who remain within the bounds of the Japanese American community. The former (56 percent) express a greater interest in politics than do the
latter (37 percent). Likewise, the former are more likely to be looked to for
political advice than the latter. It is not too farfetched to say that even though
more integrated, Sansei who have Caucasian friends are in a better position, than
those who lack them, to represent the interest of the Japanese American community, from which, in a traditional way, they appear to be so alienated.

Further to the point: It is the more integrated, not the less, who reflect
upon the relocation period with more disgruntlement. Fifty-one percent of the
more integrated have unfavorable views of relocation, compared with 37 percent
of the less integrated. We also asked this question:

> "During the World War II relocation, some Nisei worked to make
> relocation as orderly and comfortable as possible, while others pro-
> tested the injustice of the relocation and tried to have it declared
> unconstitutional. Which kind of leader do you *now* think employed
> the better approach?"

Now, it is true that 75 percent of the Sansei vote for the leader who tried to
make relocation as orderly and comfortable as possible. But it is also true that

28 percent of the more integrated Sansei vote for the leaders who made a protest, compared with 17 percent of the less integrated.

We suggest that the more militant Sansei today are drawn not from the ranks of the traditional community, but from the ranks of those, who through socialization and training, have broken away from that community. They form no tightly bonded community themselves, and tend to identify with the larger American scene. Even so, their private identities would tend still to be as Japanese Americans.

Typological Differences

Another way of viewing the Sansei data on immersion in the Japanese American community, on the one hand, and integration into the larger society, on the other, is to form a typology, as we have already done with the Nisei.

TABLE 8.20

Typologies of Social Relations: Visits with Relatives and Integration into American Society

Measure	Nisei Visits	
	Few (0–4)	Many (5 or more)
Integration		
Low (0, 1)	1. Disengaged = 28%	2. Monocultural Japanese Americans = 17%
High (2–4)	3. Monoculturally Americans = 37%	4. Bicultural = 18%
	Sansei Visits	
Best friends		
Both are Japanese Americans	1. Disengaged = 14%	2. Monocultural Japanese Americans = 12%
One or both are Caucasians	3. Monocultural Americans = 54%	4. Bicultural = 20%

In Table 8.20, we compare the Nisei and Sansei typologies. Granted that the measures of integration differ between the generations, the data still indicated a growth, in the third generation, in the proportion who can be classified as monocultural "Americans"—that is, those making few visits to relatives, and having one or two non-Japanese American close friends. Fifty-four percent of the Sansei fall into this category, and 37 percent of the Nisei. Otherwise, the most significant intergenerational changes are the drop in the proportion of the disengaged (Sansei who neither visit relatives nor have non-Japanese American friends), followed by a small reduction in the proportion of monocultural Japanese Americans. This latter is significant, for it means intergenerational continuity in the proportionately small, hard-core Japanese American community noted for intensive patterns of visitation and exclusiveness in friendship patterns. The bicultural form a fifth of the Sansei generation.

In Table 8.21, we sum up the major differences among the Sansei types. We concentrate on the two clearest types: the monocultural Japanese American and the monocultural "American." The bicultural truly have a foot in either camp, for on some measures, they are like the one pure type, and on others, like the other. The disengaged, the majority of whom are Los Angelenos, tend to be like the monocultural ethnics.

Typically, the monocultural Japanese American is a woman, a member of the older subgeneration, and married endogamously. She had proportionately few non-Japanese American friends in grade or in high school; neither did her parents urge her to take part with Caucasians, although she is in favor of this for her own offspring. She also tended to have close relations with her best-known grandparent, tends to believe the Sansei are too American, and strongly believes that minorities should preserve their own subcultures. She would be disturbed if a Japanese American girl married a Caucasian, and believes most Caucasians would be disturbed at a mixed union. If an organizational member, her favorite organization is a Japanese American one. She tends to have little interest in politics, is an avid reader of the Japanese American press, and, more likely than not, lives in Los Angeles.

In contrast to the monocultural Japanese Americans, the "Americans" are not differentiated by sex, but tend to be rather young (only 19 percent were 25 years old or older in 1967) and single (only 24 percent had wed at the time of the fieldwork). Of the married, a majority had chosen non-Japanese American partners. And of those engaged or going steady, the same holds true. Unlike the monocultural Japanese Americans, the monocultural "Americans" had non-Japanese-American friends in grade and in high school, and were urged by their parents to take part with Caucasians, just as they believe their children should. They tend toward more distant relations with grandparents, and are the least likely of the types to believe that the Sansei are too American. They are also least likely to believe that minorities should preserve their own subcultures, and least likely to be disturbed if a Japanese American girl married a Caucasian. If an organizational member, the "American" is not at all likely to belong to an ethnic association. He or she is the most likely, however, to believe that relocation leaders should have protested. In contrast to the Japanese American, the "American" is indeed interested in politics and is most frequently sought out for

TABLE 8.21

Differences among Types of Sansei

Item	Disengaged	Monocultural Japanese Americans	Monocultural "Americans"	Bicultural
Percent female	48	67	52	54
Total number	(112)	(88)	(410)	(152)
Percent 25 years old or older	22	31	19	26
Total number	(112)	(86)	(408)	(152)
Percent married	29	41	24	36
Total number	(112)	(88)	(410)	(152)
Percent outmarried	21	9	57	40
Total number	(33)	(34)	(100)	(55)
Percent engaged to or dating non-Japanese American	12	10	66	76
Total number	(25)	(21)	(107)	(33)
Percent college graduates	26	23	26	23
Total number	(112)	(88)	(410)	(152)
Percent that have non-Japanese friends in grade school	40	53	73	67
Total number	(111)	(88)	(408)	(152)
Percent that have non-Japanese friends in high school	17	27	68	65
Total number	(112)	(88)	(408)	(152)
Percent whose parents urged them to take part with Caucasians	38	38	65	62
Total number	(110)	(88)	(405)	(149)
Percent who believe own children should take part with Caucasians	72	74	84	79
Total number	(111)	(87)	(406)	(150)
Percent whose parents stressed that dishonor should not be brought to Japanese American community	64	68	54	60
Total number	(89)	(80)	(362)	(136)

	A	B	C	D
Percent who had distant relations with the best-known grandparent	26	26	42	25
Total number	(111)	(88)	(408)	(151)
Percent who believe Sansei are too American	38	48	33	41
Total number	(110)	(88)	(394)	(145)
Percent who believe minorities should preserve own cultures	63	73	58	74
Total number	(110)	(88)	(404)	(148)
Percent who would be disturbed if Japanese American girl married Caucasian	61	66	47	52
Total number	(112)	(84)	(397)	(150)
Percent who believe Caucasians would be disturbed if Japanese American boy married Caucasian girl	77	75	64	66
Total number	(112)	(84)	(395)	(148)
Percent of organizational members whose favorite one is Japanese American	55	64	21	29
Total number	(20)	(28)	(117)	(42)
Percent who believe they should adopt to continue family line	51	58	45	49
Total number	(111)	(86)	(402)	(150)
Percent who believe better relocation leader protested	17	17	31	22
Total number	(109)	(86)	(390)	(143)
Percent with no religious affiliation	12	17	23	18
Total number	(111)	(88)	(408)	(151)
Percent with little or no interest in politics	67	59	43	45
Total number	(112)	(88)	(410)	(152)
Percent who are asked for political advice	15	22	26	24
Total number	(112)	(88)	(408)	(152)
Percent who hardly ever read Japanese American newspapers	34	24	65	55
Total number	(112)	(88)	(410)	(152)
Percent living in Los Angeles	57	49	27	32
Total number	(110)	(87)	(399)	(148)

for political advice. Finally, he or she hardly ever looks at the Japanese American press, and is least likely of the four types to reside in metropolitan Los Angeles.

Intergenerational Effects

How did the more integrated Sansei, now a majority of the generation, get that way? Our data point to the conclusion that they were bred to take part in the larger American context—and not only by the Nisei, but derivatively by the Issei as well. The more educated the Issei male was, the more integrated his offspring, the Nisei, are likely to be. And the more integrated the Nisei are, the more integrated into the larger scene (as indicated by friendship choices) are the Sansei. In other words, the better-schooled Issei were better able to assay the lay of the land to which they had come, and groomed their children to become part of the mainstream of American life. The process is simply more pronounced among the Sansei, who face none or few of the barriers to their forebears faced by the Nisei. We suggest, then, that the transformation of the Japanese American community into one with fewer and fewer effective normative constraints could already have been forecast before the Issei set sail from Japan.

A FINAL NOTE: THE CHILDREN OF MIXED MARRIAGES

We had hoped to be able to compare Sansei who spring from endogamous Nisei unions with those who are the products of outmarriage. We could have expected that about 10 percent of our Sansei sample would be exogamy products. Since the exogamous Nisei tended to be rather young, however, few of their children were of age at the time of our fieldwork. In fact, we have only 13 Sansei respondents out of the 802 who are children of the intermarried.

One can tell little from 13 respondents. Suffice it to say that they tend to follow in the exogamous footsteps of their parents. Five are married, four to Caucasians and one to a Korean. Of the other eight, three are only dating casually or not dating. Of the remaining five, four are going with Caucasians and one with a Sansei. If these bare results are a harbinger, then mixed marriages would seem to breed mixed marriages.

NOTES

1. Stanford M. Lyman notes the desire of Sansei and Yonsei to recover their Japanese culture, while at the same time allocating their energies and activities to things American. See Stanford M. Lyman, "Contrasts in the Community Organization of Chinese and Japanese in North America," *Canadian Review of Sociology and Anthropology* 5 (1968): 55.

2. We plan to query Sansei who have now come of age, in order to see whether or not the younger cohort differs from their older brothers and sisters. We also have plans to interview, in depth, the children of Nisei outmarriages, especially around the issue of mixed-identity resolution.

3. Outmarriage rates have reached 50 percent in such areas as Hawaii, Los Angeles, Fresno, and San Francisco, according to Akemi Kikumura and Harry H. L. Kitano, "Interracial Marriage: A Picture of the Japanese," *The Journal of Social Issues* 29, no. 2 (1973): 67.

4. The identity data form the basis for the doctoral dissertation of Hilla Kuttenplan Israely (UCLA, 1975).

5. For a discussion of intermarriage as boundary maintenance, see John N. Tinker, "Intermarriage and Ethnic Boundaries: The Japanese American Case," *Journal of Social Issues* 29, no. 2 (1973): 49–66; and Kikumura and Kitano, "Interracial Marriage."

6. See Joe Yamamoto, "Japanese American Identity Crisis," in Eugene B. Brody, ed., *Minority Group Adolescents in the United States* (Baltimore: Williams and Wilkins, 1968), pp. 133–56, for a statement as to why Americans of Japanese descent should maintain dual identity.

7. Ima points out that although "successful," Japanese Americans' success has been qualified, and that they have been confined to the lower subordinate ranks. Kenji Ima, "Japanese Americans: The Making of a 'Good' People," in Anthony Gary Dworkin and Rosalind J. Dworkin, *The Minority Report* (New York: Praeger, 1976), p. 280.

9

CONCLUSIONS

RECAPITULATION

We have conducted a set of surveys of Japanese Issei migrants to these continental shores; of their Nisei offspring; and of the Nisei's children, the Sansei, who have by now largely come of age.[1] Our primary focus has been upon the transformation of the closely bonded, exclusive, and excluded communities of Issei (a subnation), founded mainly on the West Coast, into a more fragmented state of affairs in succeeding generations.[2]

The Issei were hemmed in by many restrictions (they were excluded from some occupations; they could not own land; they could not become citizens), by intense discrimination and virulent prejudice, by an incomplete facility with the language,[3] and by consequent poverty—in which state, however, they managed to raise relatively large, cohesive families. They were not invited to take part, except economically—and then in delimited ways—in the larger context; neither did they seek to enter the milieu that environed them. Many planned an eventual return to Japan, once their fortunes could be won. And although thousands did indeed return to the homeland, many more stayed on, sent to Japan for brides, and founded families in America.[4]

The Issei were not all of a piece, however, Although they shared common values (e.g., the primacy of familial obligations, the importance of achievement), some came to America better equipped to deal with new situations than others. Specifically, they were differentiated by their education in Japan (an indicator of class differences, of urban-or-rural origin, perhaps of achievement-oriented values)—and those who had more, and their descendants, have done better in the new setting, if success is defined in socioeconomic terms.[5]

The close-knit Issei community contained the seeds of its own destruction. By encouraging the Nisei, the older of whom still faced intense racial prejudice and discrimination, to seek education and white-collar careers (especially valued was the free professional), rather than to stay in farming or to enter into marginal small businesses, the Issei (surely not consciously) actually drove the Nisei into forming close associations and friendships in the Caucasian world. Then, too, the Japanese Americans have even constituted a small minority on the U.S. mainland, little able to isolate itself and insulate itself from outside influences. So few in number, and in proportion to the total population, even in Los Angeles, they could not, with some exceptions, choose to be, or be compelled to be, ghettoized. Almost from the start, Japanese lived in mixed or largely Caucasian neighborhoods, and have increasingly been accepted there. By now the great majority of Nisei are dispersed in largely Caucasian neighborhoods—and the Sansei have, as a result, been schooled therein and have forged mostly Caucasian associations.

After the trauma of Pearl Harbor, the concomitant relocation of some 110,000 Issei and Nisei (U.S. citizens) from the West Coast, and the gradual postwar resettlement (a majority returned to California, especially to Los Angeles), the younger Nisei found a different climate facing them. Prejudice and discrimination rapidly declined from the late 1940s on. They were accepted economically and socially in an expanding economy, in perhaps unforeseen ways. A plurality began to drift away from the old-fashioned, retrogressive bonds that had held the Issei together as a community. Although they may identify as Japanese Americans, the lives of the significant minority are spent almost wholly in the larger, Caucasian world. This is so much more so in the case of the Sansei.

Still, outmarriage, the primary indicator of assimilation, has been the exception among the Nisei.[6] Only 10 percent have married outside the fold. But that one in ten is radically different from the others: He or she tends to be highly educated, Christian, and professional; is more likely to have grown up among Caucasians; has cut ties with other Japanese Americans; and, anyway, is likely to live off the West Coast—and out of Los Angeles, the heartland of the Japanese American community.

The situation of the Sansei is radically different from that of the Nisei. Some half of the Sansei have already formed, or are contemplating forming, marital unions with Caucasians, and they express relatively little concern over this. They have, in fact, been socialized to it. Residence in largely Caucasian neighborhoods, attendance at largely Caucasian schools, social acceptance by Caucasians, and parental encouragement to associate with Caucasians have led a soon-to-be majority of Sansei to form exogamous ties. Moreover, exogamy aside, their close friendships are largely with Caucasians. The great majority are unfamiliar with the kind of Japanese American world characterized by intimate, primary, communal association and by close social control. Only a small minority live in that kind of setting, and they are vanishing breed. A larger proportion, now a majority, of the Sansei can be classified—and classify themselves—as "American." They see members of the clan rarely and associate mostly with Caucasians as friends. The ways of their Issei grandparents are alien to them—when they can comprehend what the Issei may utter in Japanese. Still and all, they express a yearning to know more about their cultural roots.

What we find, in fact, is little persistence of Japanese American communities in the classic, Issei sense. As Nisei and Sansei have entered the social and economic networks of the larger society, they have willy-nilly moved away from older-style, Japanese American identities. In this respect, they follow the fates of so many noncolored ethnic groups.

We do not mean to imply that the Nisei and, especially, the Sansei generations have ceased to define themselves, or have ceased to be defined, as Japanese Americans. We do imply that, increasingly, such a characterization matters relatively little to them and to a world that is no longer foreign to them—and hostile. They are in that world—and in it to stay. Barring some unthinkable calamity bestirring international relations between Japan and the United States, Japanese Americans, especially the younger, think of themselves as Americans, and they are considered as such by their friends, neighbors, and associates—and at least by the majority of the California public, who have had the most interaction with them.[7] Elsewhere, they may still appear foreign.[8]

Besides, there is the problem of the consequences of Sansei outmarriage. The offspring of exogamous unions may have little reason to retain any Japanese American identity at all. (And that may partly depend on appearance.) Even so, they may have incurred some psychic and other costs. In our samplings, we have about 100 children of interracial unions between Nisei and Caucasians who have reached adolescence. We plan to explore with them the problems of identity formation and the direction of subcultural commitment that they have faced. Who are these young men and women, born and bred of two worlds? What, if anything, is distinctively Japanese American about them? What pains have they suffered in trying to determine, "Who am I?" Do they have any wish to embark upon a voyage to assay whether or not their partially Japanese heritage still has any relevance?

New Blood

Even though the Japanese American community has undergone great transformations as one generation has succeeded the other, there have been potential sources of fresh blood that could potentially shore it up. First, in the post-World War II period, many American soldiers returned home with Japanese brides, some of whom, especially in Los Angeles, have become active in the old-time, Issei-forged community. The community may even function for them as a way station as they learn the foreign manners and mores, and adapt to American culture.

Second, there has been an increasing flow of Japanese Hawaiians to the mainland as their educational accomplishments in Hawaii have left them with too few economic opportunities.[9] But Japanese American Hawaiians have been less likely to acculturate or to assimilate than their mainland brethren. After all, they comprised some 57 percent of Hawaii's population in 1940; and now (1970 census), even though the proportion has shrunk to 28 percent, they tend to maintain a well-knit group[10] —which is due not only to their own ethnocentrism, but also to prejudices on the part of Caucasians, especially the haoles, who arrived later to replace them as the plurality of the Hawaiian population. Still, Hawaiians have elected a governor, a senator, and two congressmen of Japanese ancestry. Politically, Japanese Hawaiians have been far more active than their counterparts on the mainland, who have tended to shun politics. Senator Hayakawa, an older Nisei, is an exception, not the rule. For Hawaiians who have come to the mainland, too, the existence of a viable Japanese American community may be serving the latent function of helping resolve their identity problems, while also manifestly aiding them in adapting to mainland ways—and to social and economic opportunities.

Finally, the new legislation of 1952 and 1965, which made immigration more possible for Japanese, has resulted in a steady flow of Japanese immigrants to the United States, numbering about 4,000 a year since 1963.[11] To these fresh immigrants can be added the many students who come here from Japan (and many of them eventually gain immigrant status and stay), businessmen, and tourists. Japanese Americans may seem alien to the new arrivals. But to the extent that associations between the newcomers and old-timers are formed, there is necessarily mutual profit.

In short, the interchange between Japan and the United States, between Hawaii and the mainland, continues apace. Young Japanese Americans cannot help wondering what these foreigners are like—foreigners with whom they share common roots and common physical features. Actually, we know little or nothing about interaction between established Japanese Americans and the newcomers. But we can speculate. Sansei, particularly, are bound to be curious, and perhaps troubled. Have they been deprived of something valuable that might be regained? In any case, they soon find that, for example, a Japanese contemporary has far different values from, and a style of life distinct from, their Issei grandparents. The latter left Japan decades ago, when Japan was still largely a rural and feudal nation. Today, the young Sansei meet sophisticated Japanese youth who share many of their interests in music, in the arts, in sports—and yet, they are indefinably different. Language, too, is a barrier. We suggest that the very presence of Japanese immigrants and students in the United States can serve to compel even the most assimilated Sansei to question their own values, their own identity. Trips to Japan, which Sansei (not unlike other Americans) are eager to make, no doubt have the same results.

The Militants

In pluralistic America, younger members of many ethnic groups have begun to rebel against forces that would have them abandon the unique ways of their forebears.[12] That they are few in proportion to the size of their groups is attested by our data, wherein the culturally militant are scarcely evident. The militant Sansei on a campus like UCLA, for example, seem to want to know more, not less, about who they are, and how they have become what they are. They want to know how and why the relocation came about—an incident in history, like the Holocaust among Jews, that they cannot let rest. They want ultimately to know where they, collectively, are heading. Although our data show increasing assimilation among the Sansei that would lead toward the dissolution of a sense of community among them, our observations tell a contrary story. The intellectual elite of the young Japanese American world would preserve the aspects of their subculture that are most functional for solutions of their personal identity problems. Perhaps they will succeed in persuading the majority of their ethnic peers to join with them in forging a newly defined collective identity. But they pull oars against a strong tide: the economic, social, and cultural forces of late twentieth century America that sway toward the conditions of the mass society, in which each person is but an atom, and in which the protective clothing of the ethnic group will have been swept away. If viable ethnic groups serve as a buffer between the person and the state, there is every reason for the Sansei leadership to proselytize among the many apathetic ones. They may believe that a stronger Japanese American makes for a stronger America.[13]

A CLOSING NOTE ON DIFFERENCES BETWEEN MEN AND WOMEN

Nowadays, the careful social researcher is geared for the detection of sex differences that sample surveys may disclose. This was not the case earlier on— before the growing importance of the women's movement, before the campaign to achieve equal rights for women. True enough, earlier studies have taken sex into account, to explain better variations in attitudes, opinions, and behavior. As one example in the 1950s, Stouffer, in his landmark inquiry into the American public's tolerance for the activities of nonconformists, discovered that women were less tolerant than men.[14] His explanation of sex differences regarding that dimension derives from a general sociological conception, now eroding, that women have (or had) a narrower set of social relationships than men, and that they therefore are (or were) more likely to be constricted in outlook.

When the Japanese American Research Project got under way at UCLA in the early 1960s, there is no denying that a sexist slant was insinuated into the study design. An attempt was made to list all Japanese immigrants, men and women alike, who were then still alive and resident on the mainland of the United States. Eventually, some 18,000 Issei were listed, from whom a sample of over 1,000 was drawn for the survey.

From the outset, the researchers proceeded in a fashion that favored interviews with men. Largely, women were interviewed only if their husbands were incapacitated or dead. The lengthy interview focused heavily on the social and economic experiences of the male Issei—whether they were reported by the men themselves or were reported upon by the wife or widow.

Then, in early 1966, in order to conclude the Issei part of the inquiry sooner, we considerably shortened the interview schedule. At the time, it seemed appropriate to delete questions and batteries of questions not deemed central to the study. Many of the deletions related to the attitudes and the behavior of Issei women. When, in 1977, Susan McCoin Kataoka later undertook a secondary analysis of data collected from Issei women, she was considerably restricted.[15] The first third of the interviews contained many of the data she sought. Among the other two-thirds, many essential data had not been collected.

A preference for collecting data from and on men is also evident in the survey of the Nisei generation. It will be recalled that some offspring of the immigrants were designated for face-to-face interviews (and even a few for telephone interviews), while others (the majority) received compatible questionnaires in the mail. As expected, National Opinion Research Center inverviewers achieved a high completion rate among Nisei specifically sought. The return rate of the mail questionnaire was expectedly lower. But consider the order of priorities: Interviews were sought first with eldest sons, and then, if they were either not available or nonexistent, with eldest daughters. (Patently, there was also a bias in the direction of selecting for interview only children of either sex.) It was conceived that the careers of the first born, especially elder or eldest sons, would provide the best measure of a family's adaptation to the American scene. The conception, even at this late date, has yet to be confirmed or disconfirmed.[16]

Since sexist biases, however innocent and unwitting, had been built into the surveys, we are called upon to detect, generation by generation, differences between Japanese American men and women.

The Issei

To a remarkable degree, Issei men and women have similar opinions and share backgrounds, have the same perceptions, and reflect upon their experiences in the United States in a like way. For example, an equal proportion of immigrant men and women, only one-fourth, state that, upon arrival, they had originally planned to remain permanently in the United States. Regarding their backgrounds, we find that a majority of either sex—70 percent of the men, 62 percent of the women—had achieved a relatively high level of education (eight or more years) before leaving Japan. Once on these shores, Issei men and women converted to Christianity (an indicator of acculturation) at about the same rate: 68 percent of the men, 62 percent of the women. Consider another measure of acculturation: the respondent's self-selected position on the issue of Japanese American identification. Eighty-five percent of the men and 77 percent of the women are considered "American."

In certain important respects, however, there are differences between Issei men and women. Issei men were more likely than the women (32 as compared with 6 percent) to take up studies, once in the United States. This is entirely to be expected, since the men were more likely to have direct dealings with the environing Caucasian population than were women.

In another telling respect, Issei men and women differ: About six men of every ten report that they are interested in American politics, compared with only fewer than four women of every ten (see Table 9.1). Although we have no comparative data, we suspect that immigrant women of any stripe were (and are) not expected to interest themselves in the new country's politics. Issei women came of age before the rights and duties of women here and abroad had been dealt with seriously.

TABLE 9.1

Interest in U.S. Politics across Three Generations, by Sex

Generation	Percent Who Express a Great Deal, or a Fair Amount, of Interest	
	Men	Women
Issei	61	37
Total number	(684)	(345)
Nisei	55	54
Total Number	(1,197)	(1,098)
Sansei	57	46
Total number	(377)	(425)

In detectable, and expected ways, then, there are disparities between immigrant Japanese men and women. What is remarkable, however, is the finding that, in many respects, the men and women are alike. Let us proceed to examine the Nisei generation.

The Nisei

Differences between Nisei men and women are difficult to detect—and, when detectable, go in an unexpected direction. For example, the Nisei were asked a number of questions on membership in voluntary associations, both ethnic and nonethnic. Quite unexpectedly, Nisei women are more likely to belong to a nonethnic organization than men. The difference only borders on significance (61 percent of the women, 51 percent of the men), but does suggest that Nisei women, different from their mothers, are striking out to form associations in the larger community.

In the main, Nisei men and women are in accord when it comes to their interpretations of the American scene, and the place of the Japanese American community within it. Only minorities of either sex frown upon outmarriage; likewise, only minorities believe that Caucasians look with disfavor on interracial marriage. Regarding the religious indicator of acculturation, over half of either sex have converted to Christianity. Nisei men and women are alike in their reading of English-language Japanese American newspapers (eight of ten do so), six of ten, regardless of sex, reportedly speak Japanese fluently or well. And virtually all the Nisei report that they speak perfect English.

Although Issei women, few of whom had received any of their education in the United States, looked upon politics as of little concern to them, their daughters tend to take a different stand. Fifty-five percent of the Nisei men and 54 percent of the women state that they are interested in U.S. politics. In short, the Nisei women have tended to break away from the obsolete norms of their mothers in order to take a place, with women of different backgrounds, in the political process. Among the Sansei, the story becomes intensified.

The Sansei

Young Sansei men and women, in spite of their exogamous tendencies, place a high value on retaining some features of Japanese culture, especially the language, in which they profess to be deficient. Even so, their perspective is undeniably an American one—women as well as men are active participants in educational pursuits, occupational advancement, and politics. Fifty-seven percent of the Sansei men, and 46 percent of the women, report that they are interested in politics.

We conclude that on a variety of measures, Japanese American men and women are much alike. There appear to be no gender-related subcommunities among them. Although immigrant women may have conceived a differentiated role for thmselves, American-born Japanese American women stand next to the men.

FINAL THEORETICAL CONSIDERATIONS

A variety of quite different trends must be observed in the evolution of an ethnic community. Each generation has its general orientation—but within each generation are subcurrents that may become dominant streams of change, which are the evident trends, and which are submerged but may emerge to dominance.

Japanese Americans are a unique case among all the immigrant groups that have come to the United States. Social science theories that explain the processes of adjustment to American life are directed to European immigrants, who, too, are so diversified that they cannot be easily explained by one set of concepts. The Japanese Americans stand apart. They are culturally alien to Western tradition. And, they stand apart racially. Despite these differences, Japanese Americans have adapted to America not only better than other non-whites have, but also better than many European groups have.

As we and many other students of the Japanese Americans have noticed, there are many areas of value congruence between white Anglo-Saxon Protestant civilization and Japan that have made successful adaptation possible.

The first generation, the Issei, were preoccupied with economic survival and the question of how best to adapt to America. There was no thought of assimilation. The Issei saw themselves as paving the way for future generations of Japanese who, by their birth and upbringing in the United States, would enter all walks of American life.

The second generation, the Nisei, moved toward this goal. Since, however, they were reared by parents who did not really know the subtleties of American society, and since the older among them (those who entered the labor market before the war) faced a great deal of prejudice and discrimination, they were limited in entering mainstream American life. Relatively unencumbered entry was then left to the younger Nisei and to the Sansei. But neither have the Sansei totally chosen to become absolutely Americanized.

Japanese Americans—and we focus our attention on the younger—have three choices. First, they could continue to emulate the dominant white, middle-class culture, while largely discarding their Japanese roots. A second goal, an extension of the first, is amalgamation, whereby a fusion between races and cultures occurs. Absolute entry into white society would be the ultimate result. A third choice would be to move toward a pluralistic position in which components of Japanese culture would continue to influence the formation of self-identity. We see all these processes occurring in various degrees within the Japanese American community. Which one will become dominant?

First, in order to have access to the rewards of American society, a high degree of assimilation is a prerequisite; or else one is at a competitive disadvantage. In the case of Japanese Americans, competition with the majority greatly diminished during the 1950s and 1960s, when the economy was expanding and when jobs were plentiful; in the postwar period, prejudice and discrimination had been radically reduced. The preponderance of younger Nisei and of Sansei who are grown up chose to move in the direction of acculturation. We do not mean to imply that these were solely individual decisions. Social structural factors, e.g., their residence, educational pursuits, have made the individual choices ineluctable.

In the short run, the collective outcome has been fraught with contradiction. Although discriminatory barriers were lowered, they have persisted—and, in a contracting economy, can become salient. Even if subtle, the barriers are infuriating. One solution would be amalgamation. But this is a longterm solution. A person of mixed background must see his progeny and theirs undergo further fusion to lose totally every stigma of Asian identification.

A more practical solution that many Japanese Americans have chosen to follow during the stringent 1970s is the capture of enhanced self-esteem through a reinvigorated wedding of their Japanese selves with their American heritage. Their goal is not to fuse themselves, but to relate to both traditions in varying degrees. This augurs a reversal of the assimilationist trend of the older Nisei sub-generation.

But to what degree is this reversal occurring, and will it endure? Now that non-Europeans are competing with whites for society's seemingly ever scarcer rewards, they will have to confront white ethnocentrism. Before the war, Japanese Americans did not face such a confrontation, for they were largely segregated in the work environment from whites. After the war, the skills of the Nisei were sorely needed as the economy expanded. Now, with increased competition for top positions, the ethnic factor becomes a point of issue for Japanese Americans. Since the war, Japanese Americans have tried to act as if they were white, by denying any involvement or concern with, or any real knowledge of, their ethnic background. This position was meant to convey to whites the idea that Japanese Americans were totally American. However, in the stress of competition and close interaction with whites, for prominent positions, Japanese Americans have become increasingly vulnerable affectively to ethnically derived slights. Affirmative-action programs may repair some of the damage.

One way to shore up self-esteem is to develop a high regard for one's distinctive cultural roots. By denying their Japanese background, but by failing to be accepted as white, a sense of normlessness may arise. A search for individual identity may ensue, with little collective support. In such a state of anomie, the very existence of the ethnic community, however shaky a state it may be in, can serve as a positive point of reference within which the anomic can be socialized to values, attitudes, and behavior they had failed to learn before, owing to uncontrollable circumstances. The potential function of the ethnic community in providing a reference point for the building of self-esteem and for identity reformulation is present. Through absorption in the community, Japanese Americans would be better able to withstand any attacks as to their worth. In a constricted economy, ethnic life would in turn be enriched.

For all the potentialities of the Japanese American community—as an agent for socializing the new arrival from overseas; as an agent for socializing those who have become too American to face hard times, when they cannot find employment, or suffer prejudice—it must be concluded that the primary trend among Japanese Americans will, as our data have shown, be toward assimilation. For all the advantages of preserving the vigor of the Japanese American community, so as simultaneously to preserve democratic institutions, the future looks bleak, at least outside Los Angeles. The predilection of the Sansei to choose Caucasian mates spells disaster for the passing on of the traditional ways. When all is said and done, it falls heavily upon the developing Sansei leadership to carve out the means and modalities of enlisting the loyalties of the many.

Should they fail in their task, the endurance of a distinctive Japanese American community will be short.

NOTES

1. A fourth generation, the Yonsei, is beginning now to appear.

2. We cannot conceive of the Japanese Americans, cross-generationally, as a sub-nation, since our data show that so many Nisei and Sansei have left the ethnic community in terms of both associations and values. Still, the components of Petersen's concept of the subnation are useful in gauging just how far many Americans of Japanese ancestry have wandered from their ethnic roots, with no doubt many strains, in forging their personal identities. See William Petersen, *Japanese Americans: Oppression and Success* (New York: Random House, 1971), pp. 214–32.

3. Petersen notes that, according to a sample of wage earners surveyed by the Senate Immigration Commission in 1911, nearly all Issei men could read and write Japanese, and that literacy in their own language facilitated their learning of English, in comparison with some other groups. Ibid., p. 14.

4. The exact figures on Japanese immigration to, and emigration from, the United States are difficult to fix with exactitude. Ibid., pp. 14–19.

5. The Japanese Americans in the post-World War II period have been stereotyped as a highly successful, model minority. But there are potentially negative consequences of favorable stereotypes. See Stanley Sue and Harry H. L. Kitano, "Stereotypes as a Measure of Success," *Journal of Social Issues* 29, no. 2 (1973)): 83–98; Dennis Ogawa, *From Japs to Japanese: The Evolution of Japanese-American Stereotypes* (Berkeley: McCutchan Publishing, 1971).

6. We recall to the reader again, however, that in California, for example, a Nisei could not, by law, marry a Caucasian until November 1948.

7. See Hilla Kuttenplan Israely, *An Exploration Into Ethnic Identity: The Case of Third-Generation Japanese Americans* (Ph.D. diss., University of California, Los Angeles, 1975).

8. Where Japanese Americans are few and far between, a Nisei or Sansei may have difficulty in convincing residents there that he or she is ignorant of the Japanese language and owes loyalty to the United States, not to the Japanese government.

9. Given that the Hawaiians are U.S. citizens who travel without passports to the mainland, it is not possible to gauge their movements with precision. After the 1920s, there had been proportionately more Japanese Americans in Hawaii than on the mainland. In 1940, for example, there were 157,905 in the islands and 126,947 on the continent. The same disparity held in 1950. According to the 1960 and 1970 censuses, however, the balance had shifted again. There are now more Japanese Americans on the mainland—and this has not been the result of any greater fertility there. The Hawaiian flow will no doubt continue as young Japanese Americans go east to seek fortunes that cannot be made in the islands. U.S. Department of Commerce, Bureau of the Census, *U.S. Census of Population, 1940*, vol. II, pt. 1, table 6 (Washington, D.C.: Government Printing Office, 1940). Bureau of the Census, *U.S. Census of Population, 1960*, vol. II, pt. 1, table 6, "Nonwhite Population by Race," Special Report PC (2) 16 (Washington, D.C.: Government Printing Office, 1960).

10. Bureau of the Census, *Statistical Abstract of the United States, 1943*, table 55 (Washington, D.C.: Government Printing Office, 1944). Bureau of the Census, *U.S. Census of Population, 1970*, Tables 17, 18, "General Population Characteristics," Final Report PC (1)-B13 Hawaii (Washington, D.C.: Government Printing Office, 1970).

11. In 1963, for example, there were 4,056 immigrants from Japan. The figure has been virtually invariable. In 1975, 4,274 came. U.S. Department of Justice, Immigration and Naturalization Service, *Annual Report of the Commissioner of Immigration and Naturalization*, 1965, table 14, p. 65. In 1965, the law regarding the admittance of immigrants from countries around the world was changed to favor nations like Japan. *U.S. Code Annotated 8, sec. 1181*, p. 178. The change in the law, however, has not affected the number of Japanese immigrants. The low point in recent years was 1965, when 3,180 entered; the high point was 1973, when 5,461 came in.

12. The Sansei militant, the advocate of yellow power, has been examined by Minako K. Maykovich, *Japanese American Identity Dilemma* (Tokyo: Waseda University Press [in English], pp. 125–45.

13. We paraphrase here the thoughts of Justice Louis D. Brandeis, regarding Jewish youth, as later given voice by Justice William O. Douglas, in an address celebrating the 25th anniversary of the Brandeis Camp Institute, given in Beverly Hills, 1967. For a view of the liberated Sansei, whose "main concern . . . is in resolving the identity crisis from which they believe most Sansei are suffering," see Maykovich, *Japanese American Identity*, pp. 125–26.

14. Samuel A. Stouffer, *Communism, Conformity and Civil Liberties: A Cross-section of the Nation Speaks its Mind* (Gloucester, Mass.: Peter Smith, 1963), p. 132.

15. Susan McCoin Kataoka, *Issei Women: A Study in Compliance-Noncompliance* (Ph.D. diss., UCLA, 1977).

16. The trigenerational data are still being reassembled in order to construct sibling-set measures among the Nisei, and both sibling-set and cousin-set measures among the Sansei. Results of this analytic path will appear later.

APPENDIX A:
STUDIES COMPLETED AND IN PROGRESS

STUDIES COMPLETED

Books

Bonacich, Edna, and John Modell. *The Economic Basis of Ethnic Solidarity: A Study of Japanese Americans.* Berkeley and Los Angeles: University of California Press, 1980.

Chuman, Frank F. *The Bamboo People: The Law and Japanese Americans.* Del Mar, Calif.: Publishers', Inc., 1976.

Hosokawa, Bill. *Nisei: The Quiet Americans.* New York: William Morrow and Co., 1969.

Ichioka, Yuji; Yasua Sakata; Nobuya Tsuchida; and Eri Yasuhara. *A Buried Past: An Annotated Bibliography of the Japanese American Research Project Collection.* Berkeley and Los Angeles: University of California Press, 1973.

Modell, John. *Economics and Politics of Racial Accommodation: The Japanese of Los Angeles, 1900-1942.* Urbana, Ill.: University of Illinois Press, 1977.

Montero, Darrel. *Japanese Americans: Changing Patterns of Ethnic Affiliation Over Three Generations.* Boulder, Colo.: Westview, 1980.

Wilson, Robert A., and Bill Hosokawa. *East to America: A History of the Japanese in the United States.* New York: William Morrow and Co., 1980.

Articles and Papers

Bonacich, Edna. "Working Papers, Japanese American Research Project." Los Angeles: University of California, 1969-74.

Levine, Gene N. "Occupational Mobility Among Japanese Americans." Paper presented at American Sociological Association Meetings, Washington, D.C., 1970.

Levine, Gene N., and Edna M. Bonacich. "Nonindividual Units in the Analysis of Surveys: The Case of the Japanese American Research Project." Paper presented at the Annual Meetings of the Pacific Chapter of the American Association for Public Opinion Research, San Diego, 1970.

Levine, Gene N., and Darrel M. Montero. "Socioeconomic Mobility Among Three Generations of Japanese Americans." *Journal of Social Issues* 29, no. 2 (1973): 33-48.

Modell, John. "Japanese Immigrants in America: Some Fragments of a Quantitative Picture." Paper presented at Second Annual Meeting of the Conference of Asian Studies on the Pacific Coast, Los Angeles, 1967.

——. "Class or Ethnic Solidarity: The Japanese American Company Union." Paper presented at the Sixty-First Annual Meeting of the Pacific Branch of the American Historical Association, Santa Clara, 1968.

——. "The Japanese American Family: A Perspective for Future Investigations." *Pacific Historical Review* 37 (1968): 67–81.

——. "Class or Ethnic Solidarity: The Japanese American Company Union." *Pacific Historical Review* 38 (1969): 193–206.

——. "A Different Color Line: The Japanese American Response to Racism, 1900–1940." Paper presented at the Annual Meetings of the Organization of American Historians, 1970.

——. "On Being an Issei: Orientation Toward America." Paper presented at symposium, "The Overseas Japanese." Annual Meetings of the American Anthropological Association, San Diego, 1970.

——. "Tradition and Opportunity: The Japanese Immigrant in America." *Pacific Historical Review* 40, no. 2 (1971): 163–82.

Montero, Darrel M. "Assimilation and Educational Achievement: The Case of the Second Generation Japanese Americans." Paper presented at the Annual Meetings of the American Sociological Association, New York City, 1973.

——. "Correlates of Achievement Orientation Among a National Sample of Second Generation Japanese Americans." Paper presented at the Annual Meetings of the Pacific Sociological Association, 1973, San Jose, California.

——. "A Study of Social Desirability Response Bias: the Mail Questionnaire: The face-to-face Interview and the Telephone Interview Compared." Paper presented at the Annual Meeting of the American Sociological Association, Montreal, 1974.

Montero, Darrel M., and Gene N. Levine. "Third Generation Japanese Americans," Paper presented at Annual meeting of the Pacific Sociological Association meetings, San Jose, California, 1974.

Montero, Darrel M. "Response Effects in a National Survey." Paper presented at the Annual Meeting of the American Sociological Association, New York, 1976.

Montero, Darrel M., and Gene N. Levine. "The Japanese Community: A Study of Generational Changes in Ethnic Affiliation," Paper presented at annual meetings of the American Sociological Association, Chicago, 1977.

Montero, Darrel M., and Ronald T. Tsukashima. "Assimilation and Educational Achievement: The Case of the Second Generation Japanese Americans," *Sociological Quarterly*, 18 (Autumn, 1977): 490-503.

Montero, Darrel M. "Aging Among the Issei," pp. 193-205 in Donald Gelfand and Alfred Kutzik (eds.), *Ethnicity and Aging: Theory Research and Policy*. New York: Spring Pub., 1979.

———. "The Elderly Japanese American: Aging Among the First Generation Immigrants," *Genetic Psychology Monographs* 101 (1980): 99-118.

Rhodes, Colbert, and Eric Woodrum. "Contending Hypotheses of Minority Fertility: Three Generations of Japanese Americans." *California Sociologist* 32, no. 2 (Summer 1980): 166-83.

Takashi, Maeda. "A Comparative Study of the Issei, Nisei, and Sansei." *Kansai Daigaku Shakai Gakubu Kiyo* 4, no. 2 (1973): 37-59.

Woodrum, Eric, Colbert Rhodes, and Joe Feagin, "Japanese American Economic Behavior: Its Types, Determinants and Consequences." *Social Forces* 58 no. 4 (June, 1980): 1235-54.

Ph.D. Dissertations

Hate, Donald Teuro, Jr. "'Undesirable': Unsavory Elements Among the Japanese in America prior to 1893 and Their Influence on the First Anti-Japanese Movement in California." Ph.D. dissertation, University of Southern California, 1970.

Henry, Sheila. "Ethnic Community and Its Members' Achievements." Ph.D. dissertation, University of California, Los Angeles, 1973.

Israely, Hilla Kuttenplan. "An Exploration Into Ethnic Identity: The Case of Third-Generation Japanese Americans." Ph.D. dissertation, University of California, Los Angeles, 1975.

Kataoka, Susan McCoin. "Issei Women: A Study in Compliance-Noncompliance." Ph.D. dissertation, University of California, Los Angeles, 1977.

Modell, John. "The Japanese of Los Angeles: A Study in Growth and Accommodation, 1900-1946." Ph.D. dissertation, Columbia University, 1969.

Montero, Darrel M. "The Educational Achievements of Three Generations of Japanese Americans." Ph.D. dissertation, University of California, Los Angeles, 1975.

Sakata, Yasuo, "History of Japanese Emigration to the United States, 1885 to 1908." University of California, Los Angeles, 1977.

Woodrum, Eric. "Japanese American Social Adaptation Over Three Generations." Ph.D. dissertation, University of Texas, Austin, 1978.

STUDIES IN PROGRESS

Books

Iwata, Masakazu, *Agricultural History of the Japanese in the United States.*

Articles

Levine, Gene N., and Hilla Kuttenplan Israely. "Changes in Sansei Attitudes and Values Over Time."

Levine, Gene N., and Colbert Rhodes. "Sibling Sets and Cousin Sets: The Use of Collective Measures on Japanese American Data."

Modell, John. "Class, Culture and Choice: Varieties of Japanese American Education." Unpublished manuscript, 1967.

——. "Reduction of Prejudice: California and Its Japanese American Minority." Unpublished manuscript, 1967.

Rhodes, Colbert, and Gene N. Levine. "Paths to Assimilation: Japanese American Patterns of Exogamy."

APPENDIX B:
THE NISEI INTERVIEW SCHEDULE

National Opinion Research Center
University of Chicago

Survey No. 4013

JAPANESE AMERICAN RESEARCH PROJECT
University of California at Los Angeles

Survey of Japanese Americans:

Phase Two

April, 1967

This survey is supported by a grant from the
U.S. Public Health Service. The directors
of the study assume full responsibility for
the contents of this questionnaire.

165

```
┌─────────────────────────────┐
│ ENTER                        │
│ TIME INTERVIEW_____  AM     │
│ BEGAN:                PM     │
└─────────────────────────────┘
```

1. First, we would like to know whether you are single, married, divorced, separated, or widowed.

Single . . 1	10/
Married . . 2	
Divorced . 3	
Separated . 4	
Widowed . . 5	

2. How old were you on your last birthday?

_____ 11-12/

3. Where were you born? _____ _____ 13-15/
                          (City)   (State or Country)

4. ASK MALES ONLY: Were you the oldest son in your family?   Yes . 1   16/
                                                              No . 2

5. ASK EVERYONE: How many children did your parents have altogether?

_____ 17-18/

ASK Q'S. 6-8 IF EVER MARRIED; OTHERWISE SKIP TO Q. 9.

6. Where was your (wife/husband) born?

_____ _____ 19-21/
        (City)   (State or Country)

                        Don't know. 888

A. IF SPOUSE BORN IN U.S.: What is your (wife/husband)'s background? Is (she/he) a Nisei, a Sansei, a Caucasian, or of some other background?

Nisei 1	22/
Sansei 2	
Caucasian 3	
Japanese (born in Japan) . . 4	
Non-Japanese oriental 5	
Other (SPECIFY) 6	

7. How many children have been born to you and your (wife/husband), not counting stillbirths?

_____ 23-24/

8. What kind of work did your father-in-law do when your (wife/husband) was in (her/his) teens?

OCCUPATION: _____ 25-27/
               (PROBE: What did he actually do on that job?)

INDUSTRY: _____

ASK EVERYONE:

9. I'd like to know a few things about some of your other relatives.

	A. (Relative) Living here in this city.		B. Living in your neighborhood.		C. Living in this household.	
	Yes	No	Yes	No	Yes	No
A. (1) Do you have any brothers or sisters living in (city/county)?	1	0	1	0	1	0
(2) Do either of your parents live in (city/county)?. . .	2	0	2	0	2	0
(3) And have you any other relatives--including anyone you consider a relative, but not including your own children--living here in (city/county)?	4	0 28/	4	0 31/	4	0 34/

IF YES TO ANY, (1), (2), OR (3), ASK A (4) AND B.

IF NO TO (1), (2), AND (3), SKIP TO Q. 11.

(4) About how many relatives does this make altogether living in (city/county)? . . . . .

City/County:_____ 29-30/   Nbrhd:_____ 32-33/   Hshld:_____ 35-36/

B. Now, do any of all these relatives we've talked about live in the same neighborhood as you? IF YES: Which ones? CIRCLE ALL THAT APPLY [A (1), (2), AND/ OR (3)] UNDER B ABOVE, AND ASK B (1) AND C. IF NO: CIRCLE "0'S" IN COLUMN B ABOVE, AND SKIP TO Q. 10.

  (1) About how many relatives does this make, who live in your neighborhood? ENTER NUMBER IN TABLE UNDER B ABOVE.

C. And do any of these relatives live with you here in the same household? IF YES: Which ones? CIRCLE ALL THAT APPLY UNDER C ABOVE, AND ASK C (1). IF NO: CIRCLE "0'S" IN COLUMN C AND SKIP TO Q. 10.

  (1) How many relatives live with you in this household? ENTER NUMBER UNDER C.

IF R HAS ANY RELATIVES IN CITY, ASK Q. 10.

10. About how many times in the past month have you visited with or been visited by relatives living in (city/county)--(apart from those living in the same household as you)?

                                    _____ times   37-38/

11. Now about your neighborhood: Do you think of this neighborhood as your real home--the place where you really belong, or do you think of it as just a place where you happen to be living?

Really belong . 1   39/
Just a place . 2
Don't know . . 8

12. About how many of your neighbors, including relatives, are you on visiting terms with?

None 1   40/
One or two . . . 2
Three or four . . 3
Five - nine . . . 4
Ten or more . . . 5
Don't know . . . 8

13. How many years altogether have you lived here in this neighborhood?

Less than 1 year 1   41/
1 to less than 5 years . . 2
5 to less than 10 years . 3
10 to less than 15 years . 4
15 to less than 25 years . 5
25 to less than 35 years . 6
35 years or more 7
All my life 8
Don't know 9

14. Would you say that this neighborhood is made up mostly of Japanese Americans, mostly non-Japanese, or is it mixed?

Mostly Japanese Americans. 1   42/
Mixed 2
Mostly non-Japanese . . . 3
Don't know 8

15. What other kinds of groups besides Japanese Americans live in this neighborhood? DO NOT READ CATEGORIES, BUT CIRCLE ALL THAT APPLY.

Other orientals (including Filipinos) 01 43-44/
Negroes 02
Mexican Americans 03
"Caucasians" (no subgroup mentioned) 08
Subgroup of Caucasians 16
(RECORD; DON'T PROBE FOR ADDITIONAL

_____)

Others 32
(RECORD, DON'T PROBE: _____

_____)

Don't know 88

16. Now, I'd like to find out about the various cities and towns you've lived in.

    A. To start, since when have you lived here in (city/county)?

<table>
<tr><td>1967 . . . . 1</td><td>45/</td></tr>
<tr><td>1966 . . . . 2</td><td></td></tr>
<tr><td>1963 - 1965 . . . . 3</td><td></td></tr>
<tr><td>1958 - 1962 . . . . 4</td><td></td></tr>
<tr><td>1953 - 1957 . . . . 5</td><td></td></tr>
<tr><td>1943 - 1952 . . . . 6</td><td></td></tr>
<tr><td>Before 1942 . . . . 7</td><td></td></tr>
<tr><td>All my life (GO TO Q. 17) . 8</td><td></td></tr>
<tr><td>Don't know . . . . 9</td><td></td></tr>
</table>

ASK B-D FOR EACH PLACE, GOING
BACK TO R'S YEAR OF BIRTH, AND
RECORD BELOW.

B. And in what city or town did you live just before that? City and State, or Country	C. In what year did you move there? Year	D. Were your neighbors there mostly Japa- nese Americans, mostly non-Japanese, or was the neighbor- hood mixed?	SPECIAL CODING
1.		J N M	———
2.		J N M	———
3.		J N M	———
4.		J N M	———
5.		J N M	———
6.		J N M	———
7.		J N M	———
8.		J N M	———
9.		J N M	———
10.		J N M	———
11.		J N M	———
12.		J N M	———
13.		J N M	———
14.		J N M	———
15.		J N M	———

17. (You already mentioned this, but let me make sure I got it right.) Were you in a relocation center or camp during World War II?

Yes . (ASK A) . . . 1   46/

No (GO TO Q. 18) . 2

A. IF YES: How long, altogether, did you spend in relocation centers or camps?

Less than 1 year 1   47/
1 to less than 2 years . . . 2
2 to less than 3 years . . . 3
3 to less than 4 years . . . 4
4 to less than 5 years . . . 5
5 years or more 6
Don't know 8

Now, let's talk about (your/your husband's) occupation.

ASK Q'S. 18, 20, 21, AND 22 ABOUT: RESPONDENT IF R IS MALE, OR IF R IS DIVORCED OR NEVER MARRIED FEMALE;

HUSBAND OF RESPONDENT IF R IS CURRENTLY MARRIED, WIDOWED, OR SEPARATED FEMALE.

---

18. A. What kind of work (do you/does your husband/did your husband usually) do?

OCCUPATION:_____ 48-50/
    [PROBE, IF VAGUE: What (do/does/did) (you/he) actually do on this job?]

B. In what kind of business or industry (is/was) that?

BUSINESS OR INDUSTRY:_____
    (PROBE, IF VAGUE: What does that firm/organization/agency make or do?)

C. Does that mean (you are/he is) self-employed or employed by someone else?

Self-employed . . . 1   51/
Employed by others . 2
Don't know 8

ASK Q. 19 ONLY ABOUT RESPONDENT; FOR CURRENTLY MARRIED, WIDOWED, OR SEPARATED FE-
MALE, GO TO Q. 20.

19. Is there any other occupation you would prefer to be in?

Yes . (ASK A AND B) . 1   52/

No . (GO TO Q. 20) . . 2

Don't know 8

IF YES:

A. What occupation is that?

OCCUPATION: _____   53-54/

55/

B. Suppose you <u>were</u> a (<u>occupation mentioned in A</u>). What difference do you
think it would make in your life?

56/

57/

58/

59/

---

20. A. <u>IF SELF-EMPLOYED</u>: Are most of the people (you/your husband) presently
serve(s) of Japanese ancestry?

Yes 1   60/

No 2

Don't know . 8

B. <u>IF NOT SELF-EMPLOYED</u>: Is (your/your husband's) present employer a
Japanese or Japanese-American individual or concern?

Yes 1   61/

No 2

Don't know . 8

21. We've been talking about (your/your husband's) present (usual) job. Now, I'd like you to tell me about the full-time position (you/he) held just before this one, whether it was a job in the same firm or a change from another firm.

BEGIN DECK 02

OCCUPATION: _____

_____

_____ 10-12/

_____

No former job (SKIP TO Q. 23) 0

A. When (you/he) took that job, did it involve a shift in firms, or did (you/he) change duties within the same firm?

Changed firms 1   13/

Same firm 2

First job held 0

Don't know 8

B. About what year did (you/he) start on that job, and when did (you/he) leave it?

_____   _____   14-15/
(year began) to (year ended)

C. Did the change to (your/his) present job from the one we're talking about now involve a change from one firm to another?

Yes 1   16/

No 2

Don't know . . 8

D. Why did (you/he) make that change? (Any other reasons?)   17-18/

19/

172

ASK Q. 22 A, B, AND C FOR EACH JOB RESPONDENT (R'S HUSBAND) HAS HELD, WORKING BACK
TO HIS FIRST FULL-TIME JOB.

22. And now I'd like you to tell me about all (your/his) other past full-time jobs--
whether or not a change in firm was involved. Let's take this back to (your/
his) first full-time position.

A. What job did (you/he) hold before the one we just talked about?	B. What year did (you/he) take that job?	C. Was that a different firm from the one (you/he) worked for just before that?		SPECIAL CODING
	Year	Same	Different	
1.		S	D	
2.		S	D	
3.		S	D	
4.		S	D	
5.		S	D	
6.		S	D	
7.		S	D	
8.		S	D	
9.		S	D	
10.		S	D	
11		S	D	
12.		S	D	
13.		S	D	
14.		S	D	
15.		S	D	

ASK Q'S. 23 AND 24 ONLY FOR CURRENTLY SELF-EMPLOYED RESPONDENTS (HUSBANDS) WHO RE-
PORT SAME JOB SINCE 1960.   INCLUDE FARMERS UNLESS THEY ARE AGRICULTURAL LABORERS.
FOR OTHERS, SKIP TO Q. 25.

23.   Since 1960 has the size of your (husband's) (holdings/establishment) increased,
      decreased, or remained about the same?

                                          Increased . 1   20/
                                          Same . · · . . 2
                                          Decreased . 3
                                          Don't know . 8

24.   Since 1960, have your (husband's) earnings from (your/his) (holdings/estab-
      lishment) on the whole increased, decreased, or stayed about the same?

                                          Increased . 1   21/
                                          Same 2
                                          Decreased . 3
                                          Don't know . 8

ASK EVERYONE:

25.   About what proportion of the people (you/your husband) see(s) regularly at
      work on (your/his) present job are Japanese Americans--nearly all, about
      three-quarters, about half, about a quarter, almost none, or none at all?

                                          Meets no one at work . 0   22/
                                          Nearly all 1
                                          About 3/4 2
                                          About 1/2 3
                                          About 1/4 4
                                          Almost none 5
                                          None 6
                                          Don't know 8

26.   Now, about the people (you/your husband) see(s) at work--(do you/does he)
      meet them off the job often, sometimes, or almost never?

                                          Often . . . 1   23/
                                          Sometimes . 2
                                          Almost never 3
                                          Don't know . 8

174

ASK Q. 27 ONLY IF <u>CURRENTLY MARRIED</u>; OTHERWISE GO TO Q. 28.

<u>ASK ABOUT RESPONDENT IF FEMALE.</u>
<u>ASK ABOUT WIFE IF R IS MALE.</u>

27. (Does your wife/Do you) work?

Yes . . (ASK A) . . . 1   24/

No . (GO TO Q. 28) . 2

    A. <u>IF YES</u>: Is that a full-time or a part-time job?

Full-time 1   25/

Part-time 2

---

28. A. Please give me the letter next to the category on this card which includes your present total family income. HAND RESPONDENT CARD 1. Please include income from rents, investments, interest and earnings of all family members--in other words, the approximate total income as recorded on your last income tax.

    B. And which letter represents what you think your family income will be in five years?

		A. Total Family Income	B. Income in Five Years
A.	Under $2,500	1 26/	1 27/
B.	$2,500 - $4,999	2	2
C.	$5,000 - $7,499	3	3
D.	$7,500 - $9,999	4	4
E.	$10,000 - $14,999 . . .	5	5
F.	$15,000 - $19,999 . . .	6	6
G.	$20,000 - $29,999 . . .	7	7
H.	$30,000 or more	8	8
	Don't know	9	9

Now I have some questions about your education.

29.

	A. What was the highest grade you completed in school?		B. (1) IF YES TO B. Highest grade in Japan?	
Never attended school	0	28/	0	29/
1-4 grades/years	1		1	
5-7 grades/years	2		2	
8 grades/years	3		3	
9-11 grades/years	4		4	
12 grades/years (high school grad.)	5		5	
13-15 years (some college) . . .	6		6	
16 years (completed college) . .	7		7	
More than 16 years (beyond college graduation)	8		8	

ASK B AND C ONLY OF RESPONDENTS WHO HAVE PREVIOUSLY MENTIONED A JAPANESE RESIDENCE.

B. Did you receive any schooling in Japan?

IF YES, ASK (1) AND C.

IF NO, CIRCLE "0" IN COLUMN B. (1) ABOVE.

(1) What was the highest level of schooling you completed in Japan? CIRCLE CODE IN COLUMN B.(1) ABOVE.

(C) How many years of school did you attend in Japan, altogether?

_____ 30-31/

---

30. Did you attend Japanese language school when you were young?

Yes 1   32/

No 2

Don't know . 8

IF EVER MARRIED, ASK Q. 31; OTHERWISE SKIP TO Q. 32.

31. A. What was the highest grade your (wife/husband) completed in school?

Never attended school 0	33/
1-4 grades/years 1	
5-7 grades/years 2	
8 grades/years 3	
9-11 grades/years 4	
12 years 5	
13-15 years (some college) . . 6	
16 years (completed college) . 7	
Graduate work 8	
Don't know 9	

B. Did (she/he) receive any schooling in Japan?

IF YES, ASK (1). IF NO, CIRCLE "0" IN (1) BELOW.

(1) How many years of school did (he/she) attend in Japan, altogether?

_____ 34-35/

Received no schooling in Japan . . 0

32. Did anyone in your or your (spouse's) family ever give (you/your husband) any...

	Yes	No or Don't know	
A. ...advice in choosing a career?	01	00	36-37/
B. ...work for pay, even part-time, in a business or farm owned by members of the family?	02	00	
C. (ASK ONLY OF THOSE WHO HAVE EVER BEEN FARMERS) ...help in acquiring a farm? . . .	04	00	
D. (ASK ONLY OF THOSE WHO HAVE EVER OWNED A BUSINESS) ...help in acquiring a business?	08	00	
E. ...help in getting a job?	16	00	
IF NO TO ALL OF THESE, CIRCLE CODE ————————>		32	

177

33. Now, would you tell me whether there has been anyone from <u>outside</u> the family who has given you (your husband) help in (your/his) advancement--either in any of these same ways, or in other ways?

                                      Yes . (ASK A - E) . . . 1   38/
                                      No . . (GO TO Q. 34) . . 2
                                      Don't know (GO TO Q. 34) 8

IF YES:

A. Who (is/was) that? <u>HAND RESPONDENT CARD 2</u>. (Is/Was) his relationship to (you/your husband) any one of those on the card? (IF MORE THAN ONE: Who is the person who helped you the most?) CIRCLE ONLY ONE CODE.

                    Friend of family or of in-laws 001   39-41/
                    Teacher or school official 002
                    Work superior 004
                    Work peer 008
                    <u>Genro</u>; community sage 016
                    Individual with community influence . . 032
                    Political leader 064
                    Recruiter from business; talent scout . 128
                    Other (SPECIFY) 256
                    Don't know 888

B. When was this? About how old (were you/was he) when that person <u>first</u> started to help (you/him)?

                                      _____ years   42-43/

C. Did that person help (you/him) in this   Only once 1   44/
   way (these ways) only once, or did he   A number of times . . . 2
   do so a number of times, or does he   Still helps sometimes . 3
   still continue to help (you/him)   Don't know 8
   sometimes?

D. What kind of help did he give (you/him)? FIELD CODE AND CIRCLE AS MANY AS R MENTIONS.

                    Advice in choosing a career 01   45-47/
                    Work, even part-time 02
                    Help in acquiring a farm or business 04
                    Help in getting a job 08
                    Bring (R's/husband's) work to atten-
                        tion of others 16
                    Support in school or college 32
                    Other (SPECIFY) 64
                    Don't know, can't say 88

E. And was this person a Japanese American?

                                      Yes 1   48/
                                      No 2
                                      Don't know . . 8

34. When you were in high school, would you say there was any particular occupation your parents hoped you would enter?

$$\begin{array}{ll} \text{Yes} \quad . \ . \ . \ . \ 1 & 49/ \\ \text{No} \ . \ . \ . \ . \ . \ 2 \\ \text{Don't know} \ . \ 8 \end{array}$$

---

35. Parents often try to influence their children when it comes to marriage. Was
this true of your parents in your case?

$$\begin{array}{ll} \text{Yes} \ . \ . \ . \ . \ (\text{ASK A}) \ . \ . \ . \ 1 & 50/ \\ \text{No} \quad . \ (\text{GO TO Q. 36}) \ . \ . \ . \ 2 \\ \text{Don't know; don't} \\ \quad \text{remember} \ . \ . \ . \ . \ . \ . \ 8 \end{array}$$

A. IF YES: What did they urge you to do? (What was the situation?)

51-52/

53-54/

---

36. How about yourself? (Have you or will you/would you) try to influence your
children when it comes to marriage?

$$\begin{array}{ll} \text{Yes} \ . \ . \ . \ . \ (\text{ASK A}) \ . \ . \ . \ 1 & 55/ \\ \text{No} \quad . \ (\text{GO TO Q. 37}) \ . \ . \ . \ 2 \\ \text{Don't know} \ . \ . \ . \ . \ . \ . \ 8 \end{array}$$

A. IF YES: What (have/would) you urge them to do?

56-57/

58-59/

179

37. For each of the principles I will now read to you, tell me whether or not your parents stressed it when you were growing up.

	Stressed it	Didn't	Don't recall	
A. You must behave properly to avoid bringing shame to the family	1	2	8	60/
B. To lose a competition is to be disgraced	1	2	8	61/
C. One must make returns for all kindnesses received	1	2	8	62/
D. You must act so as not to bring dishonor to the Japanese American community	1	2	8	63/

38.

	A. While you were growing up, would you say that your parents wanted you to take an active part with Caucasians in their activities, or to stick pretty much with Japanese Americans?		B. (Do you) (Would you) want your own children to take an active part with Caucasians in their activities, or to stick pretty much with Japanese Americans?	
Active part with Caucasians . . .	1	64/	1	65/
Stick to Japanese Americans . . .	2		2	
Neither; both; nothing in particular	3		3	
Don't know	8		8	

39. While you were in grade school, were most of your close friends Japanese Americans, non-Japanese, or about an equal number of both?

No friends 0   66/
Mostly Japanese Americans . 1
Equal number 2
Mostly non-Japanese 3
Don't know 8

40. And what about when you were in high school? (Were most of your close friends Japanese Americans, non-Japanese, or about an equal number of both?)

No friends 0   67/
Mostly Japanese Americans . 1
Equal number 2
Mostly non-Japanese 3
Don't know 8

41. Now let's talk about the people who are presently closest friends outside your immediate family--I mean the people whom you see most often or feel closest to.

BEGIN DECK 03

A. So that I don't mix them up, please tell me the first name of each friend. RECORD NAMES AND ASK B-D FOR FRIEND 1. THEN ASK B-D FOR FRIEND 2.	B. Does (friend) live on the same block as you do, in the same neighborhood, in the same city (county), or further away?				C. Is (he/she) an Issei, a Nisei, a Sansei, a Caucasian, or of another background?				
	Blk.	Nbhd.	City	Further	Is-sei	Ni-sei	San-sei	Cauca-sian	Other (SPEC-IFY)
FRIEND 1:	1	2	3	10/ 4	1	2	3	4	12/ 5
FRIEND 2:	1	2	3	11/ 4	1	2	3	4	13/ 5

D. What is (first friend's) occupation?

OCCUPATION: _____   14-16/

_____

What is (second friend's) occupation?

OCCUPATION: _____   17-19/

_____

42. A. About how many groups or organizations do you belong to? I mean groups which have a more or less regular membership and meet more or less regularly. In the count, please don't include the church you belong to; we'll come to that later.

	A. Total number of groups.		B. Number of Japanese American groups.	
None . (GO TO Q. 43)	0	20/	0	21/
One . . (ASK B-D)	1		1	
Two . . (ASK B-D)	2		2	
Three . (ASK B-D)	3		3	
Four-Five (ASK B-D)	4		4	
Six-Nine (ASK B-D)	5		5	
Ten-Twenty-four (ASK B-D) . .	6		6	
Twenty-five or more (ASK B-D).	7		7	
Don't know (GO TO Q. 43) . . .	8		8	

IF BELONGED TO ANY GROUPS:

B. (Does that group have mostly Japanese American members?)
(Of these groups, how many have mostly Japanese American members?)
CODE ABOVE UNDER COLUMN B.

C. Are you now an officer or a committee member of any of the organizations you belong to?

Yes . . . 1   22/

No 2

D. Of all the organizations you belong to, what is the name of the one to which you devote the most time? (IF ACTIVITY OR FUNCTION NOT CLEAR FROM NAME, ASK: Could you tell me what that organization does?)

_____ 23-24/

_____ 25/

43. Suppose (you/your husband) were given an extra one month's salary which you could spend in any way you wanted. How would you spend it?

26-27/

44. In your opinion, which is more often to blame if a person is poor--a lack of effort on his own part or circumstances beyond his control?

Lack of own effort	1	28/
Circumstances beyond control	2	
Both	3	
Don't know	8	

45. Who do you think has higher social value--people who make, buy, or sell things of practical use, or people like scholars and artists?

Practical use	1	29/
Scholars and artists	2	
Don't know	8	

46. If you think a thing is right, do you think you should go ahead and do it even if it is contrary to usual custom, or do you think it's better to follow custom?

Go ahead	1	30/
Follow custom	2	
Don't know	8	

47. If you did not have any children, do you think you ought to adopt a child to continue the family line even if the child were not related to you, or do you think you need not do that?

Should adopt	1	31/
Need not adopt	2	
Other (SPECIFY)	3	
Don't know	8	

48.

	A. Would you say that generally the Nisei are not American enough, too American, or just about right?		B. And what about the Sansei?	
Not American enough	1	32/	1	33/
Just about right	2		2	
Too American	3		3	
Don't know	8		8	

183

49. Would you say that in general the Nisei are more like the Issei or more like the Sansei?

More like Issei (ASK A) . . 1	34/
Equally similar to both . . 2	
More like Sansei (ASK A) . . 3	
Don't know 8	

    A. IF MORE LIKE ISSEI OR SANSEI: In what ways are they more like (Issei/Sansei) than (Sansei/Issei)?

                                                               35/

                                                               36/

                                                               37/

---

50. For each of the following statements, I would like you to tell me whether you think it is definitely true, probably true, probably not true, or definitely true.

		Definitely True	Probably True	Probably Not True	Definitely Not True	Don't know	
A.	In general, the Issei generation worked harder than the Nisei.	1	2	3	4	8	38/
B.	In general, the Issei weren't enough concerned about what Caucasians would think of them.	1	2	3	4	8	39/
C.	In general, the Nisei were brought up too strictly by the Issei.	1	2	3	4	8	40/
D.	In general, the Nisei generation is less willing than the Issei to push ahead with risky ventures.	1	2	3	4	8	41/

---

51. HAND RESPONDENT SELF-ADMINISTERED QUESTION SECTION.
Here is a page of questions which you can fill out more easily yourself. All we want to know is whether you agree or disagree with each of the statements on the sheet. Please circle an answer code for each question, even if you are not sure of your answer. There are no right or wrong answers. All we want is the answer that comes to your mind first.

TAKE BACK SHEET. Thank you very much. Now I'll ask you some more questions concerning your opinions.

52. HAND RESPONDENT CARD 3. Tell me which item on this list you would want most (for your husband) on a job. Now, would you rank the others in the order of importance to you (for your husband)? (PROBE: Which comes next? Which third? Which fourth? Which fifth? And which last?)

		Ranks first	Ranks 2nd	Ranks 3rd	Ranks 4th	Ranks 5th	Ranks 6th
A.	Income is steady	1 42/	1 43/	1 44/	1 45/	1 46/	1 47/
B.	Income is high	2	2	2	2	2	2
C.	There is no danger of being fired or unemployed	3	3	3	3	3	3
D.	Working hours are short, lots of free time . .	4	4	4	4	4	4
E.	Chances of getting ahead are good	5	5	5	5	5	5
F.	The work is important and gives a feeling of accomplishment	6	6	6	6	6	6
	Don't know; no opinion .	8	8	8	8	8	8

IF MARRIED TO JAPANESE AMERICAN, ASK Q. 53; OTHERWISE GO TO Q. 54.

53. How much do you think that being a Japanese American has hindered your (husband's) advancement--not at all, only a little, somewhat, or very much?

Not at all 1		48/
Only a little . . . 2		
Somewhat 3		
Very much 4		
Has helped 5		
Don't know 8		

185

54. Of all the Japanese Americans you have known or known about in the communities where you have lived, think of the one person who stands out in your mind as the most important leader. We don't need to know his name, but we do want to know if you know him personally, or if you know of him only by reputation?

Know personally . . . . . (ASK A AND B) . . 1   49/

Know by reputation only . (ASK A AND B) . . 2

Don't know of any leader (SKIP TO Q. 55) . 0

IF KNOWS OF LEADER:

A. In your opinion, why was he a leader?

50/

51/

B. And, as best you can remember, what was his occupation during the prime of his life?

52-53/

55. Now, a few more questions about leadership and the Japanese American people. HAND RESPONDENT CARD 4.

	A. Which one of the five things on this card is most important for a Japanese American community leader today, as you see it?		B. And which one do you think is least important today?	
A. Gaining concrete improvements for the Japanese American community.	1	54/	1	55/
B. Joining with other groups to make a better America.	2		2	
C. Leading a virtuous life	3		3	
D. Settling disputes and squabbles in the Japanese American community	4		4	
E. Winning the respect of Caucasians	5		5	
Don't know	8		8	

56. During the World War II relocation, some Nisei worked to make relocation as orderly and comfortable as possible, while others protested the injustice of the relocation and tried to have it declared unconstitutional. Which kind of leader do you _now_ think employed the better approach?

Orderly and comfortable 1   56/
Protest 2
Can't generalize; both; neither . 3
Don't know 8

---

57. Just as during the relocation period there were differences among Japanese Americans about how to act, we've heard that nowadays there are differences of opinion about how to handle important issues facing the group. Do you yourself believe that such differences exist now?

Yes (ASK A) . . 1   57/
No (GO TO Q. 58) 2
Don't know . . 8

   A. IF YES: What are these differences of opinion about? (PROBE.)

58/

59/

---

58. A. Do you suppose that most Caucasians in America would be disturbed if...

	Yes	No	Don't know	
...a Japanese American girl married a son of theirs? . .	1	2	8	60/
...a Japanese American boy married a daughter of theirs?.	1	2	8	61/

   B. And do you suppose that _you_ would be disturbed if...

...a son of yours married a Caucasian girl?	1	2	8	62/
...a daughter of yours married a Caucasian boy?	1	2	8	63/

59. As I read some ways in which discrimination against the Japanese Americans is said to have occurred, will you please tell me, for each one, whether or not in the past ten years or so you or your immediate family... ASK A AND THEN EITHER B OR C FOR EACH ITEM (1) THROUGH (4).

FOR EACH NO TO A, ASK B. FOR EACH YES TO A, ASK C.

	A. ...have experienced it personally?			B. IF NO TO A: Have you heard about cases in which other Japanese Americans experienced it within the past ten years?			C. IF YES TO A: Were you taken by surprise when you experienced (discrimination)?		
	Yes (ASK C)	No (ASK B)	Don't know	Yes	No	Don't know	Surprised	Not surprised	Don't know
1) Discrimination in housing?	1	0	8	2	0	8 10/	1	2	8 11/
2) Discrimination in schools?	1	0	8	2	0	8 12/	1	2	8 13/
3) Discrimination in jobs?	1	0	8	2	0	8 14/	1	2	8 15/
4) Police brutality?	1	0	8	2	0	8 16/	1	2	8 17/

60. Members of many minority groups in America have complained that their groups are not being treated as full and equal Americans. Which of the groups I will read to you can rightfully complain that they are not being treated as full and equal Americans today?

	Can rightfully complain	Cannot	Don't know	
A. Negroes?	1	2	8	18/
B. Italian Americans? . .	1	2	8	19/
C. Japanese Americans? .	1	2	8	20/
D. Chinese Americans? . .	1	2	8	21/
E. Jews?	1	2	8	22/
F. Mexican Americans? . .	1	2	8	23/
G. Puerto Ricans?	1	2	8	24/

61. A. Negroes are interested in bettering their position in American society. What advice would you give Negroes, as a race, to achieve their goals?

B. How long do you think it will take for the Negroes to achieve their goals? DO NOT READ CATEGORIES. CIRCLE ONLY ONE CODE.

They've already achieved them . . . . . . (GO TO Q. 62) 0 28/
Less than a year; "a very short time" (GO TO Q. 62) 1
1 to less than 5 years; "a few years" . . . (ASK C) 2
5-9 years . . . . (ASK C) . . . 3
10-24 years . . . . (ASK C) . . . 4
25-49 years "a generation" . . . . (ASK C) . . . 5
50-99 years "two generations"; "a couple of generations" (ASK C) . 6
100 years or more . . . . (ASK C) . . . 7
Never . . . . (GO TO Q. 62) 8
Don't know; can't say . . . . (GO TO Q. 62) 9

C. IF 1-100 YEARS: What will keep them from achieving their goals sooner? (PROBE: What else?)

Now I'd like to find out something about your religious affiliations.

62. Are you a Buddhist, a Protestant,
a Roman Catholic, a nonbeliever,
or something else?

Nonbeliever 1	32/
Buddhist 2	
Protestant 3	
Roman Catholic 4	
Konko Kyo (Shinto) . . . 5	
Ba'hai; World Messianity;	
Seicho-No-Ie 6	
Other (SPECIFY) 7	

63. Have you at an earlier time been a member
of a (different) religion?

Yes . . . (ASK A) 1   33/
No . . (GO TO Q. 64) . . 2

A. IF YES: What religion was that?
(IF MORE THAN ONE, RECORD FIRST
BELONGED TO.)

Nonbeliever 1   34/
Buddhist 2
Protestant 3
Roman Catholic 4
Konko Kyo (Shinto) . . . 5
Ba'hai; World Messianity;
Seicho-No-Ie 6
Other (SPECIFY) 7

IF RESPONDENT NOW BUDDHIST, HAND HIM CARD 5 AND ASK Q. 64 A.
IF RESPONDENT NOW PROTESTANT, ASK Q. 64 B.

64. A. You said you now are a Buddhist.
Which of these sects are you a
member of?

(1) Jodo Shinshu (Nishi   35-
    Hongwanji) 41   36/
(2) Jodo Shinshu (Higashi
    Hongwanji) 42
(3) Jodo Shu 43
(4) Nichiren Shu 44
(5) Zen 45
(6) Shingon Shu (Koyasan) . 46
(7) Other 47

B. You said you are a Protestant.
What denomination do you belong
to?

Methodist 02
Presbyterian 03
Episcopal 04
Seventh Day Adventist . . . 05
Churches of Christ 06
Congregationalist 07
Holiness 08
Lutheran 09
Mormon 10
United Church of Christ . . 11
Baptist 12
Other (SPECIFY) 17
None 77

190

IF CLERGYMAN, CODE Q. 65 WITHOUT ASKING.

65. How often do you usually attend religious services--once a week, a few times a month, once a month, or less often than that?

Once a week or more . . 1   37/
Few times a month . . . 2
Once a month 3
Less often than that . . 4
Never 5
Don't know; can't say . 8

ASK EVERYONE:

66. Aside from attendance at religious services, how important would you say religion is to you--very important, fairly important, or not important at all?

Very important 1   38/
Fairly important 2
Not important at all . . 3
Don't know; can't say . 8

67. What religion does your (wife/husband) belong to? Is (she/he) a Buddhist, a Protestant, a Roman Catholic, a non-believer, or something else?

Nonbeliever 1   39/
Buddhist 2
Protestant 3
Roman Catholic 4
Konko Kyo (Shinto) . . . 5
Ba'hai; World Messianity;
   Seicho-No-Ie 6
Other (SPECIFY) 7
Don't know 8

Just a few more questions about yourself now.

68. Which political party do you generally support in national elections?

Democratic 1   40/
Republican 2
Independent 3
Other (SPECIFY) 4
Don't vote 8

69. Generally speaking, how much interest would you say you have in politics--a great deal, a fair amount, only a little, or no interest at all?

A great deal 1   41/
A fair amount 2
Only a little 3
No interest at all . . . 4

191

70. During the last few months, has anyone outside your family asked you for advice about politics or public affairs?

Yes 1   42/
No 2
Don't know . 8

71. What magazines do you subscribe to or regularly read? (Any others?)

None . . . 000

1. _____   6. _____   43/
2. _____   7. _____
3. _____   8. _____   44/
4. _____   9. _____
5. _____   10. _____   45/

72. Do you ever read any Japanese American newspapers?   Yes . (ASK A) . 1   46/
No (GO TO Q. 73) 2

A. Do you read them regularly, occasionally, or hardly ever?

Regularly . . . 1   47/
Occasionally . . 2
Hardly ever . . 3

ASK EVERYONE:

73. Are you able to speak Japanese quite fluently, pretty well, only a little, or not at all?

Quite fluently . . . 1   48/
Pretty well 2
Only a little 3
Not at all 4

74. Are you able to read Japanese?

Yes 1   49/
No 2

75. IF HAS CHILDREN: Do you think your children ought to know how to speak Japanese?

IF HAS NO CHILDREN: If you had children, do you think they ought to know how to speak Japanese?

Yes 1   50/
No 2
Not certain . . 8

76. Have you ever visited Japan [aside from the time(s) you lived there]?

Yes 1   51/
No 2

---

77. Have you (or your wife/husband) ever been a member of a labor union?

Yes 1   52/
No 2
Don't know . 8

---

78. IF EVER MARRIED: (Have you/Has your husband) ever served in the United States armed forces, active or reserve?

Yes . . . (ASK A) . . . 1   53/
No . . (GO TO Q. 79) . . 2
Don't know (GO TO Q. 79) 8

A. IF YES: In what year did (you/your husband) first enter the service?

Before 1941 . . 1   54/
1941-1945 . . . 2
1946-1949 . . . 3
1950-1953 . . . 4
1954-1963 . . . 5
1964-present . . 6
Don't know . . . 8

---

79. IF EVER MARRIED AND HAS CHILDREN, HAND RESPONDENT SANSEI LISTING SHEET.

As you know, we are doing a study of three generations of Japanese American families--the Issei, the Nisei, and the Sansei. We will need, therefore, information about your children. Here is a sheet for you to fill out. Would you please enter the name, sex, age, and address of all your children, whether or not living at home? Also please enter whether each of your children is of this or a previous marriage, and whether he is natural or adopted. You only have to enter the family name where it is different from yours; and it will be sufficient for those children living with you in the home, simply to enter "at home."

SAY TO EVERYONE:

Thank you very much for your time and cooperation. You have been an invaluable help. And I hope you have enjoyed the interview.

ENTER HERE | _____ AM | TIME INTERVIEW ENDED.   55/
            | PM |

193

A. TYPE OF INTERVIEW: Face to face . . 1   56/

                                           Telephone . . . 2

B. SEX OF RESPONDENT: Male 1   57/

                                           Female 2

FILL OUT THE FOLLOWING ITEMS, C - M, AS SOON AS POSSIBLE AFTER COMPLET-
ING THE INTERVIEW, SO THAT IT IS STILL FRESH IN YOUR MIND.

C. DWELLING TYPE: Unknown: telephone interview . 0   58/

                          Single family 1

                          Two family 2

                          Multiple dwelling:

                              1 - 9 units 3

                              10 - 24 units 4

                              25 or more units 5

                          Rooming house 6

                          Hotel 7

                          Other (SPECIFY) 8

D. FLUENCY IN ENGLISH: Perfect 1   59/

                                            Nearly perfect . . 2

                                            Some difficulty . 3

                                            Much difficulty . 4

E. COOPERATIVENESS:
                                       Very cooperative 1   60/

                                       Fairly cooperative . . . 2

                                       Uncooperative 3

F. INTEREST:
                                            Great interest . . 1   61/

                                            Some interest . . 2

                                            Little interest . 3

G. RECORD RELATIONSHIP TO RESPONDENT OF ANYONE ELSE PRESENT DURING INTERVIEW OTHER THAN RESPONDENT AND INTERVIEWER.

62/

H. NOTE ANY INTERRUPTIONS IN, DISTURBANCES DURING, OR PECULIAR CIRCUM-STANCES OF, THE INTERVIEW.

63/

I. NOTE ANY QUESTIONS THE RESPONDENT SEEMED TO HAVE PARTICULAR DIFFI-CULTY UNDERSTANDING.

J. Do you think it made any difference in the responses you got that you were not a Japanese American?

Yes (ANSWER K) . 1   64/

No 2

K. How did it make a difference? On what questions and to what extent?

L. Date interview completed:

| | | | 6 | 7 | 65/
Month   Date   Year

M. Your signature: _____ 66-68/

Thank you for your cooperation!

PSU NO:

| | | |
69   70   71

195

APPENDIX C:
THE SANSEI: MAIL QUESTIONNAIRE

FAMILY ID#

JAPANESE AMERICAN RESEARCH PROJECT

University of California at Los Angeles

YOUR NAME: _____

NUMBER AND STREET: _____

CITY AND STATE: _____

DATE YOU FILLED OUT THIS
QUESTIONNAIRE: _____

This survey is supported by a grant
from the U.S. Public Health Service.
The directors of the study assume
full responsibility for the contents
of this questionnaire.

199

TO OUR RESPONDENT:

Most of the questions we are asking you to answer in this questionnaire ask you for *facts* about yourself or others you know: please answer each of these to the best of your ability. We appreciate accuracy, but it will not be necessary for you anywhere on this questionnaire to refer to your records. Just use your memory as best you can. Some other questions ask for your *opinions*. On these questions, obviously, there are no right or wrong answers. What we want to know is *just what you think*. When you aren't quite certain what your answer should be, please give us the choice that appeals to you more at the moment. Please record any additional comments you may have about particular questions or the questionnaire as a whole. Such comments are often invaluable in interpreting your answers to other questions.

None of the questions should be hard or tricky; you will find most are both short and easy. Please remember that it is *you* we are trying to find out about. It will be best, therefore, if you fill out the entire questionnaire *before* you discuss any of the questions with anyone else. After you are finished with the questionnaire, please feel free to discuss it; but be sure you promptly return the filled-out questionnaire to us in the envelope provided.

Instructions for answering each question are printed in CAPITALS along with the question. You are asked to record your answers in one of three ways for any given question. Please always record your answers as neatly as possible.

(1) Most questions require you only to place a *check* in the box representing the answer.

Yes . . . . . ☑

No . . . . . ☐

(2) Some questions ask you to *fill in* an appropriate number, word, or phrase on a line.

23 years

(3) A few questions ask you to *write your answer out freely* in a large space provided.

Some questions are to be answered by some but not all people. Explanations are provided in every case, sometimes with arrows drawn in to assist you.

You may wonder about the numbers in the right-hand column on each page and near the checkboxes. These numbers are there to aid us in tabulating your responses statistically.

THANK YOU VERY MUCH. WE HOPE YOU ENJOY THE QUESTIONNAIRE, AND WE LOOK FORWARD EAGERLY TO RECEIVING YOUR ANSWERS.

1. What is your sex? **(CHECK ONE)**

Male . . . . ☐¹

Female . . . . ☐²

2. How old were you on your last birthday? **(FILL IN NUMBER BELOW)**

_____ years

3. Where were you born? **(FILL IN BELOW)**

_____ , _____
(City)   (State)

4. Are you single, married, divorced, separated, or widowed? **(CHECK ONE)**

Single . . . . ☐¹

Married . . . . ☐²

Divorced . . . . , ... ☐³

Separated . . . . ☐⁴

Widowed . . . . ☐⁵

IF YOU WERE EVER MARRIED, ANSWER QUESTIONS 5 AND 6. OTHERWISE ANSWER QUESTION 7.

5A. Where was your spouse born? **(FILL IN BELOW)**

_____ , _____
(City)   (State)

5B. What is your spouse's background? Is (he/she) a Nisei, a Sansei, a Yonsei, a Caucasian, or of some other background? **(CHECK ONE)**

Nisei . . . . ☐¹

Sansei . . . . ☐²

Yonsei . . . . ☐³

Caucasian . . . . ☐⁴

Other background **(PLEASE SPECIFY AT LEFT)** . . . . ☐⁵

6. How many children have been born to you and your spouse, not counting stillbirths? **(FILL IN NUMBER OF BOYS AND GIRLS BELOW; ENTER "0" WHEN NONE)**

_____ boys   _____ girls

A. **(IF YOU HAVE HAD ANY CHILDREN)** How old is your oldest child? **(FILL IN BELOW)**

_____ years

201

IF YOU HAVE *NEVER* BEEN MARRIED, ANSWER QUESTION 7. OTHERWISE SKIP TO QUESTION 8.

7. Are you currently engaged, going steady with one person, dating casually, or not dating at all?
   (CHECK ONE)

   Engaged **(ANSWER A)** . . . . ☐¹

   Going steady **(ANSWER A)** . . . . ☐²

   Dating casually **(GO TO QUESTION 8)**. . ☐³

   Not dating **(GO TO QUESTION 8)** . . . . . ☐⁴

   A. Is the person you are engaged to or go steady with a Nisei, a Sansei, a Yonsei, a Caucasian, or of some other background? **(CHECK ONE)**

   Nisei . . . . ☐¹

   Sansei . . . . ☐²

   Yonsei . . . . ☐³

   Caucasian . . . . ☐⁴

   Other background **(PLEASE SPECIFY AT LEFT)** . . . . ☐⁵

EVERYBODY ANSWER:

8. What do you think is the ideal number of children for a married couple to have in America today?
   (FILL IN NUMBER BELOW)

   _____ children

9. Do your own parents live in the same household as you do, or do they live somewhere else in the same neighborhood, or somewhere else in the same metropolitan area or county as yourself, or do they live farther away than that? **(CHECK ONE)**

   Same household . . . . ☐¹

   Same neighborhood . . . . . ☐²

   Same metropolitan area
   or county . . . . ☐³

   Farther away . . . . ☐⁴

10. Aside from your parents and your own spouse and children, about how many other relatives –
    including *anyone* else you *consider* a relative – live in the same metropolitan area or county as yourself? **(IF ANY)** And about how many live in the same neighborhood as yourself? **(IF ANY)** And how many of these live in the same household as you? **(FILL IN TABLE BELOW)**

	In metro area or county	In neighborhood	In household
Number of relatives	_____	_____	_____

THOSE WITH RELATIVES LIVING IN THE SAME METROPOLITAN AREA OR COUNTY, ANSWER
QUESTION 11. OTHERS SKIP TO QUESTION 12.

11. About how many times in the past month have you visited with or been visited by relatives living in the
same neighborhood or metropolitan area or county as you? Please do *not* include visits from any relatives who live in the same household as you. (FILL IN NUMBER BELOW)

_____ times

EVERYBODY ANSWER:

12. Now we want to find out about the various *cities and towns* you have lived in. For the metropolitan
area or county you *now* live in (line 1, below), please fill in the date you moved there. Then please
go back, step by step, to your birth place, answering for each metropolitan area or county you have
lived in, questions A, B, and C. (FILL IN TABLE BELOW)

A. Name of each city or town, and state each is located in. (FILL IN BELOW; LINE 1 REPRESENTS THE METROPOLITAN AREA OR COUNTY YOU *NOW* LIVE IN)	B. In what year did you move to each? (APPROX-IMATE DATES IF YOU CAN'T REMEMBER EXACTLY)	C. Were your neighbors there mostly Japanese Americans, mostly non-Japanese Americans, or was the neighborhood mixed? (CHECK ONE FOR EACH)			SPEC COD
		Mostly Japanese Americans	Mostly non-Japanese Americans	Mixed	
1. Metropolitan area or county you live in *now*.		☐	☐	☐	
2.		☐	☐	☐	
3.		☐	☐	☐	
4.		☐	☐	☐	
5.		☐	☐	☐	
6.		☐	☐	☐	
7.		☐	☐	☐	
8.		☐	☐	☐	
9.		☐	☐	☐	
10.		☐	☐	☐	

13. Now about the neighborhood you live in now: do you think of this neighborhood as your real home — the place where you really belong, or do you think of it as just a place where you happen to be living? **(CHECK ONE)**

Really belong .... ☐¹

Just a place .... ☐²

14A. Would you say that this neighborhood is made up mostly of Japanese Americans, mostly non-Japanese Americans, or is it mixed? **(CHECK ONE)**

Mostly Japanese Americans .... ☐¹

Mixed .... ☐²

Mostly non-Japanese Americans....... ☐³

14B. What other kinds of groups besides Japanese Americans live in this neighborhood? **(ANSWER BELOW)**

Now we want to find out some things about your career to date and about your plans for your career.

15A. What occupation would you *most like* to make your life work — the work you hope to be doing throughout your career? **(DESCRIBE THE OCCUPATION BELOW; PLEASE BE AS SPECIFIC AS YOU CAN AND TELL A LITTLE ABOUT THE DUTIES THIS OCCUPATION ACTUALLY INVOLVES)**

15B. In this occupation, do you expect you would be working for yourself all the time, working for someone else all the time, or sometimes working for yourself and sometimes for someone else? **(CHECK ONE BELOW)**

Working for yourself .... ☐¹

Sometimes for yourself, sometimes
for someone else .... ☐²

Working for someone else .... ☐³

16. How likely do you think it is that you will *actually* be doing that work, say in ten or twenty years? Do you think it is almost certain, pretty likely, about fifty-fifty, pretty unlikely, or highly unlikely that you will be doing that? **(CHECK ONE BELOW)**

Almost certain **(SKIP TO QUESTION 17)** . . ☐¹

Pretty likely **(SKIP TO QUESTION 17)** . . . ☐²

About fifty-fifty **(ANSWER A AND B)** . . . . ☐³

Pretty unlikely **(ANSWER A AND B)** . . . . . ☐⁴

Highly unlikely **(ANSWER A AND B)** . . . . . ☐⁵

A. For what reason or reasons do you think that in ten or twenty years you might *not* be in the occupation you would most *like* to be in? **(CHECK ALL REASONS BELOW YOU THINK MAY APPLY)**

Insufficient education . . . . ☐001

Insufficient skills or talent . . . . . . ·. . . . ☐002

Occupation too competitive . . . . ☐004

Racial discrimination . . . . ☐008

You need pull . . . . ☐016

You lack drive or ambition . . . . ☐032

You would have to move to
take the job . . . . ☐064

Family demands would be too great . . . . . ☐128

Others **(PLEASE DESCRIBE IN SPACE
TO LEFT)** . . . . ☐256

B. What other work do you think you actually *will* be doing in ten or twenty years, if you are not in the occupation you think you would most *like* to be in? **(DESCRIBE THE OCCUPATION BELOW: PLEASE BE AS SPECIFIC AS YOU CAN AND TELL A LITTLE ABOUT THE DUTIES THIS OCCUPATION ACTUALLY INVOLVES)**

17. Many people feel that they must achieve a certain standing within their occupation before they can call their career a success. Speaking just for yourself now, how high a standing do you hope you will achieve in the life work you think you actually will have? **(CHECK ONE)**

One of the top people in the occupation . . . ☐¹

Near the top of the occupation . . . . ☐²

Above average . . . . ☐³

Just about average . . . . ☐⁴

Any secure standing . . . . ☐⁵

Standing makes no difference to me . . . . . ☐⁶

205

WOMEN WHO ARE CURRENTLY MARRIED OR WIDOWED: IF YOUR HUSBAND HAS EVER HAD A FULL-TIME JOB (APART FROM VACATION EMPLOYMENT), PLEASE ANSWER QUESTIONS 18 THROUGH 22 IN TERMS OF YOUR *HUSBAND'S* OCCUPATIONS; IF YOUR HUSBAND HAS NEVER HAD A FULL-TIME JOB, AND IS STILL A STUDENT, SIMPLY ENTER "STUDENT" FOR QUESTION 18 AND SKIP TO QUESTION 23. WOMEN CURRENTLY SINGLE OR DIVORCED, PLEASE ANSWER QUESTIONS 18 THROUGH 22 IN TERMS OF *YOUR OWN* OCCUPATIONS.

MEN PLEASE ANSWER QUESTIONS 18 THROUGH 22 IN TERMS OF *YOUR OWN* OCCUPATIONS. IF YOU ARE CURRENTLY A STUDENT AND HAVE NEVER HAD A FULL-TIME JOB (APART FROM VACATION EMPLOYMENT), SIMPLY ENTER "STUDENT" IN QUESTION 18 AND SKIP TO QUESTION 23.

18A. What kind of work do you or did you do most recently? **(MARRIED WOMEN:** What kind of work does your husband do or did he do most recently?) Please be as specific as possible, and tell us briefly what duties the job actually involves and which industry it is part of. **(ANSWER BELOW)**

18B. (Are you/is your husband) self-employed or employed by someone else? **(CHECK ONE)**

Self-employed .... ☐¹

Employed by others ...... ☐²

19. During what years (have you held/has your husband held) this job? **(FILL IN BELOW. IF (YOU/YOUR HUSBAND)** *CURRENTLY* HOLDS THIS JOB PLEASE WRITE "NOW" FOR YEAR JOB ENDED.)

_____ to _____
(Year job began)   (Year job ended)

THOSE WHO(SE HUSBANDS) ARE *CURRENTLY* WORKING, ANSWER QUESTIONS 20 AND 21. OTHERS SKIP TO QUESTION 22.

20. About what proportion of the people (you see/your husband sees) regularly at work on (your/his) present job are Japanese Americans — nearly all, about three-quarters, about half, about a quarter, almost none, or none at all? **(CHECK ONE)**

Nearly all .... ☐¹

About ¾ .... ☐²

About ½ .... ☐³

About ¼ .... ☐⁴

Almost none .... ☐⁵

None .... ☐⁶

206

21. Now, about these people (you see/your husband sees) regularly at work – how often (do you/does he) meet them off the job? Often, sometimes, or almost never? **(CHECK ONE)**

Often . . . . ☐¹

Sometimes . . . . ☐²

Almost never . . . . ☐³

22. We already know about your (husband's) most recent job. Now we would like to know about all the *other full-time* jobs (you have/he has) ever held, whether or not these represented changes from one firm to another. Please go back step by step to (your/his) first full-time position, answering for *each* job questions A, B, C, and D. **(FILL IN TABLE BELOW: BE SURE TO INCLUDE CHANGES OF POSITION WITHIN THE SAME FIRM.)**

A. Name of each job and brief description of duties.	B. Year the job began? (Approximate date if you can't remember exactly)	C. About how many employees worked for this firm?	D. Was this a different firm from the one (you/he) worked for just before that? **(CHECK ONE FOR EACH JOB)**		SPEC COD
	Year	Number	Same	Different	
1.			☐	☐	
2.			☐	☐	
3.			☐	☐	
4.			☐	☐	
5.			☐	☐	
6.			☐	☐	
7.			☐	☐	
8.			☐	☐	

IF YOU ARE CURRENTLY MARRIED, PLEASE ANSWER QUESTION 23. OTHERWISE, SKIP TO QUESTION 24.

23. Does the woman of the household work full-time, part-time, or does she not work at all?

Works full-time . . . . ☐¹

Works part-time . . . . ☐²

Does not work . . . . ☐³

64

EVERYBODY ANSWER:

24. A. Please check the box to the right of the range below which includes your own *present* total family income. Please include income from rents, investments, interest and earnings of all family members — in other words, the approximate total income as recorded on your last income tax. Please *do not* include *your parents'* income. **(CHECK ONE IN COLUMN A, BELOW)**

B. And please check the box that represents what you think your family income will be in five years? **(CHECK ONE IN COLUMN B, BELOW)**

C. Finally, please check the box that represents what you think your family income will be when (you are/your husband is) at the peak of (your/his) career? **(CHECK ONE IN COLUMN C, BELOW)**

	A. Total Family Income	B. Income in Five Years	C. Peak of Career
Under $2,500	□¹	□¹	□¹
$2,500 – $4,999	□²	□²	□²
$5,000 – $7,499	□³	□³	□³
$7,500 – $9,999	□⁴	□⁴	□⁴
$10,000 – $14,999	□⁵	□⁵	□⁵
$15,000 – $19,999	□⁶	□⁶	□⁶
$20,000 – $29,999	□⁷	□⁷	□⁷
$30,000 or more	□⁸	□⁸	□⁸

25. Are you *now* a student, not presently a student but planning to enter school at a later date, or are you all finished with your schooling? **(CHECK ONE)**

Now a student □¹
Planning to re-enter school □²
All finished with schooling □³

26A. What is the highest grade you have completed so far in school? **(CHECK ONE. IF YOU HAVE EVER BEEN MARRIED, ALSO ANSWER 26B.)**

26B. What is the highest grade your spouse has completed in school? **(CHECK ONE)**

	A. Your own education	B. Your spouse's education
Less than high school graduate	□¹	□¹
12 grades (completed high school)	□²	□²
13-15 grades or years (trade or technical school or some college)	□³	□³
16 grades or years (completed college)	□⁴	□⁴
More than 16 years (beyond college graduation)	□⁵	□⁵

208

IF YOU HAVE GONE BEYOND HIGH SCHOOL, ANSWER QUESTIONS 27 AND 28; OTHERWISE SKIP TO QUESTION 29.

27. Please list below any colleges and professional or graduate schools you have attended, their location, the years during which you attended each, the major field or fields you studied, and any degrees attained in each. (FILL IN TABLE BELOW)

	Name of School	Location	Attended From	To	Major Field(s)	Degree(s) Received
1.						
2.						
3.						
4.						

28. Please tell us a little about the various organizations or groups to which you may have belonged during your college career. For each of the types of groups mentioned below, please answer questions A, B, and C. (FILL IN TABLE BELOW)

	A. How many organizations of this type did you belong to?	B. Of these, how many had primarily Japanese American members?	C. How many of this type did you hold office or committee membership in?
Political or student government organizations, and service groups			
Fraternities or sororities			
Informal circles or unorganized groups			
Other groups (for example recreational, athletic, or hobby groups)			

29. Over your entire *high-school* career, about how many clubs, fraternities, and other organizations did you belong to? (FILL IN APPROXIMATE FIGURE BELOW: IF NONE, ENTER "0")

_____ organizations

30. And of all these high school groups, in how many did you hold an office? (FILL IN APPROXIMATE NUMBER BELOW; IF NONE, ENTER "0")

_____ organizations

209

31. While you were in high school, were most of your close friends Japanese Americans, non-Japanese Americans, or about an equal number of both? **(CHECK ONE)**

Mostly Japanese Americans . . . . ☐¹

An equal number of both . . . . ☐²

Mostly non-Japanese Americans . . . . . . ☐³

32. And what about when you were back in grade school? Were most of your close friends Japanese Americans, non-Japanese Americans, or about an equal number of both? **(CHECK ONE)**

Mostly Japanese Americans . . . . ☐¹

An equal number of both . . . . ☐²

Mostly non-Japanese Americans . . . . . . ☐³

33. When you were in high school, was there any particular occupation your parents hoped you would enter? **(CHECK ONE)**

Yes **(ANSWER A AND B)** . . . . ☐¹

No. . . . . ☐²

A. What was this occupation? **(DESCRIBE AS FULLY AS POSSIBLE BELOW)**

B. How much emphasis did your parents place upon your entering this occupation? Would you say that they placed a great deal of emphasis upon it, some emphasis, only a little emphasis, or no emphasis at all? **(CHECK ONE)**

A great deal of emphasis . . . . ☐¹

Some emphasis . . . . ☐²

Only a little emphasis . . . . ☐³

No emphasis at all . . . . ☐⁴

34. While you were growing up, would you say that your parents wanted you to take an active part with Caucasians in their activities, or to stick pretty much with Japanese Americans? **(CHECK ONE)**

Take an active part with Caucasians . . . ☐¹

Stick pretty much with Japanese
Americans . . . . ☐²

35. Would *you* want *your own children* to take an active part with Caucasians in their activities, or to stick pretty much with Japanese Americans? **(CHECK ONE)**

Take an active part with Caucasians . . . ☐¹

Stick pretty much with Japanese
Americans . . . . ☐²

36. For each of the principles listed below (A to D), please tell us whether or not *your parents* stressed it when you were growing up. (CHECK THE APPROPRIATE NUMBER TO THE RIGHT OF EACH PRINCIPLE BELOW.)

	Your parents stressed it	Your parents did not stress it	You don't recall
A. You must behave properly to avoid bringing shame to the family.	☐¹	☐²	☐⁸
B. To lose a competition is to be disgraced.	☐¹	☐²	☐⁸
C. One must make returns for all kindnesses received.	☐¹	☐²	☐⁸
D. You must act so as not to bring dishonor to the Japanese American community.	☐¹	☐²	☐⁸

37. Parents often try to influence their children when it comes to marriage. Has this been true of your parents in your case? (CHECK ONE)

Yes . . . . ☐¹
No (GO TO QUESTION 38) . ☐²

IF YES, PLEASE ANSWER: A. What have they urged you to do? (ANSWER BELOW)

MEN AND UNMARRIED WOMEN: QUESTIONS 38 AND 39 ASK ABOUT YOUR *OWN* CAREER.
MARRIED WOMEN: QUESTIONS 38 AND 39 ASK ABOUT YOUR *HUSBAND'S* CAREER.

38. Here is a list (A to E) of some types of aid families can give. For each one, we would like to know whether (you/your husband) received such aid from any one in your family or in your spouse's family. (CHECK THE APPROPRIATE BOX FOR *EACH* FORM OF AID)

	Received such aid from family or spouse's family	Did not receive such aid, or do not remember
A. Advice in choosing a career.	☐01	☐00
B. Work for pay, even part-time, in a business or farm owned by members of the family . . .	☐02	☐00
C. Help in acquiring a farm	☐04	☐00
D. Help in acquiring a business	☐08	☐00
E. Help in getting a job	☐16	☐00

211

39. Now, would you tell us whether there has been anyone from *outside* the family who has given (you/your husband) help in advancement — either in any of these same ways, or in other ways? (CHECK ONE)

Yes .... ☐¹

No (GO TO QUESTION 40) . ☐²

►IF YES, PLEASE ANSWER: A. What was this person's relationship to (you/your husband)? We would like to know how this person knew (you/him) and what was his position that he was able to give help. (ANSWER BELOW)

►AND PLEASE ANSWER: B. When was this? About how old (were you/was your husband) when that person *first* started to help? (FILL IN BELOW)

_____ years

►AND PLEASE ANSWER: C. Did that person help (you/him) in this way only once, or did he do so a number of times, or does he still continue to help sometimes? (CHECK ONE)

Only once .... ☐¹

A number of times ...... ☐²

Still helps sometimes .... ☐³

►AND PLEASE ANSWER: D. What kind of help did he give? (ANSWER BELOW)

►AND PLEASE ANSWER: E. And was this person a Japanese American? (CHECK ONE)

Yes .... ☐¹

No .... ☐²

212

40. Think for a moment of the grandparent you have known the best. Would you say that you yourself have had very close relations with him or her, rather close relations, not very close, or rather distant relations? **(CHECK ONE)**

Very close relations . . . . ☐¹

Rather close relations . . . . ☐²

Not very close relations . . . . ☐³

Rather distant relations . . . . ☐⁴

---

41. Was the grandparent you have known the best born in Japan? **(CHECK ONE)**

Yes **(ANSWER A)** . . . . ☐¹

No **(SKIP TO QUESTION 42)** ☐²

A. Do you know, without looking it up, the prefecture in Japan from which he or she came? **(CHECK ONE)**

Yes . . . . ☐¹

No . . . . ☐²

EVERYBODY ANSWER:

42. How familiar would you say you are with the experiences your Japanese grandparents had in getting settled in the United States? Would you say you are very familiar, somewhat familiar, or mainly unfamiliar? **(CHECK ONE)**

Very familiar . . . . ☐¹

Somewhat familiar . . . . ☐²

Mainly unfamiliar . . . . ☐³

43. In question 36 we asked you about some principles your parents may have stressed. Now would you, for each of these principles, tell us whether or not *any* of your *Japanese grand-parents* stressed it when you were growing up. **(CHECK THE APPROPRIATE BOX TO THE RIGHT OF EACH PRINCIPLE BELOW.)**

	Your grandparents stressed it	Your grandparents did not stress it	You don't recall
A. You must behave properly to avoid bringing shame to the family.	☐¹	☐²	☐⁸
B. To lose a competition is to be disgraced.	☐¹	☐²	☐⁸
C. One must make returns for all kindnesses received.	☐¹	☐²	☐⁸
D. You must act so as not to bring dishonor to the Japanese American community.	☐¹	☐²	☐⁸

44. Would you say that *in general* the Nisei are more like the Issei or more like the Sansei? (CHECK ONE)

More like Issei . . . . ☐¹

Equally similar to both . . . . ☐²

More like Sansei . . . . ☐³

45. Would you say that generally the Nisei are not American enough, too American, or just about right? (CHECK ONE)

Not American enough . . . . . ☐¹

Just about right . . . . ☐²

Too American . . . . ☐³

46. And what about the Sansei? Would you say that generally they are not American enough, too American, or just about right? (CHECK ONE)

Not American enough . . . . . ☐¹

Just about right . . . . ☐²

Too American . . . . ☐³

47. Some people are talking about Sansei marrying Caucasians. How *important* a question do you think this is for the Sansei? Very important, rather important, rather unimportant, or very unimportant? (CHECK ONE)

Very important . . . . ☐¹

Rather important . . . . ☐²

Rather unimportant . . . . . . ☐³

Very unimportant . . . . ☐⁴

48. Speaking just for yourself now, do you think that on the whole the effect of Sansei marrying Caucasians is *good* for the Japanese Americans, *bad* for them, or do you think this will make *little difference* one way or the other? (CHECK ONE)

Good for them . . . . ☐¹

Make little difference . . . . ☐²

Bad for them . . . . ☐³

49. In your opinion, should minority groups in America try to preserve something of the culture of their own group, or should they blend their culture into the mainstream of American life? (CHECK ONE)

Preserve own culture . . . . . ☐¹

Blend culture into
mainstream . . . . ☐²

214

50. A. Do you suppose most Caucasians in America would be disturbed if a Japanese American girl married a son of theirs? (CHECK ONE)

Caucasians would be disturbed . . . . ☐¹

Caucasians would not be disturbed . . . . . . ☐²

B. What if a Japanese American boy married a daughter of theirs? (CHECK ONE)

Caucasians would be disturbed . . . . ☐¹

Caucasians would not be disturbed . . . . . . ☐²

51. Now, we want to know a few things (A to C) about the people who are presently your closest friends outside your immediate family — that is, the people whom you see most often or feel closest to. Think for a moment of the *two* people you would say are your closest friends. PLEASE ENTER JUST THE *FIRST* NAME OF ONE OF THESE TWO FRIENDS ON THE TOP OF THE FIRST COLUMN IN THE SPACE PROVIDED, AND THE FIRST NAME OF THE OTHER ON TOP OF THE OTHER COLUMN. NOW ANSWER FOR *EACH* FRIEND THE THREE QUESTIONS TO THE LEFT OF THE TWO COLUMNS.

	First name of first friend:	First name of second friend:
A. How did you get to know your friend? Did you become friends with him at school, at work, in some organization, in the neighborhood, in your family, through friends, or somewhere else. (CHECK ONE FOR EACH FRIEND.)	School......................... ☐¹ Work .... ☐² Organization .... ☐³ Neighborhood .... ☐⁴ Family .... ☐⁵ Friends .... ☐⁶ Another place .... ☐⁷ (IF OTHER, WHAT? _____)	School......................... ☐¹ Work .... ☐² Organization .... ☐³ Neighborhood .... ☐⁴ Family .... ☐⁵ Friends .... ☐⁶ Another place .... ☐⁷ (IF OTHER, WHAT? _____)
B. Is your friend a Nisei, a Sansei, a Yonsei, a Caucasian or of another background? (CHECK ONE FOR EACH FRIEND)	Nisei .... ☐¹ Sansei .... ☐² Yonsei .... ☐³ Caucasian .... ☐⁴ Other .... ☐⁵ (IF OTHER, WHAT? _____)	Nisei........................... ☐¹ Sansei .... ☐² Yonsei .... ☐³ Caucasian .... ☐⁴ Other .... ☐⁵ (IF OTHER, WHAT? _____)
C. What is your friend's occupation? Please tell a little about what he actually does on his job, and what industry he works in. (ANSWER FOR EACH FRIEND IN APPROPRIATE BOX TO RIGHT)		

52. About how many groups or organizations do you belong to which have a more less regular membership and meet more or less regularly? In the count, please don't include any of the school organizations you have already told us about, or the church you may belong to: we'll come to that later. **(FILL IN NUMBER BELOW)**

_____ groups

53. **IF YOU BELONG TO ANY SUCH GROUPS, PLEASE ANSWER QUESTIONS 53 A, B, AND C; IF YOU BELONG TO NO GROUPS, SKIP TO QUESTION 54.**

A. Of the groups you belong to, about how many have mostly Japanese American members? **(FILL IN NUMBER BELOW)**

_____ groups

B. Are you now an officer or a committee member of any of the organizations you belong to? **(CHECK ONE)**

Yes . . . . □¹

No . . . . □²

C. Of all the organizations you belong to, which is the one to which you devote the most time? **(PLEASE ENTER NAME OF THIS ORGANIZATION BELOW, AND DESCRIBE BRIEFLY WHAT IT DOES.)**

54. A. Which of the five things (**A** to **E**) listed below is _most_ important for a Japanese American community leader today, as you see it? **(CHECK ONE IN LEFT-HAND COLUMN BELOW)**

B. And which one do you think is the _least_ important today? **(CHECK ONE IN THE RIGHT-HAND COLUMN BELOW)**

	A. Most important	B. Least important
A. Gaining concrete improvements for the Japanese American community	□¹	□¹
B. Joining with other groups to make a better America	□²	□²
C. Leading a virtuous life	□³	□³
D. Settling disputes and squabbles in the Japanese American community	□⁴	□⁴
E. Winning the respect of Caucasians	□⁵	□⁵

216

55. For questions A to DD on this and the next page, all we want to know is whether in general you agree or disagree with each of the statements. Please check an answer for each question, even if you are not sure of your answer. There are no right or wrong answers. All we want is the answer that comes to your mind first.

PLEASE DECIDE WHETHER *ON THE WHOLE* YOU AGREE OR DISAGREE WITH EACH STATEMENT. CHECK THE LEFT-HAND BOX IF YOU AGREE WITH THE STATEMENT, OR THE RIGHT-HAND BOX IF YOU DISAGREE.

		Agree	*Disagree*
A.	Most people in government are not really interested in problems of the average man	$\square^1$	$\square^2$
B.	I often get angry, irritated, or annoyed	$\square^1$	$\square^2$
C.	All a man should want out of life in the way of a career is a secure, not too difficult job, with enough pay to afford a nice car and eventually a home of his own	$\square^1$	$\square^2$
D.	The best way to judge a man is by his success in his profession	$\square^1$	$\square^2$
E.	The average man is probably better off today than he ever was	$\square^1$	$\square^2$
F.	I can usually just shrug my shoulders at misfortune	$\square^1$	$\square^2$
G.	If you try hard enough you usually get what you want	$\square^1$	$\square^2$
H.	Nowdays a person has to live pretty much for today and let tomorrow take care of itself	$\square^1$	$\square^2$
I.	When it comes to spending time, family demands come first	$\square^1$	$\square^2$
J.	When a man is born, the degree of success he is going to have is already in the cards, so he might just as well accept it and not fight against it	$\square^1$	$\square^2$
K.	Even today, the way you make money is more important than how much you make	$\square^1$	$\square^2$
L.	I often feel guilty about the things I do or don't do	$\square^1$	$\square^2$
M.	The art of work is finding an easier way	$\square^1$	$\square^2$
N.	Americans put too much stress on occupational success	$\square^1$	$\square^2$
O.	A man shouldn't try to change fate but to live with it	$\square^1$	$\square^2$
P.	I often worry about possible misfortunes	$\square^1$	$\square^2$
Q.	Most people can still be depended upon to come through in a pinch	$\square^1$	$\square^2$
R.	The secret of happiness is not expecting too much out of life and being content with what comes your way	$\square^1$	$\square^2$
S.	The family often asks too much of a person	$\square^1$	$\square^2$
T.	Next to health, money is the most important thing in life	$\square^1$	$\square^2$
U.	Although things may look hard at a particular moment, if you just bear up, things will usually improve	$\square^1$	$\square^2$

217

V. Today success demands quantity, not quality	□¹	□²
W. The most important qualities of a real man are determination and driving ambition	□¹	□²
X. I sometimes can't help wondering if anything is worthwhile any more	□¹	□²
Y. I often feel frightened or afraid of things	□¹	□²
Z. The most important thing for a parent to do is to help his children get further ahead in the world than he did	□¹	□²
AA. Most people will go out of their way to help someone else	□¹	□²
BB. It's hardly fair to bring a child into the world today the way things look for the future	□¹	□²
CC. The best man is the one who puts his family above everything	□¹	□²
DD. Anything I do I try to do well	□¹	□²

56. Below on the left is a list of statements (**A** to **F**) about jobs. In the first column, please decide which *one* of these you would want *most* in a job (WOMEN EVER MARRIED: in a job for your husband) and check the appropriate box. Choose which *one* you would want second most, and check the appropriate box. Go on ranking the remaining choices until you have recorded the *one* item you would want *least* in a job by checking one of the boxes in the right-hand column. **(CHECK A BOX REPRESENTING A *DIFFERENT STATEMENT* FOR EACH OF THE SIX RANKINGS.)**

	Most important	2nd most important	3rd most important	4th most important	5th most important	Least important
A. Income is steady	□¹	□¹	□¹	□¹	□¹	□¹
B. Income is high	□²	□²	□²	□²	□²	□²
C. There is no danger of being fired or unemployed	□³	□³	□³	□³	□³	□³
D. Working hours are short, lots of free time	□⁴	□⁴	□⁴	□⁴	□⁴	□⁴
E. Chances of getting ahead are good	□⁵	□⁵	□⁵	□⁵	□⁵	□⁵
F. The work is important and gives a feeling of accomplishment	□⁶	□⁶	□⁶	□⁶	□⁶	□⁶

BREATHE DEEPLY. THANK YOU.

57. In your opinion, which is more often to blame if a person is poor – a lack of effort on his own part or circumstances beyond his control? **(CHECK ONE)**

Lack of own effort. . . . . . . ☐¹

Circumstances beyond
control . . . . ☐²

58. Who do you think has higher social value – people who make, buy, or sell things of practical use, or people like scholars and artists? **(CHECK ONE)**

Practical use . . . . ☐¹

Scholars and artists . . . . . ☐²

59. If you think a thing is right, do you think you should go ahead and do it even if it is contrary to usual custom, or do you think it's better to follow custom? **(CHECK ONE)**

Go ahead . . . . ☐¹

Follow custom . . . . ☐²

60. If you did not have any children, do you think you ought to adopt a child to continue the family line even if the child were not related to you, or do you think you need not do that? **(CHECK ONE)**

Should adopt . . . . ☐¹

Need not adopt . . . . ☐²

We want to find out a little about what you think about the history and position of the Japanese in America.

61. Below is a list of some ways (A to D) in which discrimination against Japanese Americans is said to have occurred. Will you please try to remember whether in the past ten years or so you or your immediate family have experienced any of these forms of discrimination *personally?* Next, for any of these forms of discrimination you haven't experienced personally, would you please try to remember if you have *heard about* cases in which other Japanese Americans experienced it within the past ten years? **(CHECK THE BOX IN THE APPROPRIATE COLUMN FOR EACH OF THE FORMS OF DISCRIMINATION)**

	Experienced *personally*	*Not* experienced, but *heard* about	*Neither* experienced *nor* heard about
A. Discrimination in housing	☐¹	☐²	☐³
B. Discrimination in schools	☐¹	☐²	☐³
C. Discrimination in jobs	☐¹	☐²	☐³
D. Police brutality	☐¹	☐²	☐³

62. How much do you think that being a Japanese American has hindered your advancement – not at all, only a little, somewhat, or very much? (CHECK ONE)

Not at all . . . . ☐1

Only a little . . . . ☐2

Somewhat . . . . ☐3

Very much . . . . ☐4

63. How much do you think that being Japanese American has hindered *your parents'* advancement – not at all, only a little, somewhat, or very much? (CHECK ONE)

Not at all . . . . ☐1

Only a little . . . . ☐2

Somewhat . . . . ☐3

Very much . . . . ☐4

64. Observers have offered many different explanations for hostility shown to the Issei in the period after they arrived in this country. How do *you* account for this hostility? (ANSWER BELOW)

65. After the United States entered World War II, Japanese Americans from the West Coast were placed in relocation camps. As you think back about what you know of this action, why would you say it was done? (ANSWER BELOW)

66. During the World War II relocation, some Nisei worked to make relocation as orderly and comfortable as possible, while others protested the injustice of the relocation and tried to have it declared unconstitutional. Which kind of leader do you *now* think employed the better approach? (CHECK ONE)

Orderly and comfortable . . . ☐¹

Protest . . . . ☐²

67. Members of many minority groups in America have complained that their groups are not being treated as full and equal Americans. Which of the groups listed below (A to G) can rightfully complain that they are not being treated as full and equal Americans today? (CHECK ONE FOR EACH GROUP)

	Can rightfully complain	Cannot rightfully complain
A. Negroes.	☐¹	☐²
B. Italian Americans	☐¹	☐²
C. Japanese Americans	☐¹	☐²
D. Chinese Americans	☐¹	☐²
E. Jews	☐¹	☐²
F. Mexican Americans	☐¹	☐²
G. Puerto Ricans	☐¹	☐²

68. Assume that you are a houseowner and a qualified Negro wished to buy your house:

A. If your neighbors didn't disapprove would you sell your house to a Negro? (CHECK ONE)

Yes . . . . ☐¹

No . . . . ☐²

B. If your neighbors disapproved of your selling your house to such a Negro, would you sell it to him? (CHECK ONE)

Yes . . . . ☐¹

No . . . . ☐²

C. Would *you* disapprove if a neighbor wished to sell *his* house to a qualified Negro?

Yes . . . . ☐¹

No . . . . ☐²

221

69. Now assume that it was a qualified Mexican American who wished to buy your house:

    A. If your neighbors didn't disapprove would you sell your house to a Mexican American? **(CHECK ONE)**

                                              Yes . . . . ☐¹

                                              No. . . . . ☐²

    B. If your neighbors disapproved of your selling your house to such a Mexican American, would you sell it to him? **(CHECK ONE)**

                                              Yes . . . . ☐¹

                                              No . . . . ☐²

    C. Would *you* disapprove if a neighbor wished to sell *his* house to a qualified Mexican American?

                                              Yes . . . . ☐¹

                                            No . . . . ☐²

70. A. Negroes are interested in bettering their position in American society. What advice would you give Negroes, as a race, to achieve their goals? **(ANSWER BELOW)**

    B. How long do you think it will take for the Negroes to achieve their goals? **(FILL IN BELOW)**

                                _____ years

    C. What will keep them from achieving their goals sooner than this? **(ANSWER BELOW)**

71. People nowadays are talking about "black power." Would you say that on the whole you are very favorable to the idea of "black power," somewhat favorable, somewhat unfavorable, or very unfavorable; or would you say you have no opinion one way or the other? **(CHECK ONE)**

                                    Very favorable . . . . ☐¹

                                    Somewhat favorable . . . . . ☐²

                                    Somewhat unfavorable . . . . ☐³

                                    Very unfavorable . . . . ☐⁴

                                    No opinion . . . . ☐⁵

72. Now, we want to find out something about your religious affiliations. Are you a Buddhist, a Protestant, a Roman Catholic, or something else; or do you not identify yourself with any religion?

Buddhist . . . . ☐ 1

Protestant . . . . ☐ 2

Roman Catholic . . . . ☐ 3

Other (what?) . . . . ☐ 4

No religious
  identification . . . . ☐ 5

73. Have you at an earlier time been a member of a different religion? (CHECK ONE)

Yes . . . . ☐ 1

No (GO TO QUESTION 74) . . . . ☐ 2

→IF YES, ANSWER: A. What religion was the *first* one you belonged to? (CHECK ONE)

Buddhist . . . . . . : . . . . . . ☐ 1

Protestant . . . . ☐ 2

Roman Catholic . . . . ☐ 3

Other (what?) _____

_____ ☐ 4

IF YOU ARE NOW A BUDDHIST, ANSWER QUESTION 74A. IF YOU ARE NOW A PROTESTANT, ANSWER QUESTION 74B. IF YOU ARE NEITHER A BUDDHIST NOR A PROTESTANT, SKIP TO QUESTION 75.

74A. Which Buddhist sect are you a member of? (FILL IN BELOW)

_____
(sect)

74B. Which Protestant denomination are you a member of? (FILL IN BELOW)

_____
(denomination)

75. How often do you usually attend religious services – once a week, a few times a month, once a month, or less often? (CHECK ONE)

Once a week or more . . . . . ☐¹

Few times a month . . . . . . ☐²

Once a month . . . . ☐³

Less often than that . . . . . ☐⁴

76. Aside from attendance at religious services, how important would you say religion is to you – very important, fairly important, or not important at all? (CHECK ONE)

Very important . . . . ☐¹

Fairly important . . . . ☐²

Not important at all . . . . . ☐³

IF YOU HAVE EVER BEEN MARRIED, ANSWER QUESTION 77. OTHERWISE SKIP TO QUESTION 78.

77. What religion does your spouse belong to? Is he (she) a Buddhist, a Protestant, a Roman Catholic, or something else; or does she have no religious identification? (CHECK ONE)

Buddhist . . . . ☐¹

Protestant . . . . ☐²

Roman Catholic . . . . ☐³

Other (what?) . . . . ☐⁴

No religious
identification . . . . ☐⁵

EVERYONE ANSWER:

78. Which political party do you generally favor in national elections? (CHECK ONE)

Democratic . . . . ☐¹

Republican . . . . ☐²

Independent . . . . ☐³

Other (what?) _____

_____ ☐⁴

79. Generally speaking, how much interest would you say you have in politics – a great deal, a fair amount, only a little, or no interest at all? (CHECK ONE)

A great deal . . . . ☐¹

A fair amount . . . . ☐²

Only a little . . . . ☐³

No interest at all . . . . ☐⁴

80. During the last few months, has anyone outside your family asked you for advice about politics or public affairs? **(CHECK ONE)**

Yes . . . . $\square^1$

No . . . . $\square^2$

81. What magazines do you subscribe to or regularly read? **(FILL OUT LIST BELOW)**

1. _____ 6. _____

2. _____ 7. _____

3. _____ 8. _____

4. _____ 9. _____

5. _____ 10. _____

82. How often do you read Japanese American newspapers? Do you read them regularly, occasionally, hardly ever, or do you never read a Japanese American newspaper? **(CHECK ONE)**

Regularly . . . . $\square^1$

Occasionally . . . . $\square^2$

Hardly ever . . . . $\square^3$

Never . . . . $\square^4$

83. Are you able to speak Japanese quite fluently, pretty well, only a little, or not at all? **(CHECK ONE)**

Quite fluently **(GO TO QUESTION 84)**. . . . $\square^1$

Pretty well **(ANSWER A)** . . . . $\square^2$

Only a little **(ANSWER A)**. . . . . $\square^3$

Not at all **(ANSWER A)** . . . . $\square^4$

A. Do you wish you could speak Japanese better than you do? **(CHECK ONE)**

Yes . . . . $\square^1$

No . . . . $\square^2$

84. Have you ever been to Japan?

Yes . . . . $\square^1$

No . . . . $\square^2$

85. While you were growing up, how much training or instruction in Japanese culture would you say you had: a great deal, some, only a little, or none at all?

A great deal . . . . ☐¹

Some . . . . ☐²

Only a little . . . . ☐³

None at all . . . . ☐⁴

PLEASE ANSWER: A. Did you receive this training or instruction at home, outside the home, or both in and outside the home?

At home . . . . ☐¹

Outside the home . . . . ☐²

Both in and outside
the home . . . . ☐³

86. Do you think you know enough about Japanese culture, or do you believe that you ought to know more than you do?

Know enough . . . . ☐¹

Ought to know more . . . . . ☐²

87. Has you or your spouse ever been a member of a labor union? **(CHECK ONE)**

Yes . . . . ☐¹

No . . . . ☐²

88. Has you or your spouse ever served in the United States armed forces, active or reserve? **(CHECK ONE)**

Yes . . . . ☐¹

No . . . . ☐²

89. We are interested in knowing whether, before filling out this questionnaire, you had heard anything about the *actual content* of some of the questions on it. **(CHECK ONE)**

Heard about content of some of
the questions . . . . ☐¹

Had not heard about content . . . . ☐²

A peek at the facing page will reveal that YOU ARE FINISHED. We cannot sufficiently thank you for your contribution to our study. We apologize for putting you through so much, but hope you have had some fun, too. As you know, we are EAGER to receive your finished questionnaire.

PLEASE BE SURE YOU PLACE THE QUESTIONNAIRE RIGHT AWAY INTO THE POSTAGE-PAID RETURN ENVELOPE, AND MAIL IT AS SOON AS POSSIBLE. YOUR FILLED-OUT QUESTIONNAIRE IS INVALUABLE TO US.

Please use the COMMENTS page to enlighten us further, to protest individual questions, or to curse us, as you wish. THANK YOU AGAIN.

BIBLIOGRAPHY

Benson, L. E. "Mail Surveys Can Be Valuable." *Public Opinion Quarterly* 10 (1946): 234–41.

Bernard, Jesse. *The Sociology of Community.* Glenview, Ill.: Scott, Foresman, 1973.

Bonacich, Edna M. "A Theory of Ethnic Antagonism: The Split Labor Market." *American Sociological Review* 37 (1972): 547–59.

———. "A Theory of Middleman Minorities." *American Sociological Review* 38 (1973): 583–94.

Brooks, Melvin S., and Ken Kunihiro. "Education in the Assimilation of Japanese: A Study in the Houston Area of Texas." *Sociology and Social Research* 37 (1952): 16–22.

Bureau of Statistics, Japan. Nihon Teikoku Tokei Nenkan, December 31, 1898, vol. 19. Tokyo, 1900.

Bush, Lewis. *77 Samurai: Japan's First Embassy to America.* Tokyo and Palo Alto, Calif. Kodansha International, 1968.

Cannell, Charles F., and Floyd J. Fowler. "Comparison of a Self-Enumerative Procedure and a Personal Interview: A Validity Study." *Public Opinion Quarterly* 27, no. 2 (1963): 250–64.

Cannell, Charles F., and Robert L. Kahn. "Interviewing." In *Handbook of Social Psychology,* vol. 2, edited by Gardner Lindzey and Elliot Aronson. Reading, Mass.: Addison-Wesley, 1968, pp. 526–95.

Caudill, William. "Japanese-American Personality and Acculturation." *Genetic Psychology Monographs* 45 (1952): 3–102.

Caudill, William, and George DeVos. "Achievement, Culture and Personality: The Case of the Japanese Americans." *American Anthropologist* 58 (1956): 1102–26.

Note: All citations to works growing out of the Japanese American Research Project enterprises appear in Appendix A.

.

Chuman, Frank F. *The Bamboo People: The Law and Japanese Americans*. Del Mar, Calif.: Publishers' Inc., 1976.

Cicourel, Aaron. *Method and Measurement in Sociology*. New York: Free Press, 1964.

Coleman, James S., et al. "Equality of Educational Opportunity." Department of Health, Education, and Welfare. Washington, D.C.: Government Printing Office, 1966.

Colombotos, J. "The Effects of Personal Versus Telephone Interviews on Socially Acceptable Responses." Paper presented at the annual meetings of the American Association for Public Opinion Research, 1965.

——. "Personal Versus Telephone Interviews: Effect on Responses." *Public Health Report* 84 (1969): 773–82.

Conrat, Masie, and Richard Conrat. "Executive Order 9066: The Internment of 110,000 Japanese Americans." Los Angeles: California Historical Society, 1972.

Conroy, Hilary, and T. Scott Miyakawa, eds. *East Across the Pacific*. Santa Barbara, Calif.: CLIO Press, 1973.

Cook, S., and C. Selltiz. "A Multiple Indicator Approach to Attitude Measurement." *Psychological Bulletin* 62 (1964): 36–55.

Cox, Henrietta. "Study of Social Class Variations in Value Orientations in Selected Areas of Mother-Child Behavior." Ph.D. dissertation, Washington University, St. Louis, 1964.

Crain, Robert L., and Carol Sachs Weisman. *Discrimination, Personality, and Achievement: A Survey of Northern Blacks*. New York: Seminar Press, 1972.

Crockett, Harry J., Jr. "The Achievement Motive and Differential Occupational Mobility." *American Sociological Review* 27 (1962): 191–204.

Crowne, D. D., and D. Marlowe. *The Approval Motive*. New York: John Wiley and Sons, 1964.

Daniels, Roger. *The Politics of Prejudice*. New York: Atheneum, 1968.

Davis, James A. *Elementary Survey Analysis*. Englewood Cliffs, N.J.: Prentice-Hall, 1971.

DeFleur, Melvin L., and Chang-Soo Cho. "Assimilation of Japanese-Born Women in an American City." *Social Problems* 4, no. 3 (1957): 244–57.

Dohrenwend, Bruce P., and Robert J. Smith. "Toward a Theory of Acculturation." *Southwestern Journal of Anthropology* 18 (1962): 30–39.

Edwards, Allen L. *The Social Desirability in Personality Assessment and Research*. New York: Dryden, 1957.

———. *Techniques of Attitude Scale Construction*. New York: Appleton-Century-Crofts, 1957.

Ellis, Albert. "Questionnaire Versus Interview Methods in the Study of Human Love Relationships." *American Sociological Review* 12 (1947): 451–553.

———. "Questionnaire Versus Interview Methods in the Study of Human Love Relationships, II: Uncategorized Responses." *American Sociological Review* 13 (1948): 61–65.

Endo, Russell. "Japanese Americans: The 'Model Minority' in Perspective." In *The Social Reality of Ethnic America*, edited by Rudolph Gomez et al. Lexington, Mass.: D.C. Heath and Co., 1974.

Erikson, Erik H. *Childhood and Society*. New York: W. W. Norton and Co., 1963.

Fellows, Donald K. *A Mosaic of America's Ethnic Minorities*. New York: John Wiley and Sons, 1972.

Frazen, R., and P. F. Lazarsfeld. "The Mail Questionnaire as a Research Problem." *Journal of Psychology* 20 (1945): 293–320.

Glazer, Nathan, and Daniel P. Moynihan. *Beyond the Melting Pot*. Cambridge: M.I.T. Press, 1970.

Gordon, Milton. *Assimilation in American Life: The Role of Race, Religion and National Origins*. New York: Oxford University Press, 1964.

Greenwood, Leonard. "Japanese Brazilians." Los Angeles *Times*, pt. IV, October 20, 1974, p. 6.

Hagburg, Eugene C. "Validity of Questionnaire Data: Reported and Observed Attendance in an Adult Education Program." *Public Opinion Quarterly* 32 no. 3 (1968): 453–56.

Hansell, Stephen, and Fred L. Strodtbeck. "Ego Development Scores Obtained During Home Visits and in Concomitant Phone Interviews." Unpublished manuscript, University of Chicago, 1973.

Hansen, Marcus L. *The Problem of the Third Generation Immigrant*. Rock Island, Ill.: The Augustana Historical Society, 1937.

——. "The Third Generation in America." *Commentary* 14 (November 1952): 492–503.

Heise, David R. "Separating Reliability and Stability in Test-Retest Correlations." *American Sociological Review* 34 (1969): 93-101.

Herberg, Will. *Protestant, Catholic, Jew.* New York: Doubleday, 1955.

Hillary, George A., Jr. "Definitions of Community: Areas of Agreement." *Rural Sociology* 20 (1955).

Homans, George C. *The Human Group.* New York: Harcourt, 1950.

——. *Social Behavior: Its Elementary Forms.* New York: Harcourt, 1961.

Horinouchi, Isao. "Educational Values and Preadaption in the Acculturation of the Japanese Americans." *Sacramento Anthropological Society*, Paper 7 (1967): 1-60.

Horton, John. "Order and Conflict Theories of Social Problems as Competing Ideologies." *American Journal of Sociology* 71 (1966): 701-13.

Hyman, Herbert; W. J. Cobb; J. J. Feldman; C. W. Hart; C. H. Stember. *Interviewing in Social Research.* Chicago: University of Chicago Press, 1954.

Ichihashi, Yamato. *Japanese Immigration: Its Status in California.* San Francisco: Marshall Press, 1915.

——. *Japanese in the United States.* Stanford: Stanford University Press, 1932.

Ima, Kenji. "Japanese Americans: The Making of a 'Good' People." in *The Minority Report: An Introduction to Racial, Ethnic, and Gender Relations*, edited by Gary and Rosalind J. Dworkin, pp. 254-96. New York: Praeger, 1976.

Iwata, Eddie. "Sansei Move into Arts, Rock Music, Film, Law." Los Angeles *Times*, P. VI, September 28, 1980, pp. 1 ff.

Kahn, R. L. "A Comparison of Two Methods of Collecting Data for Social Research: The Fixed-Alternative Questionnaire and the Open-End Interview." Ph.D. dissertation, University of Michigan, 1952.

Kiefer, Christie W. *Changing Cultures, Changing Lives: An Ethnographic Study of Three Generations of Japanese Americans.* San Francisco: Jossey-Bass Publishers, 1974.

Kikumura, Akemi, and Harry H. L. Kitano. "Interracial Marriage: A Picture of the Japanese-Americans." *Journal of Social Issues* 29, no. 2 (1973): 67-81.

Kitagawa, Daisuke. "The Japanese-American Community: A Profile." In *Knowing and Understanding the Socially Disadvantaged Ethnic Minority Groups,* edited by Staten W. Webster, pp. 408-11, Scranton, Pa.: Intext Educational Publishers, 1972.

Kitano, Harry H. L. "Japanese Americans: A Middleman Minority?" *Pacific Historical Review* vol. 43, no 4 (1974): 500-19.

——. *Race Relations.* Englewood Cliffs, N.J.: Prentice-Hall, 1974.

——. *Japanese Americans: The Evolution of a Subculture.* Englewood Cliffs, N.J.: Prentice-Hall, 1969, 1976.

Kitano, Harry H. L., and Akemi Kikumura. "The Japanese American Family." In *Ethnic Families in America: Patterns and Variations,* edited by H. Mindel and Robert W. Habenstein, pp. 41-60. New York: Elsevier Scientific Publishing Co., 1976.

Knudsen, D. D.; H. Pope; and D. P. Irish. "Response Differences to Questions on Sexual Standards: An Interview-Questionnaire Comparison." *Public Opinion Quarterly* 31, no. 2 (1967): 290-97.

Kramer, Judith R. *The American Minority Community.* New York: Thomas Y. Crowell, 1970.

Lazarsfeld, P. F. "The Use of Mail Questionnaires to Ascertain the Relative Popularity of Network Stations in Family Listening Surveys." *Journal of Applied Psychology* 24 (1940): 802-16.

Lenski, Gerhard E., and John C. Leggett. "Caste, Class, and Deference in the Research Interviewer." *American Journal of Sociology* 65, no. 5 (1960): 463-67.

Levine, Gene N., et al. "Affiliations of Los Angeles Jewry: A Sample Survey of the Metropolitan Area." *Jewish Sociology and Social Research* 2 (1976): 4-9.

Light, Ivan H. *Ethnic Enterprise in America: Business and Welfare Among Chinese, Japanese, and Blacks.* Berkeley and Los Angeles: University of California Press, 1972.

Lind, Andrew W. *Hawaii's People.* 3rd ed. Honolulu: University of Hawaii Press, 1967.

Lyman, Stanford M. "Contrasts in the Community Organization of Chinese and Japanese in North America." *Canadian Review of Sociology and Anthropology* 5 (1968): 51-67.

———. "The Asian in the West." *Social Science and Humanities Publication No. 4.* Reno and Las Vegas: University of Nevada Press, 1970.

Maccoby, Eleanor E., and Nathan Maccoby. "The Interview: A Tool of Social Science." In *Handbook of Social Psychology,* vol. 1, edited by G. Lindsey. Reading, Mass.: Addison-Wesley, 1954.

Masuda, Minoru; Gary H. Matsumoto; and Gerald M. Meredith. "Ethnic Identity in Three Generations of Japanese Americans." *Journal of Social Psychology,* vol. 81, 2d half (1970): 199–207.

Maykovich, Minako K. *Japanese American Identity Dilemma.* Tokyo: Waseda University Press, 1972.

McDonagh, Edward C., and A. Leon Rosenblum. "A Comparison of Mailed Questionnaires and Subsequent Structured Interviews." *Public Opinion Quarterly* 29, no. 1 (1965): 131–36.

McGuire, W. J. "Personality and Susceptibility to Social Influence." In *Handbook of Personality Theory and Research,* edited by E. F. Borgatta and W. W. Lambert. Chicago: Rand McNally, 1968.

Merton, Robert K. "Intermarriage and Social Structure: Fact and Theory." *Psychiatry* 4 (1941): 361–74.

Miyakawa, T. Scott, and Yasuo Sakata. "Japan in Dislocation and Emigration." In *Perspectives in American History,* vol. 1, edited by Donald Fleming and B. Bailyn. Cambridge: Harvard University Press, 1974.

Miyamoto, S. Frank. *Social Solidarity Among the Japanese in Seattle.* Seattle: University of Washington, Publications in the Social Sciences, vol. II, no. 2, 1939.

Miyamoto, S. Frank, and Robert O'Brien. "A Survey of Some Changes in the Seattle Japanese Community Since Evacuation." *Research Studies of the State College of Washington* 15 (1947): 147–54.

Montero, Darrel. *Vietnamese Americans: Patterns of Resettlement and Socioeconomic Adaptation in the United States.* Boulder, Colo.: Westview, 1979.

Morgan, R. "Follow-up Letters Disclose Trends Following Opinion Surveys." *Public Opinion Quarterly* 13 (1949): 686–88.

Nakane, Chie. *Japanese Society.* Berkeley and Los Angeles: University of California Press, 1970.

Newman, William M. *American Pluralism: A Study of Minority Groups and Social Theory.* New York: Harper and Row, 1973.

Nisbet, Robert A. *The Quest for Community.* New York: Oxford University Press, 1953.

———. *The Sociological Tradition.* New York: Basic Books, 1967.

———. *The Social Philosophers: Community and Conflict in Western Thought.* New York: Crowell, 1973.

Ogawa, Dennis. *From Japs to Japanese: The Evolution of Japanese-American Stereotypes.* Berkeley: McCutchan Publishing, 1971.

Park, Robert E., and Herbert A. Miller. *Old World Traits Transplanted.* New York: Harper and Brothers, 1921.

Parsons, Talcott. *The Social System.* Glencoe, Ill.: Free Press, 1951.

Petersen, William. "Success Story: Japanese American Style." In *Minority Responses*, edited by Minako Kurokawa, pp. 169-78. New York: Random House, 1970.

———. *Japanese Americans: Oppression and Success.* New York: Random House, 1971.

Phillips, Derek L., and J. J. Clancy. "Response Biases in Field Studies of Mental Illness." *American Sociological Review* 35, no. 3 (1970): 503-15.

———. "Some Effects of Social Desirability in Survey Studies." *American Journal of Sociology* 97 (1972): 921-40.

Prodipto, Roy. "The Measurement of Assimilation: The Spokane Indians." *American Journal of Sociology* 67 (1962): 541-51.

Schuman, Howard, and Otis Dudley Duncan, "Questions About Attitude Survey Questions." In *Sociological Methodology*, edited by Herbert L. Costner, pp. 232-51. San Francisco: Jossey-Bass, 1973-74.

Schwartz, Audrey James. "Traditional Values and Contemporary Achievement of Japanese-American Pupils." Center for the Study of Evaluation, Report No. 65, University of California, Los Angeles, 1970.

———. "The Culturally Advantaged: A Study of Japanese-American Pupils." *Sociology and Social Research* 55, no. 3 (1971): 341-53.

Schwartz, M. S., and C. G. Schwartz. "Problems in Participant Observation." *American Journal of Sociology* 60 (1955): 343-54.

Scott, Christopher. "Research on Mail Surveys." *Journal of the Royal Statistical Society* 24, pt. 2, ser. A (1961): 143–95.

Selznick, Gertrude J., and Stephen Steinberg. *The Tenacity of Prejudice: Anti-Semitism in Contemporary America.* New York: Harper and Row, 1969.

Sharp, Harry. "The Mail Questionnaire as a Supplement to the Personal Interview." *American Sociological Review* 20, no. 6 (1955): 718.

Siegel, Paul M., and Robert W. Hodge. "A Causal Approach to the Study of Measurement Error." In *Methodology in Social Research*, edited by H. M. Blalock and A. B. Blalock. New York: McGraw Hill, 1968.

Simirenko, Alex. *Pilgrims, Colonists, and Frontiersmen: An Ethnic Community in Transition.* Glencoe, Ill.: Free Press, 1964.

Steiner, Jesse F. *The Japanese Invasion.* Chicago: A. C. McClung, 1917.

Stouffer, Samuel A. *Social Research to Test Ideas.* New York: The Free Press of Glencoe, 1962.

———. *Communism, Conformity and Civil Liberties: A Cross-section of the Nation Speaks its Mind.* Gloucester, Mass.: Peter Smith, 1963.

Strodtbeck, Fred L. "Family Interaction, Value and Achievement." In *Talent and Society.* Edited by D. C. McClelland, A. L. Baldwin, U. Bronfenbrenner, and F. L. Strodtbeck. New York: D. Van Nostrand, 1958.

Sue, Stanley, and Harry H. L. Kitano. "Stereotypes as a Measure of Success." *Journal of Social Issues* 29, no. 2 (1973): 83–98.

Taft, Ronald. "A Psychological Model for the Study of Social Assimilation." *Human Relations* 10 (1957): 141–56.

Takagi, Paul T. "The Influence of Parental Origin Upon Nisei Educational Attainment." Revised version of paper presented to the Kroeber Anthropological Society, Tenth Annual Meeting, 1966.

Thomas, Dorothy S., and Richard Nishimoto. *The Spoilage.* Berkeley and Los Angeles: University of California Press, 1969.

Tinker, John N. "Intermarriage and Ethnic Boundaries: The Japanese American Case." *Journal of Social Issues* 29, no. 2 (1973): 49–66.

Toennies, Ferdinand. *Community and Society.* Translated by Charles P. Loomis. East Lansing: Michigan State University Press, 1957.

U.S. Department of Commerce. Bureau of the Census. *United States Census of Population: 1940.* Vol. II, pt. 1, table 6. Washington, D.C.: Government Printing Office, 1943.

———. *Statistical Abstract of the United States, 1943,* table 55. Washington, D.C.: Government Printing Office, 1944.

———. *United States Census of Population: 1950.* Vol. II, *Nonwhite Population by Race,* Special Report P-E No. 3B, pt. 1; pt. 52, tables 8, 18. Washington, D.C.: Government Printing Office, 1953.

———. *United States Census of Population: 1960. Detailed Characteristics,* United States Summary, Final Report PC (1)-1D. Washington, D.C.: Government Printing Office, 1963.

———. *United States Census of Population: 1960.* Vol. II, *Nonwhite Population by Race,* Final Report PC (2)-1C, pt. 1, table 6. Washington, D.C.: Government Printing Office, 1963.

———. *United States Census of Population: 1970. General Population Characteristics,* U.S. Summary PCV (2)-1. Washington, D.C.: Government Printing Office, 1970.

———. *United States Census of Population: 1970. Detailed Characteristics,* Final Report PC(1)-B13, Hawaii, tables 17, 18. Washington, D.C.: Government Printing Office, 1971.

———. *United States Census of Population: 1970. Occupation by Industry, 1972,* table 1. Washington, D.C.: Government Printing Office, 1972.

———. *United States Census of Population: 1970. Detailed Characteristics,* United States Summary, Final Report PC(1)-D1, tables 203, 221, 250. Washington, D.C.: Government Printing Office, 1973.

———. *United States Census of Population: 1970.* Subject Reports, Final Report PC(2)-1G. "Japanese, Chinese, and Filipinos in the United States," table 1. Washington, D.C.: Government Printing Office, 1973.

U.S. Department of Justice. Immigration and Naturalization Service. *Annual Report of the Commissioner of Immigration and Naturalization.* Washington, D.C., 1975.

United States Code Annotated, Title 8: Aliens and Nationality. St. Paul, Minn.: West Publishing Co., 1970.

Uyeki, Eugene S. "Correlates of Ethnic Identification." *American Journal of Sociology* 65, no. 5 (1960): 468–74.

Weiss, Carol H.; L. J. Bauman, and T. F. Rogers. *Respondent Interviewer Interaction in the Research Interview: Abstracts.* Springfield, Va.: National Technical Information Service, 1971.

Wicker, Allen W. "Attitudes Versus Actions: The Relationship of Verbal Overt Behavioral Responses to Attitude Objects." *The Journal of Social Issues* 25, no. 4 (1969): 41–48.

Yamamoto, Joe. "Japanese American Identity Crisis." In *Minority Group Adolescents in the United States,* edited by Eugene B. Brody, pp. 133–56. Baltimore: Williams and Wilkins, 1968.

INDEX

acculturation, 1-2, 7-8, 9, 33-35, 40
assimilation:
   continuing trend toward, 153
   cultural, 12
   and cultural pluralism, 13
   and Japanese Americans, 14-15
   structural, 12-13
   theory of, 12

Childhold and Society (Erikson), 6
cultural pluralism, 13
   and assimilation, 13
   and Japanese Americans, 14-15,
      117

divorce, paucity of, among Japanese
     Americans, 25, 29, 38, 55,
     101, 110

English language, knowledge and use
     of, by Issei, 35
ethnic identity, 6
ethnic minorities, general experience
     of, 1-2
Erikson, Erik, 6
exogamy among Japanese Americans,
     36, 39, 64-66, 88, 104, 145
   age an inverse factor, 65
   education and, 66
   relation to Japanese community
     adherence, 72, 101
   Sansei experience, 109, 110-13,
     133
   sex not a factor, 65-66

family:
   basic unit of Japanese society, 8-9
   community an extension of, 9-10
   importance to Japanese American
     community, 54-66, 69-71

Japanese view of, brought to
     America, 9-10
   and marital stability, 55
   size of: among Issei, 29, 39, 55
     among Nisei, 39, 55
   social contacts with greater, 56-
     66, 74, 77
   age and education, relation of,
     60-61
   exogamy and, 64-66
   opportunity and proximity,
     effects of, 61-62
   regional variations in, 63-64
   Sansei experiences, 125-32
   types of relatives visited, 64
   visiting patterns, 57-66
Field California Polls, 112, 122, 123

Gentlemen's Agreement (1908), 3
Glazer, Nathan, 13
Gordon, Milton, 12, 13

Hansen, Marcus, 15
Law of Return, 109

Issei, 2, 7, 145-46
   America, life in, 28-36
   Americanization, 33-35
   anti-Japanese discrimination,
     31-33
   Caucasians, friendships with,
     35
   earnings, level of, 30
   English language, use of, 35
   family size among, 39
   further education, little at-
     tempt at, 29, 51
   jobs, types of, 29-30
   marriages, 29, 65
   and Nisei marriage patterns, 36

239

ABOUT THE AUTHORS

Gene N. Levine is professor of sociology at UCLA. Trained at Columbia, he earlier had been research associate at the Bureau of Applied Social Research and project director at the United Nations Research Institute for Social Development. Since the mid-1960s he has studied American, Chicano, and Jewish ethnic groups, as well as Japanese.

Colbert Rhodes is an associate professor of sociology at the University of Texas of the Permian Basin located in Odessa, Texas. He received his BA from the University of California, Berkeley, and his MA and Ph.D. from UCLA. His specialties include sociological theory, race/ethnic relations, industrial sociology, and social gerontology. Dr. Rhodes has published articles on sociological theory and on Japanese Americans. He is continuing his research on Japanese Americans by examining the determinants for outmarriage among the second and third generations.